Some Sunny Day

b' Blair is the son of an RAF navigator who flew in
Campaign and a WAAF mother who was stationed
Park in the Second World War. He was educated at
Ellesmere Port Grammar Schools and began his
weekly papers. He moved to the *London Evening*
fore emigrating to Canada, where he worked for
itizen, then on to Hong Kong. After two years with
hina Morning Post Group he returned to London
rty years with Mirror Group Newspapers.

years he has visited more than ninety countries,
dia, Myanmar (formerly Burma), Malaysia (Malaya),
Thailand, Hong Kong, Cambodia, Laos, Vietnam,
van, Borneo, the Philippines and Indonesia.

Some Sunny Day

A nurse. A soldier.
A wartime love story.

MADGE LAMBERT
with Robert Blair

PAN BOOKS

First published 2018 by Pan Books
an imprint of Pan Macmillan
20 New Wharf Road, London N1 9RR
Associated companies throughout the world
www.panmacmillan.com

ISBN   978-1-5098-5937-5 PB
ISBN   978-1-5098-9327-0 HB

1 3 5 7 9 8 6 4 2

A CIP catalogue record for this book is available from the British Library.

Typeset by Palimpsest Book Production Ltd, Falkirk, Stirlingshire
Printed and bound by CPI Group (UK) Ltd, Croydon, CR0 4YY

For my husband, Basil –
I love him as much today as when we
first met during the Burma Campaign
— Madge Lambert

This book is dedicated to the finest
generation in British history
— Robert Blair

Contents

Prologue 1

1 The India Office 5

2 Friday Meant Steak and Kidney Pudding 18

3 War is Declared 25

4 Becoming a Nurse 35

5 Rules and Regulations 50

6 The Journey Begins 71

7 Passage to India 81

8 Life Jackets and Pith Helmets 92

9 Arriving in Bombay 102

10 Chittagong, Here We Come 117

11 56 Indian General Hospital 128

12 Learning About Indian Life 143

13 Madge Goes Dancing 152

14 The Gurkhas' Holy Man 160

15 Letters From Home 172

16 Captain Basil Lambert 181

17 Christmas in Chittagong 196

18 Auld Lang Syne 212

19 A Moonlight Serenade 217

20 Nursing the Japanese 230

21 Holiday in Calcutta 246

22 A Painful Goodbye 262

23 The Casualty Clearing Station 276

24 The Himalayas at Sunrise 297

25 The Japanese Surrender 312

26 Homeward Bound 318

27 Wedding Bells 334

Epilogue 346

Glossary 355

Acknowledgements 358

Prologue

Madge felt as if she'd only just dropped into an exhausted sleep when the rustle of the tent flap jerked her awake again.

'Good morning, girls. It's time for duty. We've got a very busy few hours ahead of us,' the staff sister said, her flickering hurricane lamp held high.

Operating on autopilot, Madge pulled the single sheet free of her camp bed and opened a gap in the heavy-duty mosquito net, before bending to turn her shoes upside down to ensure tarantulas or snakes hadn't snuck in during the night. Finally she slipped on her khaki nursing uniform. She could hear the other nurses around her doing the same, everyone quietly getting ready to face the new day.

The nurses were staffing a casualty clearing station in Burma, close to the front line, where Lieutenant General William Slim's 14th Army were involved in brutal hand-to-hand combat as they forced the Japanese back south towards the capital of Rangoon.

It was two hours before dawn but it was already humid

as Madge and five other nurses carefully picked their way down the slope on which their tent was pitched. The Arakan jungle surrounded them, the trees looming black shapes in the darkness. They were headed for the operating theatre – another tent housing two large trestle tables on which weary doctors performed daily miracles on Allied troops, who often suffered horrendous, life-changing injuries.

The faintest of movements deep in the shadows of the valley caught Madge's eye as the nurses approached the tent. Soldiers ran from their camouflaged guard posts to help the exhausted bearers, who came into sight carrying a wounded comrade on a stretcher.

The injured man was taken straight into the tent, where Madge helped cut his blood-soaked clothes away and cleaned him up in preparation for surgery. She recognised the severe shrapnel damage caused by a Japanese shell exploding. *Goodness me, that left arm doesn't look good*, she thought to herself as a drip was inserted in the other arm to counter the effects of dehydration.

The operating team carefully removed embedded metal fragments and fought long and hard to save the damaged limb, but they soon became resigned to the fact that the young soldier would have to spend the rest of his life with just one arm. The amputation took place shortly before dawn. Minutes later the sombre silence that had engulfed the operating tent was broken by the thunder of the 14th Army heavy artillery pounding forward Japanese positions.

'When he starts to come round, I want you to take extreme

care that he doesn't accidentally discover he's lost his arm,' the surgeon said. 'The shock to the system could be very damaging. I will tell him myself when he's in a fit state to take it in.'

Madge knew that within forty-eight hours the patient would be taken to a landing strip and flown by a DC-3 to one of the military hospitals in Chittagong or Calcutta.

On the other operating table there was a lance corporal who had been hit by a bullet that seemed to have gone straight through his shoulder. Madge didn't know whether to laugh or weep when he gave her a cheeky wink just before the anaesthetic took effect.

'The bravery of these boys is amazing,' Madge whispered to her friend Vera.

Eventually the nurses were ordered to get something to eat and grab a few hours' sleep. They had been on duty for almost twenty-four of the previous thirty hours.

When Madge was working, she was too busy to think about the danger she was in or what would happen if the Japanese overran the camp. Now, as her head hit her pillow, she was too tired to worry. Images from the shift ran through her mind – the shrapnel fragments clunking into a waste container, the young soldier's arm being amputated. She pushed them to one side and thought instead of her mother and sisters back in High Wycombe, wondering what they would be doing now.

Nurse Madge Graves was twenty-one years of age and a very long way from home.

1

The India Office

Madge woke with a knot in her stomach. Today her future would be decided. She got out of bed in her tiny room at the nurses' home at Stoke Mandeville Hospital and instantly began worrying about the questions she would be asked at the interview in London later that day. She leaned across her ageing bedside cabinet to pull the curtain back and open the window to let the fresh spring air into the little box room where she had slept since starting as a trainee in 1941, almost three years earlier.

As she made her way along the corridor for an early morning bath, Madge smiled at two fellow trainee nurses whispering anxiously together. *Perhaps they're going to London for the interviews too*, she wondered. *They look as worried as I feel.* Back in her room, she brushed her short fair hair until it shone, opened her excuse for a wardrobe and put on her freshly laundered nursing uniform. Make-up was banned when the nurses were on duty in the wards and for that reason she decided not to wear any for her interview, not even the slightest trace of lipstick. *I'm as ready as I'll ever be*, she said to herself, before strolling to the spacious whitewashed dining hall and sitting down at one of two long trestles which served as tables. Senior staff like Matron and the ward sisters sat at one trestle, along with experienced nurses from the Emergency Medical Service. Madge, who was a junior, sat at the other table with the trainees.

Madge had her usual simple breakfast of tea and two slices of toast, covered with the merest scraping of butter. How she longed for the day when rationing was over and she could have a real slathering of butter. Madge tried to calculate the last time she'd had such a luxury and worked out it had to be more than four years ago. The first round of rationing had come in January 1940, and now it was April 1944.

When she was finished, she walked the short distance from the nurses' home to the hospital reception area, where she had arranged to meet her friends Vera Clark and Phyl Irvine, who would be joining her on the early train from Aylesbury station to Marylebone. Madge smiled as her two fellow nurses, who were rarely punctual, surprisingly arrived bang on time. Vera was dark-haired, outspoken and proud to be a northerner. Phyl was fair-haired and quieter. Once the trio got to Marylebone the plan was to make their way to the India Office in Whitehall for their day-long test.

As the minutes ticked by, the three young women became increasingly worried. The green six-seater van that masqueraded as official hospital transport was notoriously unreliable. Madge was the first to hear it come coughing and wheezing round the corner.

'Thank goodness you're here, William!' she said to the driver.

'The ignition again! Sorry, girls. Squeeze in.'

'What do you think our chances are?' Madge asked the other girls as they set off for the station.

'I heard it's a jolly hard test,' said Vera. She looked uncharacteristically edgy, but still kept her sense of humour and pretended to snap at the driver when he cheerfully said she sounded like a Geordie.

'William, that is absolute heresy. I'm from Sunderland and we're Macams, not Geordies,' she said with a grin as she winked at the other girls.

The bit of fun encouraged a very nervous Phyl to chip in. 'I've never even *been* to Whitehall!'

The train was a good twenty minutes late, but Madge had wisely allowed an extra hour in case of emergencies and it gave the girls time to chat about the questions they might be asked at the India Office. All three had responded to a plea from Lord Louis Mountbatten for nurses to bolster the overworked and understaffed Allied medical units in the Burma Campaign of the Second World War.

Mountbatten, since his appointment as Commander of the South East Asia Command in 1943, had made repeated requests for more nurses but was still getting nowhere until he enlisted the help of his wife, Lady Edwina Mountbatten, Superintendent-in-Chief of the St John Ambulance Brigade.

Firebrand Edwina organised a conference of the relevant authorities at the very same India Office where the nurses' interviews were to take place and circumvented any further objections by having a quiet chat with an old friend, Winston Churchill. Sure enough, Lord Louis promptly received word that approval had been granted for the first 250 VAD nurses to travel to India.

Pamphlets were sent to hospitals nationwide and when Phyl saw one on the nurses' noticeboard at Stoke Mandeville Hospital she had a quick conflab with Madge and Vera, then arranged for them to go to a cafe on Aylesbury High Street to talk further.

'Things are so quiet at the hospital, it's definitely worth considering,' said Vera.

'All we do is clean the wards, make beds and prepare cotton wool swabs,' Madge chimed in.

'Exactly!' Vera went on. 'So all things considered, it's worth having a go.'

The girls laughed at the memory as they stood on the platform, but the conversation had dried up and the longer they waited, the more worried they became about the reason for the delay. Eventually the train arrived and the girls piled into their carriage, and for a while at least, their trepidation over the test that lay ahead was replaced by excitement.

'This feels like a real adventure!' Phyl said as they made themselves comfortable for the journey.

A number of trains and many miles of track in and out of London had been damaged in enemy air raids, but luckily the Aylesbury to Marylebone line had been spared so far. An entertaining conversation, whispered as it may have been, took place as the train approached London about the number of smartly dressed little penguins they could see from the carriage window waddling around in bowler hats. When the three young nurses spotted the India Office as they walked down the smart street of Whitehall they were almost overwhelmed by the vast three-storey building.

'I've never seen anything like it,' said Vera. 'It looks like a French chateau!'

'It's definitely imposing,' Madge agreed. She stared at the building, pleased to have something to help take her mind off the barrage of questioning they were about to face.

There was little time to enjoy the equally impressive interior of the building because the girls were quickly directed by a portly steward with his jacket sleeves overhanging his knuckles to the interview rooms, where their details were taken by a sympathetic, matronly secretary, who did her best to ease their increasing nervousness.

The young nurses had just enough time to wish one another good luck before they were taken individually to different rooms on the same floor.

'I see from the notes here that you nursed in the services section of Stoke Mandeville,' said one of the doctors who was interviewing Madge. He walked with a pronounced limp and had a hint of grey round the temples, but was very charming and relaxed.

'Yes, that's right,' she answered, before they began a lengthy discussion about how to deal with bullet and shrapnel wounds.

Eventually he asked, 'So, Nurse Graves, do you have experience of nursing abroad?'

Madge, smiling, replied, 'Not yet, but I'm keeping my fingers crossed!'

Yet still the questions came. Would she be prepared to nurse Indian soldiers? What were the early symptoms of gangrene? What was the cause of and treatment for malaria and had she read about the sterilisation of medical equipment in field-hospital conditions? Had she any experience in the use of the new wonder drug, penicillin?

After four hours of intense questioning, another particularly stern interviewer with a big, bushy moustache nodded to Madge that she could return to the waiting room. Phyl and Vera were already there, along with three other unknown nurses, who were all sitting next to one another on the hard wooden chairs looking quite stunned. Madge gave Phyl and Vera a nod as she sat down. The whole room was silent as the interviewees reflected on the past few hours. A secretary brought in tea and biscuits as they waited to hear what their fate would be.

As Madge nibbled on a bit of shortbread, she began to wonder if she was doing the right thing after all. It dawned on her all of a sudden that if she was successful, she'd soon be leaving England for the first time, moving away from her family. She'd already let Stoke Mandeville know that she was applying, and in addition had promised her sisters Doris and Doreen her winter clothes when she left because she had the strangest of feelings that she would not be returning to

England any time soon, if at all. She was too young to really believe that she might die, but still she vowed to keep a diary of her adventures abroad for her sisters so they would have something to remember her by if she didn't make it back.

Madge thought the interview had gone well, but as the minutes turned to an hour she started to fret. At last the door swung open and every nurse in the room sat bolt upright as a woman with immaculately coiffed hair, scarlet lipstick and a sharply pressed St John Ambulance Brigade uniform walked in. Madge gave an audible gasp as she realised it was Lady Mountbatten! She had seen photographs of her in magazines but she was far more striking in person. The nurses watched, starstruck, as Lady Mountbatten took her place at the imposing desk, her pristine white gloves placed neatly alongside a leather-embossed folder. The regulation St John Ambulance black-and-white hat was worn at a jaunty angle and the white epaulettes sewn to her jacket's shoulders stood in vivid contrast to the immaculately tailored black uniform. She smiled kindly at the young nurses in front of her.

There was a twinkle in her eyes as the society beauty hesitated for a moment, almost as if she was gently teasing them, but then announced, 'Congratulations, ladies, you've all passed the selection test.' Vera had her hand in front of her face to try and stifle the tears of joy. Phyl simply beamed from ear to ear and Madge was elated – could this be real? But her thoughts were interrupted by Lady Mountbatten, who fixed them each with a serious face and announced rather sternly, 'Be sure to ask yourself, ladies, if you will be able to stand the heat.' Madge was somewhat puzzled. She hadn't been north of Watford, let alone overseas, so she couldn't begin to imagine what the heat would be like in the Far East. On a good day in Dover, where she had lived until starting work at Stoke Mandeville, it was possible to see Calais, but a long journey was a bus ride to Folkestone and the sun was never more than warm.

Lady Mountbatten shook hands with each of the girls and they were escorted down a level and along the corridor to the Military Department of the India Office to sign a set of papers. An unsmiling official handed Vera her documents and then gave Phyl hers. Madge looked at him expectantly but he just peered over his circular, black-rimmed glasses and said without a hint of apology, 'You are not legally eligible for service overseas because you have yet to reach the age of twenty-one. Permission is refused.'

'But . . . But . . .' Madge stammered as her stomach dropped.

'I'm afraid that's final, miss,' the official said, before pointedly turning back to his filing.

'Oh, that's too bad, Madge,' Vera said sympathetically, while Phyl gave her arm a squeeze. Madge willed herself not to cry.

As they made their way back to Stoke Mandeville she gave the matter some thought. On the one hand, when Mountbatten's plea was issued, life at Stoke Mandeville Hospital had been very quiet and that had been a major factor in her decision to volunteer for service overseas. On the other hand, there had been huge troop movements for weeks. Nurses and doctors alike were muttering that the 'big one' was coming and that they needed to be ready. Perhaps, Madge thought, she'd be able to help just as much at Stoke Mandeville. And at least that way she'd be able to stay close to her family.

All the same, during dinner, Madge struggled to keep a smile on her face, and that night as she snuggled into bed she had to try her hardest to convince herself that staying in Britain was the best thing after all.

After a sleepless night, a somewhat dispirited Madge made the short walk from the nurses' home to the hospital to begin her 8 a.m. shift. Even on that five-minute stroll numerous people asked how the interview had gone. She had a late lunch with her two friends who were understandably buzzing about the exciting, brave new world that beckoned. Phyl said she had looked at an atlas and couldn't believe just how huge India was.

'It's such a shame you're not coming with us,' she told Madge. 'That horrid old man in the Military Department of the India Office shouldn't be allowed to make such ridiculous decisions.'

The kindness and support of both Vera and Phyl left Madge in somewhat of a quandary. She loved the fact that Mum and her sisters were just a short bus ride from the hospital, but she also felt that the way she had been treated was totally unfair.

That night, yet again lying awake in bed, thoughts whirling through her mind, she made a decision. *I am simply not prepared to be pushed around like this, not under any circumstances. First thing tomorrow I'm going to set to work convincing them to change their minds, and I won't stop hounding them until they let me go!*

Over the next few days, Madge repeatedly tried, and failed, to navigate the maze that was the India Office telephone system until the kindly hospital telephonist, Mrs Hutchinson, stepped in to help. Day after day, Madge spoke to officials but simply could not persuade the India Office to overturn their decision.

Weeks passed into months and Madge became resigned to the fact that she would be staying at Stoke Mandeville after all. The rumours of a 'big one' sadly came true and Madge was kept madly busy with the volume of casualties arriving from the D-Day landings on 6 June. Many of those boys were in a terrible state and Madge found a renewed sense of purpose as she tended to their wounds and made them as comfortable as they could be.

It was a warm summer's day and Madge had been on her feet all morning when she checked her pigeonhole for word from her sisters, Doris and Doreen, who loved receiving and sending little notes. Instead of the slim letter she was expecting, there was a thick envelope with 'On His Majesty's Service' emblazoned across it and 'India Office' printed on the bottom left-hand side. Madge's hands trembled, sure this would be final confirmation of the India Office rejection. She ripped open the envelope and read.

Madam,
  I am directed by the Secretary of State for India to
inform you that your acceptance as a member of the VAD

for employment in India has been approved with effect from
16 June 1944, under the conditions set out in the enclosed
memorandum.

Madge's heart leapt. She'd done it! She was in! All her phone
calls had paid off. She read on:

You will be entitled to pay at the inclusive rate of £134 per
annum from the date of your acceptance until the date of
your arrival in India. Issue of allotment will commence on the
first day of the month following that in which you embark,
and you should therefore conduct your private financial
arrangements in this knowledge.

You should be prepared to embark for India at short notice.
Detailed instructions will be forwarded as soon as possible
and you should inform this department immediately of any
change in your address.

It cannot be too strongly stressed that the utmost secrecy
must be observed since disclosure by a member of her destin-
ation, location of assembly place or time of departure not
only endangers the life of the member concerned, but also the
lives of comrades. It is of particular importance that no
baggage or personal belongings should bear inscriptions or
initials of the destination other than the place of assembly.

I am, madam,
Your obedient servant,
H. G. Bull

Madge read the letter three times. Then went straight to the little room that housed the switchboard and was put through to Whitehall 8140. She waited for what seemed like an age before Mr Bull himself came to the telephone and blandly explained that whilst indeed their original decision to refuse Madge's application was correct, on review, it was pointed out that the sea journey to India would take several weeks, during which time Miss Graves would celebrate her birthday, meaning that she would be of age by the time she reached her destination.

'The application has been approved and, yes, you really are going,' Mr Bull told her.

Madge was standing in somewhat of a daze with the letter in her hand as Vera walked past on her way to lunch.

'Are you OK or have you just seen a ghost?' she quipped, and tried to sneak a look at the document. All she could see, however, was a line that read: *Miss Madge L. Graves, W5101845, VAD 125 IGH (C), SEAC*. 'What on earth is that all about?' asked Vera. 'It looks like a secret code.'

Madge was bubbling with excitement. 'You'll never believe it,' she said, as she handed the letter over and added, 'I'm going to be joining you!'

Vera's whoop of joy was so loud that heads turned to see what the noise was all about, but she didn't care.

'I'll get Phyl and we can all go into Aylesbury for a celebration lunch,' she almost shouted.

Madge laughed and said she loved the idea, 'But not today because I must tell a very important person first.'

As luck would have it, driver William was sitting outside the hospital in his battered old van and happily drove her into Aylesbury, and from there she caught the bus to High Wycombe.

By pure coincidence, as Madge got off the bus her mum Lily was waiting at the bus stop to go shopping. Madge was bursting with excitement and pride as she told her mum the news.

'Your father didn't like India at all when he was posted there during the Great War,' her mother said, the shock clear on her face. 'Do you think it's a wise idea? Oh, but listen to me, you'll have a wonderful time and you'll be doing something truly amazing. I'm incredibly proud of you, love.'

Tears glistened as she wrapped her arms around Madge to give her a long and loving hug and then they walked back to the family home in Dashwood Avenue arm in arm so Lily could make her beloved eldest daughter a cup of tea.

2

Friday Meant Steak
and Kidney Pudding

Madge was only too aware that her service overseas would involve a number of personal sacrifices, and that the most painful of those would be being separated from her mum and her sisters Doris and Doreen, who were aged eighteen and thirteen respectively. Not to mention leaving behind the warmth and comfort of the family kitchen or, indeed, the mouth-watering family meals, so she made a point of spending as much time as possible with her family in the few days left before the start of her passage to India.

One day, as Madge and her mother sat chatting in the back garden of the family home, Lily talked for the first time about the early years of her marriage to husband Charles. Lily was born in High Wycombe and Charles in Dover in 1897, the year in which Queen Victoria celebrated the Diamond Jubilee of her accession to the throne.

'Did you know,' she told Madge, 'the Great War broke out in 1914, when your dad was just seventeen. He wanted to do the right thing for his country so he joined the Royal Field Artillery. Most of his next six years in the army were spent in India. We got married soon after he was demobbed, but, as you know, he seemed to suffer from some sort of flu from then on . . .'

Madge went in to make a pot of tea and when she returned Mum said that after he came back from India Dad started work as a flour miller in Dover, 'and we felt really blessed when you arrived. Then there was Doris and, five years later, Doreen. I was never happier than when your dad was playing the piano or the mandolin at your birthday parties,' said Lily. 'Do you remember how everyone wanted him to play at their parties? He could tinkle out most of the popular songs of the day, but he couldn't read music. It was all played from memory!'

Madge knew all of this already but she loved to hear it again. She smiled and said her early memories were of the mouth-watering aromas and tastes from the Graves' cosy kitchen, which was always the centre of the household.

'Everything went on in there and you were forever baking or cooking something, but however busy you were, you always had time to sort out a problem, or kiss a bruised knee better,' she said with a fond smile.

Of all the days of the week, Friday was by far the best because the Graves family always had steak and kidney pudding for lunch. By 6 a.m. on a Friday morning, Lily would have the sauce steaming away on the stove and six hours later the beef was so tender it would just melt in your mouth. The girls would come home from school at midday, as they did every day, and their father Charles would arrive not long after. Fridays meant that Charles would be in a good mood because steak and kidney pudding was his favourite, too, and every time he would have second helpings.

'You know, I'm not sure if I'll miss steak and kidney pudding the most or the smell of newly baked bread,' Madge said, thinking of the homely, comforting aroma that regularly wafted round their cosy kitchen.

As the eldest, she was allowed to help her busy mum by slicing the bread once it had cooled and that meant she was first in the queue for a crust. But being the eldest also meant she had responsibilities. From the age of ten one of Madge's jobs had been the weekly walk to the baker's shop where old Mr Goodwin sold yeast, which, as Lily had explained to her, was the essential ingredient to make bread rise, and Mr Goodwin's yeast was the best in Dover. One day, Lily was shocked to pull the bread from the stove and discover a flat loaf.

'Maybe it's a problem with the oven, Mum,' Madge said, shuffling her feet.

'Maybe . . . I'm sure it can't be Mr Goodwin's yeast,' her mother said dubiously.

But the next day they had the same problem and Lily was certain that Mr Goodwin hadn't given them their full tuppence's worth.

'I wouldn't put him for a scoundrel, Madge, but we have to do something.' And with that she dragged a very reluctant Madge to the shop. The old boy protested indignantly that he wouldn't dream of short-changing a customer, especially one he had known for so many years. Madge watched as her mother started to raise her voice. It was awful! She couldn't bear it any longer.

'Mr Goodwin isn't to blame, Mum . . .' Madge felt herself going bright red and the rest of her words came out in a tumble. 'I had a little nibble of the yeast. I'm very sorry!' Madge's stomach sank as she watched her mother's face go as red as her own when she began apologising profusely to Mr Goodwin.

'Not to worry, Mrs Graves,' Mr Goodwin said, as the pair tumbled out the door.

Madge was given a stern ticking-off on her way home and she dreaded her next visit to the bakery. It took her a quarter of an hour longer than it usually would to walk there as she dragged her feet, and by the time she arrived she was almost in tears.

'Ah, look, if it isn't our little yeast snaffler,' Mr Goodwin said as she walked in. Madge thought she might be sick she was so ashamed but was surprised to hear Mr Goodwin break out into kindly laughter. 'How on earth can you bear to eat raw yeast?'

Madge gave him a grateful smile as he handed over the Graves' weekly yeast portion in a little parcel that this time was securely tied up.

'Hold on,' he said, and picked up a block of yeast, sliced off a slither and handed it to her as a treat to eat on the way home.

Mum laughed at the memory of that little escapade and slowly drifted to sleep in the afternoon sun to leave Madge thinking about some of the other events of her childhood. She remembered a time when the arrival of a new headmistress caused a bit of a stir. There had been whispers all around the school and Mum had told her, not entirely approvingly, that this one was 'a very different kettle of fish'. Madge adored Miss Radford at first sight. She wore a black suit, high heels and make-up. She taught history to Madge's class and told them that her brother was Basil Radford, the actor who starred in many films, including Alfred Hitchcock's *The Lady Vanishes*. Madge hadn't seen that film – in fact, her mum hadn't taken her to the cinema yet – but it all sounded very glamorous!

Miss Radford talked to the pupils about the Great War and she told the class that in his training, her brother had to stick a bayonet into a sack of straw and that he kept on having mental images of blood pouring out. One of the girls surprised Madge by almost fainting at the very thought of blood spurting from a sack, but Miss Radford calmed her down and went on to explain that the war had been a difficult time, particularly for the men who had to go off and fight. Madge looked down at her desk as she thought about *her* dad and wondered what he had thought about the war. She knew that he'd been to India, though all he said was that it was jolly hot.

'This week,' Miss Radford said, 'I'd like you all to take part in recording your own bit of history. Please ask your fathers and write half a page about their war experience, and please bring it back next week.'

Madge looked up. She was determined to make her history project the best in the class. When school finished she rushed home and started planning her questions. Charles had barely been through the door a minute when Madge told him about the project.

His face paled and Madge knew instantly that she had made a mistake. He marched straight upstairs and wouldn't come down for dinner. Madge knew he was furious because she could hear him telling her mother through the walls that he was going directly to the school in the morning to register a complaint.

'That was the war to end all wars and it should never even be mentioned!' he said to her mother. 'There will never ever be another war like it and I don't want her worrying about that sort of thing.'

It was the first and last time Madge raised the subject; she never wanted to see her father that worked up again.

By the time Madge was a teenager her father was suffering from more and more of his flu bouts, with nausea and very high fevers. During these episodes, he would shake so much that his bed banged violently against the bedroom wall. It was frightening for the family, who had never seen anyone quite so ill, but the doctors said he was just unusually susceptible to the illness.

At the end of November 1938, when Madge was fifteen years old, her father was struck by yet another bout of fever which worried the doctor so much he was admitted to the Royal Victoria Hospital in Dover. After a short stay there, Charles was transferred to the Royal Free Hospital in Hampstead, London, where he died just a few days later on 8 December.

Lily was determined not to let her grief at the loss of her beloved husband affect her three daughters and bravely insisted that life should continue as normal. To avoid even more emotional upset within the household she decided it would be better if Madge, Doreen and Doris didn't attend the funeral. The girls were distraught at the loss of their father, but carried on as normally as they could, albeit with a sadness in their hearts that hadn't been there before. Madge, still a teenager but that bit older than her sisters, was far from convinced by the doctor's diagnosis that flu was the cause of her father's death.

The fun-filled childhood that the three sisters had so enjoyed came to an abrupt end with the sudden loss of their father. Christmas Day 1938 should have been a time of merriment with a chorus of neighbours and friends crowded around Charles's piano for hours on end. Instead there was just silence and sadness.

3

War is Declared

The new year came and Madge vowed that she'd help Mum and her sisters recover from Dad's death. As the months passed they all tried to put on a brave face, but couldn't help but notice the gap at the head of the table where Dad used to sit.

On 3 September 1939, Madge, as usual, took her sisters to Sunday school in the stark Wesleyan chapel near their home, and found herself staring out of the window as she day-dreamed. She had left school that summer, aged sixteen, and had enrolled at a commercial college to learn skills that included shorthand and typing. Madge had always wanted to be a hairdresser but you had to pay a hundred pounds to serve an apprenticeship and that sort of money was out of the question. Dad hadn't left them much and Mum was struggling to get by as it was.

She suddenly realised the rest of the Sunday school pupils had begun whispering. The teacher was usually very strict about talking in class but she wasn't at her desk in front of the board. Instead, she was huddled around the radio along with some of the other volunteers.

'Turn it up, I can't hear,' someone said.

Prime Minister Neville Chamberlain's clipped voice echoed loud and clear around the hall.

'*I am speaking to you from the Cabinet Room in 10 Downing Street. This morning the British ambassador in Berlin handed the German government a final note stating that unless we heard from them by eleven o'clock they were prepared at once to withdraw their troops from Poland, a state of war would exist between us. I have to tell you now that no such undertaking has been received and that consequently this country is at war with Germany.*'

Madge's stomach dropped and she couldn't help but think about the Great War and what Miss Radford had told them about her brother imagining blood pouring out of the straw sack and the way her dad had looked when she'd asked him about the history project. She didn't normally pay much attention to the news but she had overheard her mother's worried conversations with the neighbours about Hitler and everything awful that was happening in Germany.

Madge saw their teacher's face blanch and, as the announcement finished, she quietly told the group to go straight home. Madge gathered her things and walked out with her sisters.

'What do you think will happen now?' asked Doreen.

Doris opened her mouth to speak but was cut short because they had barely walked out of the doors when an air-raid siren started shrieking. The sisters looked at one another, eyes wide in fear.

'Leg it!' Madge said, and the girls ran back home, encountering many panicked neighbours on their way, and hid under the dining room table.

'Will there be bombs, Madge?' asked Doreen.

'Probably not, don't worry, I'm sure it's just a drill,' Madge said, although she wasn't sure at all.

The sisters stayed under the table, huddling close together, for what felt like forever, even after the siren had stopped howling. All three of them jumped as they heard the front door lock turn and rushed to hug Lily as she walked through the door.

'It was the awful noise that really frightened us,' said Madge, as Doris and Doreen burst into tears of relief at the comforting sight of Mum standing in the hallway. 'Thank goodness you're home. We didn't know what to do.'

'Oh, girls, you poor things,' said Mum. Lily had been just one year older than Madge when the Great War started in July 1914, so she knew all too well the fear they were feeling. 'Everything's OK. It's over now. Let's all have a nice cup of tea and some biscuits.'

A little while later Madge caught Mum on her own in the kitchen preparing dinner. 'I told Doris and Doreen I thought it would be better if they didn't go out to play,' she told Lily. Mum nodded in agreement. 'I'm scared, Mum. What do you think's going to happen?'

'Oh, love. I don't honestly know,' she replied. 'We'll just have to wait and see.' She sighed deeply before turning back to peeling the potatoes, and Madge could see the concern etched on her face.

By the following morning rumours about what the Germans were and weren't going to do were rife throughout Dover. Just a few days later, the authorities began letting families know that instructions would soon be issued for the mandatory evacuation of school-age children from the area, probably to Wales. Raids by German bombers were expected sooner rather than later.

In fact, just two months before the outbreak of hostilities with Germany, the Civil Defence Service had issued a leaflet, 'Evacuation – Why and How', that explained the steps that would be taken in the event of war. Because Doris was thirteen and Doreen was eight and Dover was such an important port, making it a prime target for German bombers, Lily accepted the inevitability of another family upheaval. However, after losing her husband Charles, Lily certainly wasn't going to let the authorities take her precious daughters away. As the early months of the war got underway, Wales and the West Country were being named as safe havens, but Lily had already decided on another venue for when the time came. She waited until Doris and Doreen had gone to bed one night and talked the situation over at length with Madge.

'I think we should go to High Wycombe,' she told her eldest daughter. Madge knew that was where her mum had grown up. 'It was a safe place during the Great War and that's where I would like to take your sisters when the evacuation orders come through,' she said. 'And I would very much like you to come with us.'

The discussion went on long into the night because Madge, after completing the course at the commercial college, had just recently started a job with excellent prospects at Wiggins Teape, the paper manufacturers. John Husk, a friend of her father, had contacts at the company and had been very helpful in pointing her in the right direction. Of more importance was Madge's ability to take shorthand at 180 words a minute and she was already a valued member of the company.

'This job has real prospects, Mum,' Madge sighed. 'The truth is, I really want to stay in Dover and see if I can make a success of it. I'll miss you all but I don't want to be a financial burden on you any longer,' she added. 'It's about time I made my own way.'

Mum reluctantly agreed to let Madge remain on condition that she lived with Beatrice and Mark Spice, her aunt and uncle. As a midwife, Mrs Spice was well known in Dover and always got a cheery wave from the many young mothers she had cared for.

Auntie Bea was a veritable font of local knowledge and told Lily that she had heard that plans were in place to flatten every single building on Dover's waterfront so the army would have a direct line of fire if the invasion fleet of German Grand Admiral Karl Doenitz's *Kriegsmarine* ever hove into view. That was the final straw for Mum. She took Doris and Doreen soon after to live in her brother William's house at 97 Dashwood Avenue in High Wycombe.

*

Lily's decision to take her youngest daughters away from danger proved to be a wise move. Within months the vibrant south coast port became the target of Luftwaffe bombing raids and soon become known as 'Hellfire Corner'. When the night raids happened and the sirens howled, Madge often found herself wishing she had followed her family to High Wycombe. She would run to the air-raid shelter, looking up but unable to see the bombers in the pitch-black sky, and huddle up to her aunt and uncle who, like her, flinched every time they heard an explosion. As well as bringing life into the world as a midwife, Aunt Bea also became the neighbourhood 'layer out' of the bodies of people killed in the bombing and shelling.

Wailing sirens and strictly enforced blackouts became the norm and so intense were the bombing raids that there were spells of a fortnight or more before Madge finally got a night in her own bed instead of the Anderson air-raid shelter at the bottom of Auntie Bea's garden. It wasn't very comfortable but Madge soon found herself accepting it as part and parcel of everyday life. It almost became an adventure after a while!

During the day she was so busy with work and helping Auntie Bea around the house that she barely had time to miss her family. But after so many months apart, every time she thought of Mum, Doris and Doreen there was a tug at her heart strings. Auntie Bea was an expert at sensing even the slightest of emotional changes and over dinner on one of the few nights they weren't in the air-raid shelter she very gently and diplomatically mentioned that she had been thinking of Lily and the girls and wondered how they had settled in.

'I bet your mum is missing you,' she said. 'Do you think it might be time for a little visit to High Wycombe?'

'Oh yes,' said Madge, the thought bringing a big smile to her face. 'I'd love to see them all again and have a bit of fun with my sisters.' She sighed and the smile faded. 'But getting there will be the problem. You never really know when the trains are going to be running these days.'

As luck would have it, a neighbour, John Husk, son of John Husk Senior, heard that Madge was planning a visit and kindly offered to give her a lift up to Buckinghamshire where his wife and children were also sheltering from the bombs of Dover. Madge was given time off from Wiggins Teape and after just a few days' anxious wait, she set off with Mr Husk in his car.

'It's really good of you to give me a lift,' said Madge. 'Your father did me a favour over the job at Wiggins Teape and now you're being so kind as well. I'm incredibly grateful.'

'Well, we were all very fond of your dad,' said John, as he looked at his watch and apologised for the length of time the journey was taking. 'I had no idea it would be this slow.'

Road closures, checkpoints and air-raid warnings meant he had been driving for more than six hours.

'I wonder when they will put the road signs back up,' said Madge as they came to a T-junction with no signs showing.

It was almost seven hours by the time she was dropped off in High Wycombe.

'You're here!' Doris and Doreen yelled in delight as Madge walked through the door, and they ran to hug her.

'Hey, my turn!' Mum laughed as she stepped up to embrace

her daughter in a tight hug. 'It's so wonderful to see you, love. It feels like forever since we were last all together. And John,' she said, 'you must stay for a quick cuppa as a thanks for being so kind.'

The few days back as a family passed all too quickly and Doris and Doreen quizzed Madge relentlessly about the German bombers, and anything else they could think of.

'Have you got a boyfriend?' asked Doris, who was told by a laughing Madge that it was none of her business.

She played endless games of Snap with the girls and they even got Mum to have a go with a skipping rope in the back garden. It was almost like those happy days when Dad was still alive. Almost, but not quite.

Once the girls had gone to bed on Madge's last night with the family, Mum grilled her on just how bad the damage was in Dover.

'Come on, love, tell me truthfully. I've heard some terrible things are going on down there. And it nearly broke my heart hearing about all those hundreds of kiddies being evacuated to Wales and taken away from their parents. Auntie Bea said that the mothers were weeping even more than the kids. I'm so glad I brought Doris and Doreen up here when I did,' she added.

'Oh, it's really not that terrible,' Madge said, trying to stay as cheerful as possible before changing the subject, not wishing to worry Lily. 'I've had such a lovely time seeing you all but I suppose I'd better pack for the journey back tomorrow.'

'I don't think so, Madge,' Mum replied, fixing her gaze on

Madge's shocked face. 'Everyone down the greengrocer's was just saying that the Germans are going to land up on the south coast and there's no way in hell you'll be there on your own when the Nazis arrive.'

'Mum, come on, they're just rumours, and in any case, I've got Uncle Mark and Auntie Bea!'

But Lily had put her foot down and no amount of pleading from her eldest daughter would change her mind. There was simply no way that Madge was going to be allowed to return to Dover and that was that!

Because the port of Dover had been designated as a 'Restricted Zone' it was many weeks before Madge was granted official permission to make the journey back to pick up her clothes. By the time she eventually got there, the population of the town had halved as worries over a German invasion increased, causing people to pack onto trains carrying more than 800 people at a time away from the coast. Dover Priory station was eerily quiet and the journey had taken almost twice as long as normal.

Madge was shocked to see that many of the shops on her way back to the family house were boarded up, if not blasted to bits. She looked around in horror and clutched her suitcase with white knuckles as she came to the streets on which she'd grown up. In a nearby road there was a space where Mrs Hanley's house should have been.

Madge stumbled on rubble as she walked towards her childhood home and, finally, stood in shock. The brick walls were still standing, albeit almost completely blackened, but the front door was open and some windows had been blown in. Madge felt a lump in her throat as she thought of all the happy times they'd had there as a family, before Dad had died. She peered into where the window had been and there, on the dust-coated piano, were her mother's brown leather gloves, a treasured gift from husband Charles.

Madge stood outside the blast-damaged house as she remembered how Dad told the sisters that he had bought a special present for Mum's birthday. After being sworn to secrecy the girls were allowed to see the gift that turned out to be the gloves, which he had bought at a shop near Dover Priory station.

'Your Mum has lovely soft hands,' he told the girls, 'and these gloves will keep them warm in the winter.'

One by one the girls had been allowed to try on the gloves and they'd all laughed when Doreen's tiny hands and wrists completely disappeared from view when Dad helped her to put them on.

'They are so soft and smell really nice,' Doris had said in awe.

Mum will be absolutely delighted when I hand these over to her in High Wycombe, Madge said to herself. *Especially as they were the last gift from Dad before he died.* She tiptoed gingerly through the wreckage, picked up the gloves and took one last look around the home that would never be quite the same again.

4

Becoming a Nurse

The first thing Madge did once her move to High Wycombe became permanent was to start looking for a job. In truth, her real ambition was still to become a hairdresser, but she knew there was no way to find the money for the apprenticeship. Instead, with the help of an impressive reference from Wiggins Teape, she quickly landed a job in the secretarial department with Ernest Turner, an electrics company.

There was an active social side to her job and Madge soon became friends with Stella Peaty, who was a few years older and spoke keenly of how wonderful it would be to help the brave, injured soldiers by becoming a nurse. Stella's passion made Madge wonder whether she might also be able to do her bit once she turned eighteen, so the pair started attending Red Cross meetings at Naphill, the headquarters of Bomber Command, where they went on a series of first aid courses and learned how to deal with medical emergencies.

They were encouraged to volunteer as nurses, but the plans were hit by a strange twist of events. During the weeks it took for the volunteer paperwork to be completed, Stella fell in love with and married Eric Moorby, an RAF officer. Just days after the marriage ceremony Stella told Madge, very calmly, that she would no longer be going to the meetings for she wouldn't be volunteering now that she was married. Madge was disappointed to be embarking on her adventure alone but she enrolled anyway and within days she received instructions to report to Stoke Mandeville Hospital to begin training as a Voluntary Aid Detachment nurse.

'Good on you, my girl,' said her mum. 'Although I'll be incredibly sad to see you moving away to live in the nurses' home but you won't be far.' Lily looked thoughtful for a moment. 'I'll tell you what, I was never too keen on that Stella. I think you'll make some much nicer friends at Stoke Mandeville. And by the way, there's something I want to say.'

'You've worried me a bit now,' said Madge. 'What is it?'

'Only that your dad would have been ever so proud of the way you're doing your bit for the country,' replied a beaming Lily before giving her a hug.

On the morning Madge first reported for training at Stoke Mandeville towards the end of 1941, she woke with a sense of nervous excitement. She couldn't wait to get started but she also seemed unable to control the feeling of butterflies in her stomach. She managed to eat only half a slice of toast, before slipping on her coat and shoes and making her way to her new job.

The hospital was divided into two sections. One was for civilian patients from Middlesex Hospital in London and the other was for the 'Services' and was staffed in the main by Emergency Medical Service nurses, a unit set up at the outbreak of war in preparation for the anticipated mass casualties.

When Madge arrived at the hospital reception, a kind-looking lady with glasses and a beaming smile greeted her warmly.

'Hello, dear. We're so pleased to have you. You young ladies are doing wonders for this country. I only wish there were more of you!' She grinned at Madge, who felt a surge of pride rising in her chest. 'Follow me, dear. You'll be working with civilians to begin with, and Rose will show you the ropes. She's been a nurse for donkey's years so there's nothing she can't teach you and she'll be pleased to have you. She has two daughters right around your age.'

Madge quickly settled in, but after following Rose around like a little duckling for a couple of days, her first unsupervised job was to clean the mouth of an old lady, teeth and all.

For Madge, this turned out to be her worst nightmare! The task made her feel so sick she instantly retched into a strategically placed bucket and had to be very careful not to let the old lady's dentures disappear into the bucket as well when she cleaned everything up. Madge was surprised how quickly she got over that little hurdle and realised with a rush of relief that she could do the job after all.

Not all aspects of life at the hospital went as smoothly as the work, though. Her very first shift just happened to fall on the day after the weekly issue of hospital rations. Nurses were given a little string bag which contained portions of sugar, jam, margarine and bread to be eaten as snacks. But when Madge went to collect her allocation there was only dry bread left, and no sugar, which was important to her!

Feeling somewhat dumbfounded, and incredibly hungry, she asked the storekeeper, 'I don't suppose there's any chance I could have a little pot of jam as an advance on next week's rations, could I?'

'Sorry, miss, there's nothing I can do because rules is rules,' he said with a pompous sniff, and proceeded to dunk a biscuit in the cup of tea he was slurping behind the counter.

Madge was far too shy to ask other nurses if she could borrow some jam and margarine, so she ended up eating dry bread until the following week's rations were handed out. *At least I know the system now*, she thought. *I won't let that happen again!*

After just a few weeks treating civilians, Madge was secretly relieved when the head nurse took her aside and said she would be transferred to the services section of the hospital. It was really just a hop across the corridor so Madge didn't think it could be that different and was surprised when she realised that the EMS nurses, which made up the majority, were mostly much older than her. She was in the middle of her first rounds when a tall, broad sister with a heavily starched white cap pulled well down over her forehead and rosy-red cheeks marched into the ward like a ship in full sail. Madge stopped still with her mouth open.

'Right then, you must be Graves,' the sister said with an

Irish accent. 'I see you've got yourself stuck in already so you'll do fine here, eh? You can call me Sister Crowley.'

Madge soon noticed that she was not the only one in awe of Sister Crowley's presence. Whenever she walked into a room not only the nurses but also the patients, whether soldiers, sailors or airmen, would fall quiet.

Sister Crowley's height and demeanour might have been intimidating but she had a twinkle in her eye and Madge learned that as long as you did what was asked, Sister Crowley wouldn't give you any grief. Her ward had to be the best in the hospital, in the country even, and that meant the nurses had a lot to live up to. Sister Crowley made endless, exhaustive checks on the ward inventory and if so much as a flannel was missing a major inquiry would begin and every nurse would be quizzed until the item was accounted for.

She was a stickler for process and insisted that all patients should be tightly tucked in. The open ends of pillowcases had to be pointing away from the ward door and if the sheets' hospital-style corners weren't absolutely perfect, the beds had to be made again. Everything had to be spick and span for Matron's round. Or else!

Madge smiled when Victoria, another trainee, told her that there was no Christmas Day respite for nurses on Sister Crowley's ward. Instead they were instructed to make sure it was 'the best decorated and happiest in the whole hospital'. Not even the young doctors dared to argue with her once they had been told it was their turn to carve the turkey. She made it

clear to everyone that the patients came first under all circumstances.

The demands of 'HMS Crowley', as the girls nicknamed
her, were the furthest thing from Madge's mind some weeks
later as dawn began to rise after an exhausting night on the
men's surgical ward, one of ten wards in the services section
of the hospital. It was one of her favourites because even
though many of the soldiers were recovering from serious
injuries they were endlessly cheerful.

Even at the end of a busy shift, Madge still had a long list of
tasks to complete. Many patients needed help to wash and
there could be thirty in the ward with only Madge to look after
them. On one particular night she realised she didn't know
where to begin – bedpans and bottles had to be cleaned and
sterilised, temperatures needed to be taken and tea and toast
for breakfast prepared. Madge sighed as she remembered sitting in the kitchen with her mum, eating bread crusts, which
Lily always described as 'chef's treat' because of the work she
had put in. On this occasion Madge had over a hundred slices
of bread to cut but there was no one around to distract her
from the boring job. At least there was a very large and sharp
bread knife which should hopefully make the job a little
quicker and easier.

Even though dawn had passed, Madge kept the ward's lights
off so patients could get as much sleep as possible. Suddenly
the sound of footsteps, unusual at that time in the morning,
made her look up and there, silhouetted in the doorway of
the kitchen, was a patient who seemed disturbingly agitated.

Madge recognised him as a man who had previously shown signs of instability after being brought in to hospital suffering from shrapnel wounds sustained on a raid in northern France. Eyes bulging, he marched over, shouting and yelling as he demanded the knife.

She had dealt with rude and grumpy patients before but never anything like this. Stepping back, she stuttered, 'W-w-w-would you like a cup of tea?'

Madge kicked herself mentally for the question but before she could move, the soldier reached out, shook the knife free from her hand, waved it menacingly in front of her chest and was gone as quickly as he had appeared.

By then the commotion had woken several other patients who had seen the man running out into the hospital grounds and security staff instantly mounted a search. Later that morning he was found sitting peacefully in the sunshine on a bench in one of the gardens.

As Madge and a worried hospital security officer stood and watched him being led away to be placed in a 'more secure environment', she said, 'I feel so sorry for the poor soul. He needs help. Who can blame him for being so unsettled after what he must have seen?'

'I know,' replied the security officer. 'It doesn't even bear thinking about what that poor boy's witnessed.'

The incident had upset many of the badly injured soldiers on the ward because they had come to adore their little teenage nurse, who bustled in on duty with a cheerful smile every day. For the duration of that shift, there were touching words of comfort as they urged her 'not to worry' and 'just forget about the whole thing' but once they realised that this remarkable young woman had taken it all in her stride the teasing began.

Vera Clark, who Madge had met shortly after starting work at the hospital and who had quickly become a friend, knew every detail after tuning in to the most efficient communication system in all hospitals – the NGL (Nurses Gossip Line).

'Are you OK, Madge?' she asked, as they queued to get bowls of the thick and creamy pea soup that was such a favourite in the canteen later that day. The concern touched Madge as she nodded in answer to the question.

'Well, if that's the case, you'd better watch out for the bogeyman again tonight,' laughed Vera.

The teasing went on when Madge's shift started again that evening. 'Fee-fi-fo-fum, I smell the blood of an English woman,' said a handsome young lance corporal as he lifted his heavily bandaged hands, pretending to be Dracula. Madge had written letters for him to his parents every week since he was brought into the ward and it was his way of letting her know just how concerned, and grateful, he was.

She was asked if the tea 'really was that awful' and was told never to be late with the breakfasts again 'because you know what might happen'. It was affectionate humour that made her feel as though the boys on the ward were as fond of her as she was of them. They were treating her, without ever overstepping the mark, as one of the gang!

Madge joined in the laughter. If even the most grievously

wounded soldiers were enjoying the fun and nonsense, she thought, then perhaps they could recover to lead a normal life once more.

Just when things seemed to have calmed down, Madge heard steps running along the corridor.

'Watch out because HMS Crowley is as mad as hell,' a laughing young Welsh nurse, Maggie, warned. 'She's on the warpath because that man ran off with a brand new pair of pyjamas from the inventory!'

For the last ten minutes of her eight-hour shift, Madge made sure to keep out of Sister Crowley's way, just in case she was in trouble. At 8 a.m., having clocked off, she walked the ten minutes back to her room and fell into bed with her uniform still on. *Well*, she thought as her eyelids drooped, *if I can survive that, I should think I can survive anything.*

Over the next six months, Madge's routine was much the same, although during that time she was taught how to use the many different medical instruments and types of bandages, and the kindest way to give injections. With the alternating shift patterns, there was not much time for fun but in her spare time she started going to the cinema in the town centre either on her own or with Vera or Phyl, who she'd also become friendly with. After six months Madge was also due a pay rise of one shilling, upping her wages to £1/11d a week. This was especially welcome as she was still paying off the cost of six thermometers that had broken when she put them in a jar that promptly fell off a shelf. That mishap took place in Madge's second month on the ward.

Nurses had to pick up their weekly wages from Matron's office, but by the time they got the money she had taken 2s 6d out for government savings stamps, which were issued in a bid to raise funds for the national coffers as part of the war effort. The Treasury never benefitted for very long, however, as the next time the nurses had a day off they went straight into the post office in Aylesbury and cashed the stamps in!

Just before her eighteenth birthday Madge woke up one morning with the worst stomach ache. She remembered how sarcastic Matron had been when Phyl had asked for the afternoon off because of her monthlies and thought better of staying in bed. Instead Madge joined the group following the surgeon on his ward rounds that morning. Matron was second in line, then came the senior nurses and, being the most junior member of staff, she was at the end.

That turned out to be the best place because the very observant surgeon took one look at Madge and baulked.

'Get that nurse to sick bay straight away,' he said. Matron gave Madge one of her most withering looks, almost as if it was all being put on. Madge flushed red at the reprimand but almost swooned with relief. Just two hours later she had her appendix removed by the very surgeon who had spotted how unwell she looked in the first place.

The following morning, she was still feeling groggy from the anaesthetic gas, which was administered via a rubber mask, when she woke to see Vera sitting beside her bed with a cup of tea and toast.

'I'm glad to see you're still here with us,' Vera smiled.

'I do hope I haven't been an awful nuisance,' Madge replied, wincing at the pain as she attempted to lift herself up to talk to her friend. She gave up and rested her head back on the pillow.

'Hardly!' Vera said. 'You were good as gold on the night shift. But you won't believe what Matron said.'

Apparently, as soon as the surgeon came out of the operating theatre, Matron had rounded on him and asked if the appendix had really been in a bad enough condition to warrant an emergency operation and take her nurse off duty.

'You'll never guess what he said!' Vera went on. 'He told her, "Madam, it was in such a dreadful condition that it is still aching in the jar," and he said it completely straight-faced!'

Madge laughed so much that she almost pulled her stitches.

She recovered well from her operation but not quickly enough to celebrate her eighteenth birthday, which she spent cooped up as a patient. There had been fleeting visits from Vera and Phyl and birthday wishes from many of the boys on the wards, but as the sunny July afternoon wore on it had all the makings of the gloomiest birthday she could remember. The anaesthetic had taken a lot out of her and Madge was taking forty winks when Mum and the girls burst into the ward singing 'Happy Birthday to You', having caught the bus over from High Wycombe once school was finished for the day.

As there were ten wards in the services section of the hospital, when the new rosters went up there was always a scramble among the girls to see where they would be next. As luck would have it, after Madge's return from sick leave she was allotted to the tightly knit team run by Professor Tommy Kilner, one of an elite group of brilliant surgeons who were practising what the hospital called 'plastic surgery'. Along with Sir Harold Gilles he was one of just two plastic surgeons in the country in the early 1920s, and by 1940 he was still one of only four such surgeons.

Pipe-smoking Professor Kilner operated frequently at Stoke Mandeville on Allied air crew, many of whom had fought the Luftwaffe over 'Hellfire Corner' in the Battle of Britain.

'Watch out, Graves,' Clarissa, one of the EMS nurses, warned when the roster went up. 'He runs his operating theatre like a military exercise.'

Madge soon found out, however, that he also loved a bit of fun.

Halfway through an operation in which he was reshaping the distorted features of a once fresh-faced young pilot he said to Madge, without looking up, 'Please remove the patient's glass eye now and put it in this wooden box. Don't drop it under any circumstances,' he added. 'It will then need to be sterilised.'

Because the patient on the operating table was unconscious after the anaesthetic there was simply no way of knowing which eye was the glass one, and when Madge realised she didn't know what to do, she felt very silly. She looked round in desperation for help and spotted one or two of the surgical team doing their level best not to laugh. Madge then looked over at the surgeon and realised he was almost smiling as well.

'Very funny,' she moaned when the penny finally dropped!

Professor Kilner made it clear to Madge and his hand-picked team that successful recuperation was a key element in patient recovery. The sight of young men walking around the hospital with new noses growing on their arms or stomachs became quite normal after undergoing operations that Professor Kilner called pedicle grafts.

Patients also had to wear an 'aeroplane splint' to keep an arm at ninety degrees while the skin that had been grafted grew straight and strong before being transplanted and shaped into a new nose. Madge found that she was in constant demand by men worried about the life-changing injuries and burns they had suffered. They weren't always the most serious, but they were unquestionably the most disfiguring and, as a result, often the ones that caused the soldiers the most trauma.

The fact that Madge had seen these boys walking round the hospital grounds meant it wasn't a complete shock when she first joined Professor Kilner's team, and she found that her endless patience was a huge asset when she stayed behind, often long after her shift was over, to write deeply personal letters to girlfriends and parents for the incapacitated war heroes. She would encourage the boys to open their hearts and help them to add a signature and two big XXs.

Archie McIndoe, a New Zealander, was another plastic surgeon who worked at Stoke Mandeville as well as at the Burns Unit at the Queen Victoria Hospital in East Grinstead. He was always very charming and courteous to staff and patients alike. He and Tommy Kilner were chalk and cheese when it came to the way they dressed for surgery. McIndoe dressed in white, from head to toe, whereas Kilner looked as if he were wearing dark green pyjamas, and his surgical cap was the same colour. The only white items he wore were his boots. Both, however, were unified in telling their patients to look upon their wounds as badges of honour, and believed that the key thing in overcoming their psychological problems was to concentrate on leading normal lives, as much as was possible.

As Madge's experience grew, she was given the responsibility of looking after several wards and became ever more certain that nursing was the route for her. The pace at the hospital increased dramatically with the influx of casualties brought home to England as brutal fighting continued in the weeks after the D-Day landings. It meant Madge was so madly busy she was almost able to forget the bitter disappointment of being rejected after responding to Lord Mountbatten's plea for nurses to serve in the Burma Campaign. When the instructions from the Military Department of the India Office arrived, however, with the news that she had finally been officially accepted, Madge was left with an overwhelming feeling of sadness.

She had witnessed acts of tear-jerking kindness as the wounded warriors in the services section strived to help one another. A soldier on double crutches hobbled the length of the ward to read a newspaper to a young airman with bandages over both eyes. Another with his left arm immobilised in a sling carefully wrote a note to an almost completely deaf and badly wounded lad from one of the artillery regiments, inviting him to play chess. The boys simply refused to give in. Their courage amazed her.

It was little wonder Madge had grown fond of this group of men who had every right to complain about their truly dreadful injuries, but simply got on with life instead.

She hadn't cried when she ran for her life as the Luftwaffe bombed and machine-gunned the good citizens of Dover. Nor had she shed a tear when the deranged soldier threatened her with the bread knife. Now, excited as she was to go on her great journey, it broke her heart to receive news that she was to walk away from a hospital she had joined as an inexperienced teenager and where she had developed into a compassionate and efficient young nurse.

An overwhelmingly delighted Vera, along with Phyl and the switchboard operator were among the first to congratulate her. Madge received endless good luck messages and so many thank-you notes from her boys on the wards that although she wanted to be going closer to the action, where she believed she could make more of a difference, she truly meant it when she resigned from Stoke Mandeville Hospital 'with considerable regret'.

5

Rules and Regulations

Madge had just eight days from the arrival of the letter from the Military Department at the India Office before she was due to report to the designated assembly point at 108 Baker Street, London, on Monday 10 July 1944. Eight days in which to complete an all-too-short notice period at Stoke Mandeville Hospital, buy clothes suitable for the heat and humidity of the Indian subcontinent, say a thousand goodbyes and keep a stiff upper lip at the farewell family supper. Madge was so overwhelmed at just how much there was to do that she couldn't dwell on the butterflies fluttering in her stomach.

Instead she began packing the cabin case and trunk that had been delivered with instructions that the maximum weight allowed would be 'one and a half hundredweight'. The weight limit amused her because they had been told by the authorities at the India Office that most English clothes would not be suitable so she hadn't the faintest idea what on earth they expected her to take to use up that enormous allowance. The letter also warned Madge again not to reveal the slightest hint about the ultimate destination when she filled in the luggage tags and that really made her smile because she didn't know where she would be ending up anyway.

The days passed in a flurry of activity and suddenly the last meal at home was upon her. As Madge would be aboard the troop carrier on her twenty-first birthday, Lily decided to turn the evening from a last supper into an early birthday celebration for her. Madge had been more than pleased to be staying for the last few nights with the family and sleeping in her own comfy bed away from that tiny room at the nurses' home. In spite of the stringent meat rationing that had been in effect for what felt like a lifetime, Lily worked a minor miracle to produce one of her mouth-watering steak and kidney puddings, but Madge noticed that she seemed distracted and was glad that the evening's conversation had been about the future and not the sadness of the past few years.

'With a bit of luck the next time the family is together we will all be back in Dover,' said Madge.

Doris and Doreen had gone to bed and Lily smiled, almost sadly, as she nodded in agreement. But then her face lit up with a flash of humour. 'You know, Doris and Doreen were planning to make you an apple-pie bed as a special going-away surprise, but they changed their minds thankfully and that's why you got those roses in your room instead!' Lily's smile faded again. 'You will watch out for those doodlebugs in London, won't you, love?'

'Of course I will, Mum. Stop fretting. I'll be fine,' said Madge warmly, placing a reassuring hand on Lily's arm.

'I know you will . . . Like you said, we'll all be together in Dover again before we know it.'

Eventually, after finishing their cups of tea, they said goodnight and made their way up to bed, each more quiet and subdued than normal as they contemplated what the unknown future would hold for their family.

The Baker Street billet, with accommodation over three floors and a spacious dining room, was one of many assembly points throughout London for the 250 VADs travelling to India. Another group of fifty were in a Salvation Army hostel in nearby Bloomsbury. Vera had positively demanded she be allowed to show Madge the sights once she arrived in London after spending the weekend up in Sunderland saying goodbye to her parents, but there was no sign of her.

There was a nice crowd in the room which Madge was to share with five other girls, including another nurse called Phyllis Yearron, a VAD who was a good five or six years older than the rest and let slip that an irreparably damaged relationship was among several reasons why she had volunteered for service in the Burma campaign. The afternoon simply flew by as Madge and Phyllis got to know each other better.

It drew to a close when Madge checked in at reception to see if there was a message from Vera but nothing had come through so she joined Phyllis and the other girls for a pot of tea and sandwiches at a Quality Inn. Then off they went to the Empire, Leicester Square, to see *Two Girls and a Sailor* with Gloria DeHaven and Van Johnson. Because of the threat posed by the very doodlebugs Lily had warned Madge about, the screening took place in the cinema's cellar as an extra safety precaution. The Germans had started using these pilotless flying bombs shortly after the D-Day landings and Londoners soon learned that once the strange buzzing noise cut out it was time to race for cover. Madge had heard that air-raid sirens often wailed all night so it was no surprise when the film was halted and ushers gave directions to the nearest air-raid shelter. Posters in the cellar cinema showed a warden blowing a whistle and the instructions 'In a raid do not run. Take cover quietly, then others will do the same.'

Madge and her new gang of friends waited to see what would happen but it soon became clear that no other person was going to leave even though the sirens were by then at full volume. Not wanting to cause a fuss, the girls looked at one another nervously and settled down to watch the rest of the film. Ten minutes later, just as gold-digger Jean (Gloria De-Haven) made a big play for the attention of sailor Johnny (Van Johnson) the film was paused once more. By the end of the third interruption, a handful of the audience eased their way to the exits but the great majority made it quite clear that even the air-raid sirens could not disturb a night in the company of gravel-voiced Jimmy Durante grinding out his much loved 'Inka Dinka Do'!

The all-clear had been sounded by the time they left the cinema and they went straight back to Baker Street in plenty of time for the 10 p.m. curfew and the nightly check to ensure all the girls were safe.

On the way back on the bus, Madge said, 'That was so much fun! It was a shame that the film wasn't in colour, but it was still wonderful. I haven't been to the pictures in ages!'

Phyllis looked preoccupied. 'What would we do if one of those doodlebugs was actually flying over us?' she asked. 'We'd all be goners if one of those things exploded near us.'

'Don't worry,' Madge replied. 'As long as you can hear them coming, you'll be fine as chances are they'll just keep on flying. It's only when the noise suddenly stops you have to worry, as they drop like stones then. The chances of that happening are really small so please don't worry so much.'

But the look on Phyllis's face told Madge that she hadn't convinced her, and she wasn't sure she had convinced herself either.

The next day, Vera finally surfaced at Baker Street, full of apologies as Madge stood shaking her head in mock dismay.

'Honestly it's not my fault this time,' said Vera with one of her big toothy grins, knowing she was notoriously late for everything. 'They cancelled all the trains because they thought that German bombers were going to have another go at the shipyards.'

Once Vera had settled in at Baker Street she suggested they go for an early dinner at a rather expensive-looking restaurant called The Curb.

'I've never even seen a place like this, let alone been in one,' said Madge as they walked through the big, wooden door that was opened by a flunky wearing a dinner jacket and bow tie.

'Vera, I don't know that I've got enough with me to pay for this!'

She knew Vera liked to spend and was more than a little concerned about ending up with half of a rather large bill.

'Oh Madge, don't be silly, it won't be more than five shillings.'

The pair sat down at a table in the corner and a smiling waiter handed over the menu. It made Madge even more dubious because no prices were listed. She knew that Vera, a shameless but wonderfully generous spendthrift, would cover her if necessary but she hated the idea of it coming to that.

'Well, what do you think India will be like then, Madge?'

'Shh!' Madge eyed the 'Careless Talk Costs Lives' poster on the wall. 'You know we're not supposed to talk about it.'

'Oh please, do you really think any of these ladies are Nazis? Honestly, Madge, we're going to be on a ship for who knows how long. Let's relax and have some fun.'

It won't be much fun if we let something out of the bag, Madge said to herself before turning her attention to the menu.

Vera noticed that Madge wasn't really sure what to choose as her main course and asked if she could help.

'I'm still looking,' said Madge. She had already decided on her first course and when a beautifully presented golden brown vol-au-vent with mushroom and chicken filling arrived she worried even more. She had never seen food like it and wondered just how much this fun would cost.

Vera had solved the indecision over their main courses by suggesting she order for both of them and saying that she would keep it as a surprise. Madge actually heard her ask the waiter for 'tarte au lapin'. She didn't know what it would be, but was certainly impressed when a rather splendid and substantial pie arrived surrounded by mashed potato, carrots and green beans.

'What is it?' she asked Vera.

'It's tarte au lapin,' replied Vera, completely straight-faced.

The waiter cut in to tell Madge the answer was actually rabbit pie, but before he could continue Vera insisted that it was guaranteed to be tasty and very tender. 'Sweet little bunnies with twitchy pink noses always are!' Madge wavered for a few seconds before tucking in to the delicious pie. Both girls also had an apple crumble as a pudding because they knew they wouldn't be enjoying such things where they were heading.

When the head waiter delivered the bill after the three-course culinary treat the surprised look on Madge's face prompted him to explain that restaurants were not allowed by law to charge more than five shillings a head.

'I assure you, madam,' he said with a condescending smile, 'that the Ministry of Food New Meals Order of 1942 includes even the Savoy and the Ritz.'

He explained that restaurants had initially been exempt from rationing but this caused upset as wealthier people were accused of supplementing their food allocation by eating out. To create a level playing field, new restrictions were introduced that meant the maximum cafes and restaurants could charge for a three-course meal was five shillings. Unless, of course, there was a cabaret show, in which case there might be an added cost!

'Well,' Madge said, 'I can't believe I haven't been eating at The Curb every night!'

Having settled the bill, the pair treated themselves to another trip to the cinema, this time to see *This Happy Breed* at the Marble Arch Pavilion, with a cast that included John Mills. It was much more pleasant to watch as the evening passed without them being interrupted by air-raid sirens. As the 10 p.m. curfew rapidly approached, the girls hurried to get back to their billet but soon found that Marble Arch underground station was being used as an air-raid shelter. Whole families were bedding down for the night on mattresses they had brought from home. There were babes in arms, toddlers, families eating their dinner. Many found they had a better, safer night's sleep in the Tube stations rather than racing back and forwards from home to the shelters when the sirens sounded.

As the girls tiptoed through, they suddenly caught sight of a large crowd.

'What on earth is that all about?' asked Vera.

'I've got no idea.'

It wasn't until they drew closer that they spotted a jolly lady of mature years in a bottle-green uniform dress and a black beret at the centre of the throng.

'Oh look, it's a WVS tea point,' Madge told Vera. 'No wonder people love these ladies,' she added, thinking of the endless hours they worked to keep the mobile canteens operational.

They watched with admiration as one of the WVS women

handed a steaming mug to a mother who looked at the end of her tether keeping two toddlers in line, then bent to sweep the naughtiest child off his feet and give him a cuddle so Mum had a few moments of peace to have a thoroughly deserved cup of tea.

After weaving their way past the sleeping bodies, mattresses, toys and gas masks that all but blocked the platform, the girls managed to get on a train to Baker Street. Back in their digs, Phyllis Yearron handed Madge a beautifully wrapped early twenty-first birthday present that turned out to be a very smart silver hairbrush with a mirrored back. She was genuinely surprised, having only met Phyllis a few days previously.

'How generous of you!' said Madge. 'Can you believe I'd forgotten to pack a mirror! What would I do without you?'

The realisation that she was perhaps not as organised as she thought she'd been encouraged Madge to make one last check on her cabin luggage case and she decided to go through the contents against the list sent from the Military Department of the India Office again:

EQUIPMENT FOR THE JOURNEY

Cabin luggage must include:
1 pair of navy blue slacks
Sports kit, including rubber-soled shoes
1 jersey or pullover
Bathing dress
1 cardigan

Extra shoes, shirts and stockings
2 pairs blue socks
White felt hat
2 nursing members dresses
Sunglasses
2 aprons
Looking glass
2 caps
Petersham belt
2 thin white shirts and navy blue skirts
Travelling rug

NOTE: VAD members will travel in their coats, navy skirts and white shirts and will carry their overcoats. Civilian clothes are NOT to be taken.

The evening was still not over because the VADs at 108 Baker Street were given their boat and destination index numbers and told to write them very clearly on the labels that were provided. The index numbers were basically a simple security system so there was no way that spies, or even nosy parkers, could find out where they were going.

When the girls were assembled in the dining room an army sergeant appeared and began giving them a short, sharp talk.

'Now, I want you to please listen, ladies. This is of the utmost importance. You must remember at all times that *careless talk costs lives*. Please take a moment to look at the posters that I have placed on the walls.'

Madge glanced at the posters. The slogan on one said 'Walls have ears'. She saw Vera looking at another poster, suppressing a giggle as she read it. It showed a big floppy black fedora decorated with a pretty yellow bow and a slogan that warned 'Keep it under your hat'. Madge smiled to herself. *Very clever*, she thought.

'Thank you, ladies. Bon voyage and goodnight,' said the sergeant as he turned on his heels and walked out of the dining room.

Vera was laughing as she turned to Madge and said there was only one thing wrong with his little pep talk. 'He's presuming we know when and where we are going. The truth is, I haven't got the slightest clue. And neither has anybody else. So who would we talk carelessly to?'

Madge held her hands up in mock surrender and said it had been such a long day it was time for bed. She was asleep within minutes of her head hitting the pillow.

A breakfast of scrambled eggs got the next day underway and the rest of the morning was spent shopping with Vera before watching an afternoon of ballet at the Royal Opera House in Covent Garden. They were well aware this would be the last week to enjoy the delights of London before service overseas so off they went to The Curb again for early evening cocktails and dinner, where Madge placed her gas mask discreetly under the table – so much more preferable to leaving it on view as a stark reminder of the terrifying times in which they were living. And the evening was rounded off with yet another trip to the theatre, this time to see Noël Coward's *Blithe Spirit* at the Duchess near Aldwych.

After many months of endless hard work at the hospital, often on the night shift, making it impossible for them to go out and have fun of an evening, the nurses were creating memories of a war-torn London that would last a lifetime. There was one little problem, however. Life was becoming very expensive all of a sudden and by Thursday morning Madge was down to her last few shillings. There was nothing for it but to make a trip to the bank in the hope that she could arrange for the Maidenhead branch to wire her last £11 to keep her going until the day of departure. What she would do if the money was not available did not bear thinking about.

'I appreciate there are many reasons for getting us together in London for almost a week before we are due to leave,' said Madge over breakfast. 'I mean, boats could be sunk or railway lines could be destroyed by German bombers, but it's certainly been an expensive few days.'

They were informed that they were going to be briefed that night by Miss Gertrude Corsar, the VAD Commandant and Chief Liaison Officer.

'She's the big boss so don't be late under any circumstances,' they were warned by one of the sisters.

'Never mind the *big boss* bit, this briefing has all the makings of being one *big bore*,' said another.

The girls grinned at one another. *I wonder if we'll be like that one day*, Madge thought to herself, glancing at Vera and Phyl.

Far from being a bore, the softly spoken, Forfar-born Scot

soon had the gathering, which included the group from the nearby Salvation Army hostel, listening intently.

'I'm not sure,' Miss Corsar said, 'just how many of you know about our history. We were founded in 1909 with the help of the Red Cross and the Order of St John and by the outbreak of the Great War we had more than two and a half thousand members. Although initially the military authorities didn't want our services on the front line, believing we would be surplus to requirements and even perhaps a hindrance, I am proud to say that time and again we proved them wrong.

'When you arrive in India it is essential that the great traditions of British nursing are upheld and that your personal behaviour is beyond reproach.

'Now we've got that out of the way,' the Commandant continued, 'let's talk about the journey by sea that may take more than a month. I've been told that it can become a little tiresome so let me recommend one or two books to read. Firstly, any by Agatha Christie, plus *Testament of Youth* by Vera Brittain and *National Velvet* by Enid Bagnold. I'm recommending those books in particular because all three authors were VADs,' she added.

'I shall be travelling on the boat with you ladies and I shall be based in New Delhi, where my door will always be open to any of you, whatever type of problem you may have. Now, I know the delights of London are much more appealing than listening to me,' she said, 'so goodnight!'

Her invigorating little pep talk received a standing ovation from nurses who were reassured to know they would have somebody prepared to stand up for them in India.

'Are we allowed one question?' asked a voice from the back of the room.

'Fire away,' replied Miss Corsar.

'When are we actually leaving?'

The reply brought the briefing to an uproarious and amusing end when Miss Corsar theatrically put her index finger across her lips, shook her head and smiled. 'Walls have ears!'

'That was one very likeable and impressive lady,' said Madge as she headed to bed.

'That she was,' agreed Vera. 'I wish I could be like her one day.'

The following morning got off to the finest of starts with a letter from Mum, packed with news of home, including an admission that she'd tried her best but failed to keep a straight face when sisters Doris and Doreen had been late home after the school dance, and, best of all, a confirmation that Madge's £11 was on its way from the bank! Of course, Madge went straight to the Royal Opera House to celebrate. Pleasant as the day was, Madge was becoming increasingly frustrated over the total lack of information about exactly when the nurses' 'big day' would be.

The sheer bliss of a lie-in meant that she missed breakfast on Friday morning but not the issue of smart, olive-coloured, felt-coated water bottles for use in India. Vera had made an early start and left Baker Street on the double so she could be at the

City branch of her bank when it opened, but had phoned the girls to confirm she would be back at 2.30 p.m. After a late lunch in the mess the nurses went to see Buckingham Palace in the hope of catching a glimpse of a royal or two.

In the early years of the war, Buckingham Palace had suffered no fewer than nine direct hits in the murderous German air attacks. Madge and Vera agreed that it was very impressive that King George VI and Queen Elizabeth had turned down officials' requests to move them to safety; like the rest of London, they refused to bend to the Blitz. A surprisingly large number of visitors had come to view the palace on the day Madge and Vera were there but they were unable to see the damage that had been inflicted by a doodlebug the previous month. Palace walls and a summer house had taken the full brunt of the explosion. Madge and Vera lingered for half an hour in the serenity of Green Park, knowing that just a few hours later, the peace would be shattered with the inevitable storm of V-1s.

Time was running short so the duo moved on to Constitution Hill before stopping for afternoon tea and a stroll into the Haymarket to see Ginger Rogers and Ray Milland in *Lady in the Dark*.

Leaving the cinema, Madge said to Vera, 'I don't know about you but I thought the film was very disappointing. I was really looking forward to seeing it too.'

Vera laughed. 'I think you've just become used to a very high standard of entertainment since coming to London, and this evening simply wasn't up to scratch!'

The pair giggled as they made their way back to Baker Street.

The evening looked to be ending on a low note until the VADs were stunned into silence when details of the 'big day' were suddenly revealed. They had just forty-eight hours to get themselves sorted, and then they'd be off. The surprise announcement left Madge in a bit of a pickle and because her mind was turning over at such speed, instead of going to bed she joined a group of VADs who reconvened for a cup of tea at the nearby Moo Cow Milk Bar. Once she was there she found she couldn't relax so she stayed for just fifteen minutes before turning in for the night, and lay awake worrying about how to solve what had suddenly become a very big problem. Madge had promised Mum that she would spend an hour or two saying goodbye to Ruby Toon, her favourite cousin, and the daughter of Dad's sister.

'It's important,' Mum had said, 'because we spent many happy summers with that side of the family when your father was alive. You must make time for all your family.'

Madge eventually fell into a fitful sleep, and dreamed about a faraway land that felt so different from anything she had ever encountered.

On Saturday morning, the usually chatty atmosphere at breakfast was replaced with a sense of urgency as the reality of what was soon to take place began to sink in. But Madge had more immediate worries and phoned Ruby shortly after 7 a.m. Those warnings about security were very much on Madge's mind as she thought about the best way to make Ruby understand the urgency of the request at such short notice without revealing the reason.

They had become very close, however, during the many happy years they had spent on those family holidays and Ruby knew her cousin well enough to instantly detect the strain in her voice.

'Hello, Ruby, do you fancy a drink in the Paxton Arms around lunchtime?' asked Madge.

'That's an invitation out of the blue,' laughed Ruby, 'but the answer is no because the Paxton is closed and so are many other places in Anerley after being hit by a doodlebug a couple of days ago.'

'Oh dear,' said Madge. 'Is there anywhere else we could meet?'

'The damage is terrible,' said Ruby, 'but how about going to see a film? Maybe in Bromley?'

They arranged to meet at 1 p.m. and once the phone call ended a relieved Madge happily waited until her bank opened so she could withdraw £5 before popping off on another shopping spree that turned out to be a disappointment. Toiletries had become increasingly difficult to find and she had run out of clothing coupons.

'This is terrible,' Madge told Ruby, as she viewed a scene of utter devastation after arriving in Anerley by bus. Gentle summer sunshine cast shadows on roofless houses and shops without windows that were yet to be boarded up because the damage was so recent.

As they ate an early lunch, Ruby asked how Auntie Lily had coped without Uncle Charles and Madge told her, with great pride, how Mum had tried so hard to make sure that Doris and Doreen had a happy life. 'She really is a wonderful woman. I'm so proud of my mum.'

They talked and talked in the little cafe where they enjoyed sandwiches and tea before heading off to the pictures to watch Merle Oberon and Laurence Olivier in *The Divorce of Lady X*. As they walked to the bus stop, Ruby couldn't help giggling when Madge said that because of security reasons she wasn't allowed to say when she was leaving.

'You sound like somebody from the Secret Service!' Ruby said. 'I take it you can't tell me where you're going either then?'

'I don't even know myself,' Madge admitted.

When they saw Madge's bus coming round the corner Ruby threw her arms round her favourite cousin in a loving and emotional farewell.

'Good luck, my darling Madge. You are just like Auntie Lily, you know – a very brave lady,' she sobbed.

On the bus Madge glanced at her watch and saw that it was 8.45 p.m. *I'll reach Baker Street in plenty of time for roll call*, she said to herself. But a bomb had landed close to St Thomas's Hospital on the Lambeth side of the Thames opposite the Houses of Parliament. There were no casualties but it wasn't the first time the hospital had been hit – twelve nurses had died in the Blitz of 1940 when it had been hit by a high-explosive bomb. The lengthy delay meant that for the first time in her days at Baker Street Madge missed the curfew that she had so meticulously observed. She found herself in trouble when her apologies and explanation for her lateness were not accepted. *I'll be pleased to be free of all these rules and regulations as of tomorrow*, she thought. But then she felt those butterflies creep back into her stomach as she realised she had no idea what she was getting herself into and what life in India would actually be like.

Sunday 16 July 1944 would become a date etched in the minds of all the 250 VADs who had volunteered in response to the plea from Lord Louis Mountbatten. It was the day on which their five-thousand-mile journey to India would begin. For Madge it meant a 6.30 a.m. start and one last check of the cabin case she had so carefully packed and repacked just to be sure. Everything she would wear and need for the sea voyage was in there and the labels that showed the ID, boat and destination index numbers were firmly secured.

Over breakfast Vera asked Madge how she felt now that the time had finally arrived.

Madge realised then how much the wait had been getting to her. 'The truth is, I'm glad to finally be getting going,' she said.

'Me, too,' agreed Vera. 'It's been a non-stop week, and lots of fun, but I think it's high time we got cracking.'

As it was their final Sunday in London they decided to attend the morning service at St Martin-in-the-Fields church in Trafalgar Square. A short way into the vicar's sermon the unmistakeable groan of a doodlebug could be heard. It became louder and louder and the girls looked at each other and raised their eyebrows. The vicar had to raise his voice to be heard but refused to let the threat interrupt his service. Suddenly there was silence, which was replaced seconds later by the surprisingly distant sound of an explosion. Throughout it all the vicar continued with an unwavering calmness that left Madge convinced somebody up there was looking down on St Martin's that day.

Rather than sit around the mess brooding for the rest of the day the girls decided to go to one last film showing to help them while away the afternoon. *Follow the Boys* was a musical film produced as a war-time morale booster and starred Marlene Dietrich alongside George Raft. But there was no hanging round once the film was over. Curfew that night had been brought forward to 6 p.m. and it was made abundantly clear that there would be very serious consequences if it was not observed by every one of the VADs.

At an early dinner provided by the Auxiliary Territorial Service, who put on a very tasty hot pot in the mess, the nurses began receiving details about the evening's departure. Then everything seemed to happen at once. Organised chaos reigned as trunks and cases were lugged downstairs from the bedrooms. Movement Control officers issued orders left, right and centre and a fleet of heavily camouflaged trucks drew up outside. Madge and all the other nurses found themselves caught up in the hubbub, following instructions and rushing from here to there making last-minute checks. But finally they were on their way.

The journey to King's Cross station was another new

experience for Madge, who had never travelled in a lorry, let alone a three-tonner with a canvas roof. As she sat alongside the other nurses from Stoke Mandeville it all became crystal clear. At long last this was it. The girls were off to war.

6

The Journey Begins

Darkness fell as the VADs joined hundreds of troops boarding the lone train at a strangely quiet but heavily guarded King's Cross station. The train stood at a platform the furthest distance possible from public view. While Madge was sorry to leave the glamour of her London life, with the cinemas, the parks and The Curb, she wouldn't miss the palpable threat that haunted every night there. She didn't feel that she was being brave heading off to India; she believed that all those people living in London with the constant threat of bombs were far braver than she'd ever be.

As everyone began filing onto the train, Madge couldn't help but recall how Field Marshall Bernard Montgomery had stated at a briefing that nurses were the most important people in the army. *Hmm, how strange then that all the male officers are being directed to the first-class carriages while we're all being herded into third class!* At least they were finally told over the tannoy that the destination would be Gourock, a west of Scotland port on the Firth of Clyde near Glasgow. The window blinds were to be kept firmly closed in the hours of darkness, and, when they weren't turned off for safety during air raids, the light bulbs on the train were blue.

An endless mass of cases, trunks and crates had to be loaded onto the train and grumbles began over the lengthy delay.

'This train is about as punctual as you and Phyl,' said a smiling Madge as they settled into the crowded third-class carriage and tried to get comfy.

'Now, girls,' said Vera, 'if any of you start snoring, there's going be a lot of trouble.'

But the delay became so tedious that eventually even the laughing and joking came to a halt.

It ended with the shrieking toot of a whistle and the wave of a green flag at precisely 11.15 p.m., and King's Cross station went into total darkness as the mighty steam-driven locomotive huffed and puffed into the night on a journey that would take close to fifteen hours.

Within an hour the comforting *clickety-click* that resounded throughout the cabin lulled the girls into a deep sleep. Madge blearily opened her eyes as dawn broke and the heavily laden locomotive pulled in to Newcastle to have its depleted coal supply replenished, but she quickly dropped off again, exhausted from her week of excitement. They stopped again at Edinburgh's Waverley station and then at Glasgow before arriving in Gourock at two o'clock in the afternoon.

The Scottish WVS ladies knew just how weary the girls would be after the fifteen-hour journey and were overwhelmingly kind as they bustled about handing out tea and sandwiches.

'Dinna worry, hen,' said one lovely old granny in a broad Glaswegian accent. 'You'll be on those wee boats soon enough.'

As the girls stood looking out across the bay they saw why there had been such intense secrecy over the details of their pending voyage. A massive convoy that would transport more than twenty-one thousand troops to theatres of war in both the Middle and Far East had begun to assemble. Code-named KMF.33, the convoy would involve fifty ships, of which twenty-one were naval escorts. The reason for the hold-up also then became apparent. The vessel on which they would play cat and mouse with Germany's killer submarine 'Wolfpacks' over the next weeks had been busy boarding hundreds and hundreds of troops. RMS *Strathnaver* was one of five similar vessels that became known as the White Sisters of the P&O shipping line. Even after being requisitioned as a troop carrier in 1939 and painted a very sombre grey it was difficult to disguise the elegance and style with which the *Strathnaver* had graced the high seas as a luxury cruise liner earlier that decade. Madge looked at the great ship with awe and the slightest bit of trepidation.

'This is going to be a bit of a struggle,' said Phyl as they approached the tenders, but there was certainly no shortage of helping hands!

'Thanks. You're such a gentleman,' laughed Vera as a burly old boy virtually lifted her into the boat. As the tender taking a group that included Madge, Vera and Phyl chugged across the short distance from the mainland they could see that the port-side bow and decks of the *Strathnaver*, 688 feet in length, were crammed with soldiers cheering and waving. The closer they got to the boat the more noise they made. The nurses had been loudly applauded by the dockers on the quayside but when they got closer to the troopship the noise was like being at a football match.

'Mmm,' said Vera, as she took a long, deep breath. 'Thank goodness that train journey is over. This fresh air is wonderful.'

'Well, it's nice to see we're welcome, even after fifteen hours on the train!' Madge said, and blew a particularly handsome blond soldier a kiss.

As she joined the rest of the girls in waving, she instantly forgot the tiredness of that never-ending train journey on which they had been packed like sardines and instead concentrated on clambering aboard the troop carrier and up a very steep gangway.

A porter greeted them. 'Welcome to the RMS *Strathnaver*, ladies. This way, please,' he said, leading them down the corridor marked 'First Class'.

Madge raised an eyebrow at Phyl. 'This must be somebody's idea of a joke.' Just then, Vera squeezed past them. 'What are you up to?' Madge asked her.

'Picking the best of the bunch,' Vera said, as she almost ran down the corridor ahead of them.

A few twists and turns of the corridor later, and it seemed it was no joke at all. The catch was there would be ten girls to a cabin that usually accommodated two. The plush beds of yesteryear had been torn out and replaced with five sets of two-level bunks. Still, there was a porthole and the bedding looked comfortable enough even if the linoleum-covered floor was a little careworn. Unfortunately, all the cabins seemed to be full.

'Maybe we won't be able to bunk together after all,' Madge said to Phyl, feeling suddenly quite worried.

'Here!' Vera's head popped round the doorway. The Stoke Mandeville girls were lucky; Vera's speed had paid off and she'd nabbed a single cabin in which there were just four bunks. For the next ten minutes the Stoke Mandeville trio actually thought they would have the cabin to themselves, until a weary-looking soul on the verge of tears knocked politely at the open cabin door.

'Hi there. I don't suppose there's space for a little one in here, is there?'

'Come in. Of course there is,' said Madge. 'I'm Madge, and my friends here are Phyl and Vera.'

'I'm Sally, Sally Mallins. You're so kind, thank you. I thought I was going to have to sleep in the corridor,' said the newcomer.

'The cabin may be smaller than a double,' said Madge, 'but we should be thanking our blessings there are just four of us sharing a bathroom instead of nine. And there is a bath, no less!'

She peered into the tiny room and picked up the soap which was labelled as being 'suitable for saltwater'. A sign on the wall declared that there would be fresh water from the basin for one hour in the morning and evening.

'I don't know *what* we'll do with our hair!' Phyl declared.

'Just to help you girls, I will very kindly delay washing my hair until that one hour in the evening,' said a laughing Madge.

'As I found this little haven in the first place, do you mind if I have a bottom bunk?' asked Vera, who was trying to keep a straight face.

To avoid cluttering up the space completely, the girls unpacked only the bare minimum from their cabin cases. With one tiny cupboard and two drawers there was simply no other option.

The nurses may have drawn the short straw with third-class travel on the train journey up to Scotland, but they were in luxury on the boat in comparison to the majority of the men. The girls heard talk of how the lower ranks had been herded in their hundreds like cattle into cargo holds that had been converted into sleeping accommodation even more cramped than the VADs'.

Madge settled in to life on the boat by having her first ever bath in salt water. Then she went with Phyl, Vera and Sally to the 8.30 p.m. dinner sitting.

'This is a bit late to eat, don't you think?' said Phyl. 'Perhaps we should try the seven p.m. one tomorrow night?'

The other girls all nodded but none of them said a word. Their mouths were too full of food as they were all so hungry after the day's excitement.

The four nurses wandered out on deck for a breath of air after dinner and Madge then wrote a letter to Mum and her sisters before tucking herself up in her bunk. She fell into a deep sleep almost as soon as her head hit the pillow.

*

For nearly three years, when on night duty at Stoke Mandeville, Madge had prepared breakfasts at 7 a.m., made tea for the ward, and helped bed-bound patients with their morning ablutions. The realisation that she had entered a very different world came when she awoke at 7 a.m. to a steward knocking ever so courteously at the cabin door.

'Breakfast will be served in the dining room at eight a.m.'

When they arrived back at the dining hall they were presented with a feast. There were bowls of sugar and jugs of milk and butter on every table. Back home, tea was limited to four ounces a week, but there was no shortage on the *Strathnaver*. *No dry toast here*, Madge thought. She couldn't remember the last time she had had a tasty, thick bacon sandwich because rationing meant that adults were allowed just four ounces each per week, along with one fresh egg. On the *Strathnaver* there were even sausages to go with as many slices of bacon as you fancied!

As they tucked in to the breakfast feast, Madge said, 'You know what I couldn't believe? That after all that lovely food last night, the tomato soup and the roast beef and those tasty roast potatoes, they brought round bananas!' Vera chuckled at this. 'I had to look twice at them,' said Madge. 'I hadn't actually seen a banana since I was a child, let alone eaten one. In fact, I could barely remember what they tasted like. But now I do remember – they're delicious!'

Once breakfast was over, she spotted a noticeboard in the corner of the dining hall. On it was a note that all mail had to be in the post box by 11.30 a.m. as the ship was due to set sail that evening. Madge dropped the letter she'd written the night before into the wooden box and wondered when she'd next be able to send word home. Then she followed the swarm of VADs as they went to the Ladies' Lounge, which looked like the inside of a great English country house she had once seen in a magazine. Gentle pastel blue curtains were set against cream and pink coloured walls that featured elegant swans on a lake. Mahogany-coloured tables were in vivid contrast to a herringboned parquet floor. The girls began chatting to while away the time, but Madge could barely focus on what they were saying. She was too busy looking around in awe.

Next, all 250 nurses were ordered to assemble on A Deck, where group Commandant, Miss Corsar, gave a short but entertaining welcome address and underlined the dos and don'ts of life on board the one-time liner that would be their home for the next five weeks.

'Some of you must be wondering,' she said, 'about the guards outside your cabin doors. There is no need for the slightest concern. They're not there to keep you ladies in. Their job is to keep the men out!'

Madge soon found out why exercise gear had been included on the equipment list as the next day all VADs were required to take self-defence classes, which were provided in case they came into contact with the enemy, but Madge couldn't help but remember Commandant Corsar's comments the previous day, especially when she noticed that soldiers were all too keen to volunteer to lend a hand. The girls were shown how to blind an assailant by jabbing their fingers deep into eye sockets, thrusting knees as hard as they could into testicles and jabbing with elbows if they were attacked from behind.

'Pay close attention, girls,' said the burly army instructor at the end of the incredibly tiring session, 'you just might learn something that will save your lives one day.'

They were flipped onto their backs, sent crashing face first into mats, grabbed from behind and squeezed in ferocious bear hugs.

Word quickly spread that there was a shop on board the *Strathnaver* and, best of all, that there was no rationing. As soon as she finished her first self-defence class, Madge was off like a shot to buy Coty face cream, Yardley shampoo, Johnson's baby powder and a great big packet of sweets.

The air of relaxation on board the ship turned to intense activity the following day, however, as tenders buzzed to and from the Gourock quayside to transport last-minute supplies and personnel. From grubby old freighters to elegant one-time cruise liners, there were dozens of boats waiting for the hours of darkness. As Madge watched the evening sun setting over the Scottish hills the huge guns on the foredeck of a battleship just a few hundred yards away captured her gaze. She found it hard to tear her eyes away; the guns were a stark reminder of the dangers they faced.

That evening was the last time she would be allowed on deck without a life jacket. Miss Corsar had just issued the first warning to the VADs that jackets must be worn at all times when on deck, a rule that officers in charge of boat drill were only too keen to reiterate. Madge had heard that they'd even confined a couple of the girls to their cabins for an afternoon!

Evening fell and the turbo generators and electric motors of the *Strathnaver* began to hum. After dinner, Madge retired to the girls' cabin. Portholes had to be covered at night meaning she wouldn't be able to see a thing once the voyage began so she put her life jacket back on and returned to the deck for a final glimpse of her homeland. *I may never see Doris, Doreen and Mum again*, she realised. Tears welled over and she carefully made her way through the moonless night back down to where her three cabin mates were already fast asleep.

A few minutes later, the twin anchors rumbled and grumbled as the *Strathnaver* began to ease away from her mooring. The noise slowly increased and the 22,238-ton vessel began the month-long voyage to Bombay. *This is it*, Madge thought to herself, feeling the ship easing away from port. *This is where my new life begins.*

7

Passage to India

Boat drill on the first day with the *Strathnaver* moored off Gourock had been a relaxed affair that left many of the VADs in fits of laughter and exasperated army instructors shaking their heads in despair.

'Excuse me, Mr Officer sir,' a girl with a delightful West Country burr had asked, 'but would you be so kind as to explain to us what on earth boat drill is supposed to be? I've not never been on a ship like this and I don't know what you're talking about.'

One of the junior instructors could barely conceal his mirth as he replied that it was all about launching the lifeboats and evacuating the vessel in the case of an emergency. 'We will also be teaching you how to put on life jackets that will help you float.'

The exercise quickly degenerated from the relaxed to the almost comical when the girls giggled away after they were told to 'fall in'.

'Is he trying to get us to jump into that freezing cold water?' asked a voice from the ranks.

The instructors courteously smiled through gritted teeth but the laughter stopped instantly when one of the sergeants warned that he was about to 'select a volunteer' and throw her over the side. The point had been made.

Typical man, thought Madge. *We're not part of the military so why should we have a clue what he's talking about?*

Once the *Strathnaver* was at sea, however, the drill took on a new seriousness. There was no joking or laughter as the instructors patiently demonstrated once again how to put on and secure the life jackets, and then jump into the sea once the lifeboats were launched. When they came back to the surface they should start swimming towards the closest lifeboat or life raft.

Madge gradually came to enjoy the drills, and there was a lot of very enthusiastic support from the inordinate number of soldiers, who seemed to be constantly walking past. What did worry Madge was that while there were hundreds of people already on board, she was far from sure if there were enough lifeboats should they be told to abandon ship.

The *Strathnaver* boasted a top speed of 23 knots an hour. If push came to shove, Captain Beck, the *Strath*'s wartime commander, could still order full steam ahead but few of the other boats could match that speed. KMF.33 progressed at the rate of the slowest vessel in the convoy.

One morning, after they had been at sea for a week, a doctor who was due to give a series of lectures to the VADs about tropical diseases joined Madge for a morning stroll on deck. He was one of a small group of doctors bound for the

Middle East and India who had boarded the *Strathnaver* at Liverpool.

After Madge confided in him that she felt a little vulnerable out at sea, having seen the size of the guns on the battleship and being well aware that German ships would be equipped with weapons just as powerful, the doctor turned to her and said, 'I can tell you something that will really cheer you up.'

'Oh, what's that?' Madge asked, intrigued.

'Before boarding this ship I worked in a hospital in the Wirral where lots of wounded soldiers told me the same thing – there is one reason why the German Wolfpack submarines are suffering such huge casualties and that's all due to the tactics of Captain Frederick John Walker. This Captain Walker devised a system that actively chases the submarines instead of waiting for them to attack the convoys, a system that has proved to be hugely successful, and they are the same tactics we are employing with this convoy. So that, miss, is why I firmly believe that this ship will not be sunk.'

'Well, that is a relief to hear, I must say,' said Madge, feeling at least mildly better.

In spite of that, the German Wolfpacks were still a threat so in addition to several destroyers, Sunderland flying boats scanned the seas to provide an extra level of security. The convoy was by now in turbulent waters heading southwest, away from the German-occupied Atlantic coast of France. Whilst the whole coast from the French border down past Spain and Portugal and round to Gibraltar was neutral the waters were still desperately dangerous.

The weather was warming and Madge, who had enjoyed her first week at sea, spent the rest of the afternoon soaking up some sunshine. Vera and Phyl, on the other hand, began to feel seasick as the *Strathnaver* started to pitch in the increasingly powerful swell and they retired to the Ladies' Lounge. Madge went back down to their cabin and used the rare bit of time on her own to have a good browse of the multi-page contract she had signed before setting off. She realised that she'd barely given the terms a cursory glance due to her excitement at being given the opportunity in the first place.

The contract showed that she would be paid £134 pounds per annum for the duration of her service which was more than double the money she received in the early days at Stoke Mandeville Hospital. A fifty-rupee Indian Allowance was added along with a 'free messing and servants' assessment' of 80 rupees. What did surprise her was the fact that the annual pay for the very senior position of VAD liaison officer was just £222 – she had heard of some factory workers who were earning more – and that of assistant liaison officer was £198. One liaison officer and two assistants were appointed to General Headquarters, New Delhi, to advise the Chief Principal Matron of the Queen Alexandra's Imperial Military Nursing Service on problems arising from the service of VADs in India.

Madge had been given an initial uniform allowance of £15 and was pleased to discover that she would also be entitled to an upkeep allowance of £5 after the first year of service, as well as an initial tropical outfit allowance of £10 plus an additional £5 after the same amount of time. Perhaps the week they had spent living the life of Riley in London hadn't been their last chance to shop after all!

Item 14 of the contract concerned travel: 'For journeys performed at government expense after acceptance, first-class railway and equivalent sea travel will be provided wherever possible and, when travelling on duty, subsistence allowance at the rates laid down for similar services in India will also be admissible.'

Madge suddenly remembered the fifteen-hour train journey from London to Gourock and laughed out loud at the first-class railway travel clause before putting the contract back in her cabin case.

Phyl, who had been suffering from a headache, was perking up a bit so Madge went with her and Sally up on deck where they joined a game of cards and a sing-song, before heading off to dinner. When it was time to make her way back down to the cabin, the sea had become so rough that she had to take a firm grip on the rails to steady herself. She was used to the fresh sea air that blew into Dover from the English Channel, but the warm afternoon sunshine, the heavy swell and a strong evening wind buffeting the *Strathnaver* worked like a sleeping pill and she fell asleep the moment she closed her eyes.

That night, Madge dreamed she was in the air-raid shelter at the bottom of Auntie Beatrice's garden in Dover sheltering while the Luftwaffe dropped bombs, but the sound of the explosion wasn't quite right. Her sleep became more and more shallow, but the explosions continued.

Madge suddenly sat up straight in the darkness. *Maybe it's another of those doodlebugs like there was in London*, she thought, but the sound it made was different. It was more of a dull thump.

'What's that, do you think?' Phyl whispered from the bottom bunk.

'Well, I thought it might be a bomb, but I'm not sure it can be out this far from land.'

Thump. Another went off to make Madge realise this wasn't a bad dream. She was now wide awake. Then there was another. She knew it wasn't one of the high-explosive bombs the Germans dropped on London. That noise was deafening. And surely they must be beyond the range of doodlebugs? It had to be the depth charges that they had been told about in the briefing the day after they boarded the troopship. Another dull crump, rather than an explosion, confirmed her initial suspicion and Madge just drifted back to sleep when things quietened down.

The atmosphere at breakfast the following morning was subdued. The girl sitting next to Madge told her that apparently one of the destroyer escorts had been sunk during the night. The thought that so many sailors may have given their lives to protect the convoy had many of the nurses in tears.

The week that followed was a quiet one as a throat infection broke out. Madge got rid of her sore throat by doing exactly what Mum had taught her as a child, which was to put two big teaspoons of salt into a glass of warm water and then gargle until it was all gone. Finally, Sunday dawned bright and beautiful as the turbulent seas of the Bay of Biscay began to calm.

The enthusiasm of the young padre who led the Sunday service raised the spirits of everyone on board as he spoke about his hopes for a kinder world for all.

The choice of the hymns during the service didn't go unnoticed at a time when the threat of German U-boat attacks was at its highest. Madge loved hymns but struggled to stop herself from smiling at the sheer irony when two particular lines of an English classic were sung with great enthusiasm:

Oh, hear us when we cry to Thee, for those in peril on the sea!

Madge spent that afternoon basking in the warmth of the sun and stayed to watch it set on the horizon. She looked over the side of the boat to see blue-green phosphorus glowing in the water alongside the *Strathnaver*. It was unlike anything Madge had ever seen but she couldn't help but be distracted by thoughts of home. The following day would be her twenty-first birthday, and the first she had spent without her family. She couldn't bear to think about what the family was doing and whether they were all safe and sound, so she went straight to bed without dinner.

'Happy birthday to you!' a not altogether unpleasant chorus of voices sang, waking her in the morning. Lined up in the narrow cabin, Phyl, Vera and Sally sang to her. They looked like schoolgirls and Madge laughed. It wasn't Dad on the piano or Mum, Doris and Doreen but she started the morning with a smile. The girls let Madge use the bathroom first even though it wasn't her turn.

Behind the door, she heard Vera whisper, 'One way or another we'll make sure that Monday the twenty-fourth of

July 1944 is a day she will remember . . . Well, after boat drill, of course,' and Madge wondered what on earth they could have planned.

The girls spent drill giggling and were told off for being so distracted. Alcohol was strictly forbidden so a glass of champagne for the birthday girl and her lunchtime companions was out of the question, but that didn't stop Vera telling everybody she came across that it was Madge's twenty-first. An older VAD performed a funny little Charleston-style dance as she walked past smiling and sang, 'Twenty-one today, twenty-one today, she's got the key of the door, never been twenty-one before.' As she turned back to wish Madge lots of luck she said, 'I read somewhere that you had to be twenty-one before you could even apply to join the service. So you must be the youngest girl on the boat, eh?'

No sooner had lunch finished than afternoon tea began. Vera, the centre of attention as usual, pretended to be a magician and pulled a heavily starched serviette off the top of a beautifully decorated birthday cake.

'All the way from Sunderland,' she said in her broad Geordie accent.

Madge was stunned. 'Vera, how did you wangle this?' she said, as she stared at the giant Victoria sponge. How Vera had managed to carry the cake from Sunderland to London, then up to Gourock and had kept it from harm as the Strathnaver ploughed through the stormy seas of the Bay of Biscay had to be a minor miracle. It turned out that Vera's mum and her neighbours had saved their ration coupons to club together for enough eggs, butter and sugar to bake a surprise Madge would never forget. The cake looked far too good to eat so it was decided to keep it for the party that evening.

The girls finally had an excuse to glam up and the young officers, who got wind of what was going to happen that evening after dinner, dressed in their khaki tropical gear, and slicked on the Brylcreem. It was stated very clearly in the contract from the Military Department of the India Office that civilian dress was not to be included in luggage so, party or no party, the girls had little option but to wear their regulation navy blue suits and thick cotton stockings, which were so unbearably hot.

As a birthday treat, before the party her cabin mates had allowed Madge the full sixty minutes of the fresh-water hour and she had opened a new packet of Coty bath cubes as well as leaving hair conditioner on for those all-important extra minutes as she enjoyed the sheer luxury of a fresh-water bath!

The result was that her fair hair glistened and the bright red lipstick she had borrowed from Vera added extra glamour to the golden tan that had developed. When Madge strode into the Ladies' Lounge that evening she felt wonderful, and even more so when a spontaneous round of applause broke out, followed by a rousing three cheers. The Ladies' Lounge was festooned with multi-coloured paper decorations and Madge knew instantly who was responsible because Vera and Phyl had mysteriously disappeared for some considerable time earlier in the day. The girls were over the other side of the room admiring a colourful cartoon that one of the soldiers, an art teacher in civilian life, had drawn. It portrayed Madge's head imposed on the body of Hollywood sex symbol Jane Russell, who was also a WW2 pin-up.

'Not too sure the artist got this quite right!' laughed Vera as Madge walked over.

A few minutes later she was watching the fun when a certain somebody tipped off a nice-looking young man with the smoothest of voices that the birthday girl adored Bing Crosby. Moments before the cake-cutting began, he started up with 'You Must Have Been a Beautiful Baby'. It was so perfect that the girls insisted on an encore and this time they all pointed meaningfully at her when he got to the 'cos baby look at you now'.

A huge cheer erupted when Madge finally cut the cake and then the party really started. A gramophone burst into life and after a moment or two of almost teenage shyness the floor was heaving as the dancing began. No Jimmy Durante and his 'Inka Dinka Doo'. This was more Glenn Miller and the Andrews Sisters. There were Bing Crosby classics and good old English songs like 'Roll Out the Barrel' and 'Doing the Lambeth Walk' with requests for 'I'll Be Seeing You' and 'Heart of My Heart'. The VADs were outnumbered by the soldiers and were danced off their feet.

Once they'd run out of records, it was decided that a singsong was in order. Three or four groups of officers were only too keen to lead the frivolities. They drew lots to see who would go first and three Welsh boys put on a performance that was an absolute credit to the 'land of song'. The harmony they produced in their version of 'Men of Harlech' was wonderful and everybody in the room joined in when they thundered out the Welsh national anthem.

Four lively Scots stepped up next and had the place in stitches by announcing that after travelling up to Gourock 'on the slowest train in Britain' they would start with 'The Bonnie Banks O'Loch Lomond'. After two Harry Lauder classics that included 'A wee Deoch an Doris' they made everybody laugh by asking if the bar was still open!

But Madge missed all of this. Once the birthday cake had been cut she had gone up on deck for a breath of fresh air. She looked out towards the back of the boat and tried to conjure up the white cliffs of Dover. She had a knot in her stomach. Phyl came up the steps.

'Are you all right?'

Madge turned her back so she wouldn't see her tears. 'Just getting a breath of fresh air. I'm fine, really! You go back in and enjoy the fun.'

'Well, if you're sure . . .'

Madge waited until she heard the door shut behind her friend. She knew the evening had been wonderful, and she felt so grateful to the girls for making her birthday as special as possible under the circumstances, but it was never going to be a true celebration without her family there too. She suddenly felt so unbearably homesick that she went straight down to the cabin and cried herself to sleep.

8

Life Jackets and Pith Helmets

With Morocco on the starboard side and Portugal fittingly on the port side security was at a maximum as the convoy began to approach the notoriously dangerous Strait of Gibraltar. After years of darkness because of blackouts in Britain it was somewhat of a surprise to see Gibraltar bathed in light in the distance. The Strait which separates the Mediterranean Sea from the Atlantic is less than nine miles wide at its narrowest point and while German U-boats had paid a fearful toll – nine had been sunk and another ten badly damaged in the area – they still posed a serious threat to Allied convoys.

Convoy KMF.33 had stood off the coast of Portugal for much of the afternoon and slipped into the Med in the darkness without incident. It was a rocky night on board the *Strathnaver* as it ran through the Strait of Gibraltar with its engines at full speed. It was a much slimmed-down version after a number of the Royal Naval escorts that had shepherded the convoy to safety from Gourock handed responsibility to other destroyers to provide protection en route to Port Said in the north of Egypt. A number of troopships had also moved away in the night, but both the *Strathnaver* and her sister ship the *Strathaird* continued on the journey to Bombay.

The calmness of the Mediterranean and the bright summer sun meant that A Deck was crowded with sun-seekers the next morning. But Madge wasn't one of them.

The VADs had already been given a general warning about the dangers of keeping a diary but the previous day one had been reprimanded in front of the entire mess hall for keeping a notebook. The army officer who was in charge of the brief-ing made it very clear that the main reason the military were banned from keeping diaries was the worry of important information falling into enemy hands. Madge had paid par-ticular notice to what was said as she was also writing regularly in her own notebook; she had promised her sisters that she would keep a diary during what she hoped would be happy times overseas. After that incident, though, she made a careful examination of the contents of her little book but remained convinced there was nothing that would be in the slightest of interest to the enemy whatsoever.

Madge kept the diary upbeat and didn't mention things like the German attack on the destroyer or the endless nightmares the nurses on board suffered over the safety of their loves in cities still being bombed back in the UK. So she happily con-tinued until the next VAD was reprimanded, in even sterner terms than the last. It was made clear that, if necessary, the ultimate sanction would be invoked and the implied threat of a court martial put an end to her diary too.

In any case, Madge had plenty of studying to keep her

occupied. A series of mandatory lectures on tropical diseases were given in the Ladies' Lounge to prepare the VADs for the medical problems in India and Burma that they would rarely have encountered at home. The first half dozen had the nurses' full attention but they became repetitive and Madge would regularly find herself staring out of the porthole, mesmerised by the blue of the sea. The lessons certainly sank in because Madge could recite by heart, among many others, the fact that onchocerciasis (river blindness) was caused by worms or sandfly, sandfly fever was a virus carried by midges, sleeping sickness was caused by tsetse flies, typhus fever was an infection carried by lice, ticks, mites, flies or rats and yellow fever was a virus transferred by the bite of a mosquito.

The 180 wpm shorthand speed Madge had achieved at the commercial college was helpful when it came to taking notes. Tedious as the lectures were, they provided early warning of the complex problems the VADs would soon be facing.

One night at supper, Madge found herself engaged in conversation with a charming ex-surveyor called Stanley. They had been exchanging light-hearted banter when suddenly his expression became intensely serious. He checked that their neighbours weren't listening and leaned in. 'If I tell you something, will you swear not to repeat it?'

'Well . . . I suppose so.'

Stanley pulled out a cutting of a *Daily Express* article from January 1943. It told the story of RMS *Strathallan*, another of the 'White Sisters', and the danger it had faced in the Mediterranean. Early in November 1942, the troop carrier had come under attack when it took the same route as the KMF.33 to take Allied personnel to Morocco and Algeria. Just after midnight on 21 December disaster struck. Two torpedoes were fired at the *Strathallan* by German U-boat *U-562*. One missed, but the other scored a direct hit and exploded in the engine room. Water flooded through a gaping hole on the port side and the ship began to keel.

Fires broke out below deck as men scrambled for safety but two Queen Alexandra nurses, Sister Julie and Sister Olive, went deep into the lower levels of the ship where they knew there would be men in the on-board hospital in desperate need of help. By now the tiny room was beginning to fill with more injured men seeking medical aid. Men with serious burns. Men coughing and choking from smoke inhalation. Men half blinded by oil that had sprayed everywhere in the engine room. The sisters treated every one of them.

The *Strathallan*, though irreparably damaged and listing at a frightening angle, simply refused to go down. The sea was calm and several Royal Navy destroyers were steaming to the rescue so a halt was called to the evacuation until first light in the morning when nearly five thousand people were saved in one of the most successful rescue operations in British maritime history.

'What a relief that so many were saved but what a terrible thing to happen!' Madge whispered when she had come to the end of the article.

There had been no mention whatsoever aboard the *Strathnaver* of the tragedy and after carefully reading the cutting, Madge gave a shudder before consigning the evening to memory and keeping her vow of silence. The fear of German submarines was bad enough as it was, she didn't want to make the other girls any more panicked.

Within days convoy KMF.33 reached Port Said and slipped into the Suez Canal, where the heat was so intense it left Madge gasping. If it was that hot in the Middle East, Madge began to wonder exactly what she would be letting herself in for in India.

Commandant Corsar was so concerned about the effects of the sun that her contingent of VADs was issued with pith helmets. The girls were told that if they were on deck between 9 a.m. and 5 p.m., the big white helmets, made of cork and covered in white cloth, must be worn at all times. Madge hadn't been given so much as a tin hat during that week of bombing in London so to be told to wear a pith helmet amused her no end.

Miss Corsar also decided that it was time for the issue of tropical kit, which was a lot cooler than the navy blue outfits that soaked up the heat even in the shade. The tropical blouses were still navy blue but made of a much lighter and cooler cotton, but the problem was that if the girls wanted to enjoy the sunshine, they now had to wear a pith helmet as well as a life jacket. It was all so cumbersome, but at least the life jacket ruling was eased when the *Strathnaver* got into the Suez Canal.

'Dear old Gertrude really has no other option,' laughed Vera. 'It's so narrow it's almost a physical impossibility to fall into the Suez Canal,' she said, eliciting giggles from the other girls.

Certainly, the biggest surprise for Vera, Phyl and Madge was not so much the 102-mile length of the canal but the width. At just 200 to 300 feet wide, Madge could look down from A Deck and just see desert either side of the boat, no water at all. After being at sea for so many weeks it was comforting to see dry land again with people and little settlements with their lights glowing in the dark.

The first evening they were on the Suez Canal, Madge, Sally, Phyl and Vera decided to take a moonlit after-dinner stroll on A Deck. The burning heat had eased and Madge was happily chatting to Vera when a cheeky-looking and unusually tiny officer gave them a mock salute and grinned. Without any invitation, he walked alongside the girls and began talking to them about the day the Suez Canal was opened.

'Is this chap going to tell us a joke?' whispered Phyl.

'No, but he sounds like a bit of fun,' said Sally as several other nurses stopped to listen and asked him to speak up because the wind was making it difficult to hear.

He said a French consortium had financed and constructed the canal and the honour of becoming the first vessel to navigate the waterway had been bestowed on the French Imperial yacht *L'Aigle*, with Empress Eugenie, wife of Napoleon III, on board.

The night before the official opening in November 1869 a huge fleet of ships, including HMS *Newport*, drew up behind it. That was until Commander George Strong Nares (Royal

Navy) ordered a total blackout on board his vessel and skilfully navigated it to the head of the queue in front of *L'Aigle*.

The French did not see the funny side when they woke to find the entrance to the canal blocked and were even less amused when the glory of becoming the first to sail from the Mediterranean to the Red Sea was snatched from their grasp by HMS *Newport*.

A sizeable crowd had gathered alongside the four girls and everyone began to cheer the fact that the Royal Navy had left the French in second place.

'There's more to come so let's have a bit of hush,' the little officer said with a grin.

When the noise had quietened, Madge's new friend added that the Admiralty were so upset over the diplomatic incident caused by Commander Nares that he was issued with an official reprimand. 'They were so irate, in fact, that a few months later Nares was promoted from commander to captain,' said the officer, who then bowed to the laughing crowd and strolled off into the darkness.

'That was great!' said Madge. 'I think he may have told that tale a few times, but it was still really entertaining.'

The mood on board the ship brightened considerably over this stage of the voyage. The VADs never tired of throwing pennies to the 'gully-gully men' who were stark naked and would happily dive from their 'bumboats' into the grubby water to retrieve the coins. In return the men had devised an ingenious way of sending up, by rope, bunches of bananas, sponges, bags of nuts and even some erotic carvings which

Madge and her friends took one look at and burst into giggles. British troops guarding both sides of the canal made a point of waving and whistling to the nurses, and the nurses were so relieved to see some new faces that they blew lots of kisses and waved back.

There was a three-day stopover in Suez, where the remaining convoy refuelled, took on new supplies and, most important of all, filled up with fresh water. That meant that Madge, after days of having to bathe in sea water, could indulge in the ultimate luxury of a long lazy soak in fresh water. The VADs weren't allowed off the boat during the short break in Suez, but the joy of a fresh-water bath full of Coty bath cubes and the lifting of blackout restrictions, which meant that the girls could continue to read after dark, helped to ease the disappointment of not being allowed to explore.

Several of the smaller ships had gone their own way after the stopover and what remained of convoy KMF.33 resumed the voyage. Because the slower vessels had left, it meant there was no need for speed restriction. Even so, it wasn't until well into the Indian Ocean and the home run across to Bombay that the full splendour of the *Strathnaver* was revealed. As the knots slowly increased and the bow lifted and plunged, Madge gripped the railings round A deck with both hands when she gazed over the side. A pod of dolphins raced with ease alongside the troop carrier and the wind was so strong it almost took her breath away. Madge, for once, was glad she was wearing a life jacket. She took deep breaths of the bracing fresh air and looked out across the horizon. *Finally, this feels like an adventure*, she said to herself.

Not so for Vera and Phyl, who once again suffered the tummy-turning misery of seasickness. Instead of staying on deck and letting the fresh air work its magic the girls went down to their cabin which made them feel even worse. Madge reminded them that the best thing to do with seasickness was to look at the horizon, never the sea. But they didn't take her advice.

In their absence, Madge got chatting to some of the other girls on board. Some were fun from the moment they got up to the last minutes of the day while some would never talk but it was clear from the sadness in their faces that they were troubled. Really troubled. Others were looking for a new start to life. There were girls determined to forget the bitterness of broken marriages and there were wives who felt that by volunteering for nursing service in the Far East they would be closer to their husbands' suffering as Japanese prisoners of war.

There were also the same social divides which blighted society back home, and it soon became apparent that some of the VADs had signed up wanting to 'do their bit' but not really to get their hands dirty.

Four weeks had passed and they were on the last leg of their journey. 108 Baker Street felt like a lifetime ago. Vera and Phyl had been holed up in the cabin on and off for almost a week, and Sally was also feeling seasick. *Poor girls, I do feel sorry for them*, Madge thought. *But I'll be damned if I let them waste their final days on board!*

On the penultimate night of the journey, Madge got up and handed her travelling companions their life jackets. Mimicking their boat drill instructor, she said, 'Fall in; we're going up on deck.' The act was so corny the cabin filled with laughter and the sickly trio stumbled to their feet and followed her. The sea had calmed to a millpond and they were just in time to enjoy a sunset of such beauty that it almost eased the nausea, and they even managed a nibble or two at dinner.

As their time on board the *Strathnaver* came to an end, promises of undying love were made. Lovers kissed tenderly under the stars. Proposals came from men on bended knees. Dreams of a future free of war and destruction were woven. Military and home addresses back in Blighty were exchanged. Couples still strolling on A Deck as midnight approached were in despair that they hadn't plucked up the courage to say the things they meant to say before time ran out.

'It was probably just as well they didn't,' Madge said to Vera and Phyl with a wry smile. 'Imagine what sort of mess some of them could have got themselves into!'

9

Arriving in Bombay

As the VADs stepped onto Indian soil for the first time they were greeted by raucous cheering and a blizzard of farewell kisses blown by troops aboard the *Strathnaver*. The wolf-whistling and waving was soon replaced by an extended round of applause which showed just how aware the soldiers were that these could be the women, in the brutal months ahead, on whom their lives might depend. With the pride of the troops behind them, the smartly dressed contingent, with their shoulders back and their heads held high, marched towards an insecure future.

Commandant Corsar had issued instructions the night before that in addition to the standard tropical kit, stockings were to be worn when it was time to disembark. The problem was that the cotton stockings made Madge's legs itch in the heat and her pith helmet was so big she had to hold her head high to stop it falling off.

'We look like extras in a Charlie Chaplin film!' she said to Phyl and Vera. She was sad to be saying goodbye to the ship after such a wonderful journey and wondered just how many of those boys would live to see their loved ones back home again.

Before she'd arrived in Bombay, Madge had visions of pink palaces, holy men, the Taj Mahal, princesses dripping in gold, elephants and the Himalayas. The reality, after the troopship docked that August, was somewhat different. Just three months earlier a freighter, the SS *Fort Stikine*, had arrived from Birkenhead on Merseyside with a cargo that included 1,395 tons of explosives, torpedoes, mines, shells, Spitfire fighter planes and £890,000 in gold bullion. Two days later, with the *Stikine* berthed in Victoria Dock, smoke from a fire that started in one of the holds was discovered, but by then it was too late and a call was issued to abandon ship. A massive explosion cut the ship in half. A second explosion was so enormous that it caused tremors which were registered more than a thousand miles away in Simla.

More than eight hundred people died in the incident. Thirteen ships were destroyed with two blown out of the water. Debris was hurled almost a mile away. Buildings burned for days and rubble-strewn streets took weeks to clear. Thousands were left homeless and the waterfront was a scene of such utter devastation that when she arrived, Madge assumed Bombay had been bombed by the Japanese. *It looks just like the destruction caused by the V-1 rocket at Anerley*, she thought.

The ruined harbour was a very sobering introduction indeed to Bombay, where the heat of the day had long since eased but been replaced by a humidity so stifling that by the time the VADs had marched the short distance to Victoria

Terminus station they dripped with perspiration. The sandwiches and iced drinks provided by the local Women's Voluntary Service were particularly welcome and reminded Madge of the time she saw the much loved WVS ladies dispensing tea and TLC on a crowded underground platform in London.

As the ambulance train left Bombay the nurses were more than grateful for the chance to freshen up and catch a quick nap. The four girls were dropped off at Kirkee station at 10.30 p.m. The drive to their destination, a transit camp, took less than fifteen minutes but it was the most exciting car ride Madge had had in almost five years because the street lighting was actually switched on and she marvelled at the sight from the window. Being late, there were many people, including children, sleeping on the pavements with only a cloth covering them. A small number were wandering along the street, while a few very old cars and lorries travelled back and forth on the main road.

When the VADs arrived at the transit camp they discovered it was an unused wing of a hospital with just fourteen beds to a ward so they had plenty of space for everybody to spread out, which made a pleasant change. In addition Madge, Vera and Phyl were once again together and by 11.30 p.m. that night three very tired but contented young nurses were all fast asleep. Sally had been billeted in another ward.

It was the first time Madge had slept under a mosquito net and the following morning they were shown how important it was not to leave the slightest crack through which even the tiniest insect could slip through.

'It is vital,' said the sister demonstrating how to seal the nets, 'that you ensure the curtains overlap because you can catch malaria from just one mosquito bite and could end up carrying it for the rest of your life. Once the curtains are overlapping make absolutely certain the bottoms are well tucked in.'

A smile crossed Madge's face as she suddenly had a vision of a sari-clad Sister Crowley at Stoke Mandeville telling her, in that lovely Irish brogue, to make sure the sheets were very firmly tucked in. Also that there was a right way and a wrong way to make hospital corners 'and then there is my way!' she would say.

At breakfast the contingent were all lined up, given a series of injections and a few hours free to recover. As they walked away from the clinic Madge said to Vera and Phyl, 'I'm used to being the one carrying out the injections, not having someone else stick needles in me.'

'I know,' Phyl agreed. 'I'm not sure that nurse had the best bedside manner either. She practically stabbed me with the syringe!' she laughed, as they all rubbed their sore injection marks.

That afternoon they were officially greeted by the Governor of Bombay's daughter, Mary Colville, who cheered them up by saying that after the heat of Bombay they would find Kirkee a little cooler.

'It's almost two thousand feet higher and the humidity is nowhere near as bad,' she explained. 'Nevertheless, you will still find the heat a lot different from home. It takes a while to acclimatise, but you will get used to it over time and you'll wonder how you ever coped with British winters!'

Miss Colville, in her cream linen shirt-dress with short sleeves and blue buttons from the neck to waistline, went on to say that there were two reasons she felt great personal pleasure in welcoming the group to India. 'The first is because you remind me of the days when I served as a VAD in Lanarkshire in Scotland. They are fond memories of mine. And the second is that the Kirkee military hospital in which you are based is where I also help, and it is desperately in need of more nurses. Your presence there will be greatly appreciated.'

Because of the tremendous shortage of nursing staff Commandant Corsar's VADs were given just three weeks to acclimatise, during which they worked one full day but otherwise only mornings. Considering the fact that newly arrived troops were given three months to get used to the new environment, Madge thought that was a pretty tall order.

A few days after their arrival the nurses were ordered to assemble in the hospital grounds. Miss Jane Amelia Patterson, Chief Principal Matron, had travelled from New Delhi to inspect the detachment.

'It is important to set a good example and show everyone that British nurses offer total commitment as well as hard work,' she said.

The smiling head of British nursing in India was in her fifties and instantly impressed Madge with her no-nonsense attitude when she told the VADs about her happy memories of training as a young nurse at Middlesex Hospital in London from 1913 to 1917. She also mentioned in passing that she had served in France in 1940. Her bravery in nursing on the front line at one of the most testing times for Allied forces during the war in Europe struck an instant chord with Madge. *I'll put everything I have into this*, she vowed to herself, feeling in awe of this inspiring woman.

After making a point of thanking everybody for volunteering, Miss Patterson explained that some of the postings would be lonely. 'Feeling homesick is inevitable. It will take time to understand the new culture and language. So if you wish to be posted alongside friends, please let the authorities know.' Madge, Phyl and Vera raised their eyebrows at one another. Miss Paterson smiled as she continued: 'There are long hours and hard months ahead so be sure to enjoy every minute of the good times in Poona, which is about half an hour away and where you should head to for a night out or to do some shopping.'

'I thought she was very impressive,' said Madge as the girls went for tea and cake after the invigorating address. 'She was modest and I liked her straight-talking honesty, and she's obviously a very brave woman. I thought she came over as very compassionate too.'

A few days later, the nurses were entertained at a dazzling formal Welcome Ball at Government House hosted by Sir John, Governor General of Bombay, and Lady Colville. There was a growing acceptance that the final years of the Raj were fast approaching but from the array of gowns and the glitter from numerous diamonds, sapphires and rubies adorning the wives of senior civil servants and army personnel, it would have been impossible to tell.

The elegant saris and the natural beauty of the wives of senior Indian personnel sprinkled the ballroom with colour and glamour in what was almost a fairy-tale setting. Crystal chandeliers, an army band playing the most beautiful Viennese waltzes and torch-lit gardens under a full moon were part of the mystique. To add to the pomp and circumstance army officers were in their dashing formal dress, which featured gold-braided scarlet jackets and a red stripe down the side of their black trousers. But it was the VADs who stole the show. They looked splendid as they marched in together wearing their caps, aprons and dresses.

'This is like being in a film,' Madge said to Vera. 'The music, the food, the beautiful gowns . . . Everything is so perfect.'

Later in the evening several of the girls strolled onto the terrace of Government House for a breath of fresh air and a cigarette or two. Phyl had never smoked before but thought if there was ever a night to give it a go, it was this one. She nudged Vera, who raised an eyebrow as she passed her a cigarette from her engraved silver case. Phyl lit it and copied the others as they inhaled then exhaled the smoke through pursed lips. After coughing and spluttering for a few seconds, she decided to give up and stubbed out the cigarette. 'It might look elegant,' she said, 'but I can't see what the fuss is all about.'

Once they were back inside they saw that they'd been bitten all over the back of their legs. The mosquitos weren't their only problem, either. The humid atmosphere meant that Madge's lipstick had melted and her skin felt like an oil slick. Madge, Vera and Phyl went to the ladies' room to blot their faces with tissue.

'I just can't get rid of the shine,' Vera complained. 'I can't look like this the whole time!'

'Aha!' An elegantly dressed older woman who Madge thought was probably an army wife overheard the conversation. 'The secret is to use as little make-up as possible. Make sure your powder compact is full. And don't make the same mistake all the others do when they first arrive. They love to sunbathe and think they look so attractive with a tan, but the sun will ruin your lovely peaches and cream complexions and you will end up a wrinkly old prune like me,' she added, before returning to the party, leaving a trail of a faintly floral perfume behind her. The girls looked at one another, astonished and smiling at the encounter.

When they returned to the grand room where the ball was being held the master of ceremonies announced that the next dance would be the last waltz, which prompted Vera to express concern that their gold carriage home would turn into a pumpkin on the stroke of midnight.

'No need to worry about that,' laughed Madge, 'but I certainly can't see any sign of four prancing white stallions either.'

'We should be so lucky,' chuckled Vera.

Instead, the perfect end to a wonderful evening came when the same fleet of station wagons that had transported the

VADs on their first night on Indian soil also took them back to Kirkee.

'I could get used to a life like this,' said Madge.

The three girls pushed their beds together and sat up late into the night talking about the ball. They made a vow there and then to follow the order to enjoy themselves to the bitter end, and they would soon find that there would be no shortage of posh afternoon teas, cocktail parties, dinners and dances. Madge was particularly thrilled to be invited to the legendary Poona races, where the social elite drank their pink gins. *Now that should be a fun day*, Madge thought once she was finally in bed. *I can see I'm going to enjoy myself here.*

Race day soon arrived and as they walked into the main enclosure, a trinket seller with bright white teeth greeted Madge's group with a beaming smile. 'Welcome to the most corrupt race track in all of India, *memsahibs!*' Madge couldn't help laughing out loud.

She looked around in wonder. The stands reminded her of cricket grounds in England, where there were impressive two-storey pavilions for the chosen few and everyone else was accommodated in what looked like open-fronted corrugated-iron sheds or simply on open-air terracing. Madge couldn't imagine any event in England other than the Derby being simultaneously glamorous and boisterous in quite the same way. Ladies wore sweeping, full-length dresses, magnificent wide-brimmed sun hats and carried patterned parasols to protect themselves from the sun. Men wore ties and stiff collars even though the temperature was almost 90 degrees Fahrenheit and the humidity was touching the 85 per cent mark. The traditional Indian love of a flutter was reflected by the ear-splitting cheering that accompanied the final furlong of almost every race. Even the fact that the girls didn't back a single winner couldn't spoil their day.

The fun continued with a dance at the Forces' Club in Poona, which started happily enough when Madge was introduced to Billy O'Gorman from Totteridge who, she soon discovered, knew her auntie Em as well as several other friends from back home.

Madge had a wonderful time and danced so much she was glad to kick off her shoes when she got back to Kirkee Hospital. Her feet were killing her, but she admitted with a beaming smile, 'This certainly is the life!'

Be that as it may, Madge wondered one morning after another particularly enjoyable dinner that went on until the early hours if some of the girls had been overdoing things. They had arrived in India with golden tans that had been carefully nurtured in the sun traps of A Deck on the *Strathnaver* but she noticed that the healthy glow had been replaced in many cases by a delicate, slightly yellow pallor.

'They've either got hepatitis or yellow fever,' Madge said to Vera, then laughed as she added, 'It's either that or the effects of the mepacrine!'

Everything suddenly clicked into place for Madge, who just two mornings earlier had been taught that one of the side effects of the anti-malaria drug they had all been taking since their arrival in Bombay was yellow colouring of the skin and eyes. She kicked herself for not working it out immediately. Perhaps she was the one overdoing things!

With her time at Kirkee coming to an end, Madge began to wonder where her new posting would be, and if there would be any shops. Just in case they were heading somewhere in the back of beyond, she and Vera caught the hospital transport to Poona from Kirkee the next afternoon where they found they were spoilt for choice by the number of fashion outlets. There were the usual stalls in front of the many shops and they steered clear of the bazaar after being warned that in hot days it was 'a little too smelly'. Instead they concentrated on clothes.

'Well, this is a surprise,' said Madge. 'There seem to be quite a few shops selling dresses, and even offering to make them within a day or so.'

'That is a plus,' said Vera, 'but it's pretty grubby as well as being dusty. I don't like the look of those bars, or those snooty colonial women in the cafes, but I suppose it's best not to look a gift horse in the mouth.'

It was the first time in years that Madge had been able to buy clothes and not worry how many ration coupons would be needed or if she had enough money.

She and Vera entered the first shop they saw. Dazzled by the display, Madge stroked the multi-coloured silks, cottons and brocades. The turbaned shopkeeper told the girls to choose any item they liked from a battered old copy of a catalogue on the counter and it would be ready the following afternoon.

Madge was tempted but opted for an off-the-hook, elegant blue and white striped piqué dress. She knew it would be perfect for afternoon tea parties, cocktails and dinners under the stars.

Vera settled for a patriotic little number in red, white and blue and a pink suit for good measure. After a few minor nips here and tucks there everything was delivered to the hospital at Kirkee the following lunchtime by a man on a bike.

'Girls back home would give their eye teeth for the chance to buy beautiful dresses at such prices,' said Madge to Vera as they admired their purchases.

'I know,' Vera exclaimed. 'Isn't this heaven!'

Fun as the social whirl of Poona was, it certainly wasn't the reason Madge had volunteered to nurse in the Burma Campaign and, as the shine wore off, she began paying more attention to her morning nursing shifts at Kirkee Hospital. This was proving to be excellent practice for treating numerous diseases, many of which they would rarely have experienced in the UK. Malaria, yellow fever, sandfly fever and typhus were all included and Madge mentally thanked the young doctor who had lectured them about those very ailments so patiently on the *Strathnaver*.

Madge was also increasingly interested in the demonstration sessions where the nurses dispensed TLC to wounded soldiers who hadn't talked to girls from home for months and, in some cases, years.

On the first Sunday in September, little more than two weeks after first treading on Indian soil, there was another reminder of the problems people were facing back home when a special service was held to commemorate the fifth anniversary of the outbreak of war. Madge had been to church both Sundays since her arrival in Kirkee, but found this service the most moving because it reminded her of the day she and her sisters had run home in terror and hidden under the dining room table after Dover's air-raid sirens were tested. She found the similarity to the Wesleyan service back home in Dover of great comfort.

The days soon seemed to blend. Mornings were spent working on the wards at the military hospital in Kirkee, and the afternoon eating a small lunch, sunbathing or playing tennis and then taking afternoon tea. Early evening cocktails were a must before dinner or a dance. It all became routine, until the girls were finally given the information they had been so impatiently awaiting for days.

'Apparently we leave on Monday,' said Madge. 'As in Monday the eleventh of September.'

'That's a surprise because it's only Wednesday today and we have plenty of time to arrange farewell dinners and things,' said Vera.

'I thought they would tell us just forty-eight hours before we go, like they did when we left Baker Street,' said Phyl.

'It's a shame all this fun is coming to an end,' said Madge, 'but I have to say, I'm actually really quite keen to get back to serious nursing.'

'Me too,' Phyl and Vera both said at the same time.

Madge was told that she would be going to an Indian

General Hospital, or IGH, in Chittagong and the best news was that she, Vera and Phyl would all be together. The bad news was they hadn't a clue where Chittagong was.

'I suppose we'll get used to not being told things in case we divulge information which we haven't the slightest knowledge of anyway,' said Madge.

'It reminds me of that song which goes something like "You're in the Army Now",' said Phyl.

To complicate matters further army security experts had lectured the VAD group about how important it was to be aware at all times of not participating in careless talk, because within a short time they would be nursing in hospitals dealing with casualties from the Burma Campaign. The nurses were instructed not to ask questions, under any circumstances, about where injured soldiers had been or what they had been doing. That was all well and good but the lecture left the Stoke Mandeville trio too worried to even ask where Chittagong was or find out how long it would take to get there. So they gave up trying to piece together the puzzle and instead concentrated on preparing themselves for what lay ahead. As departure was not scheduled until the following Monday it meant they had plenty of time to organise those all-important farewell drinks and give their cases and trunks a good dusting down.

When the Sunday morning before departure came round, Madge went for a walk, had a couple of lunchtime drinks at the Boat Club and spent the afternoon packing because all luggage was to be collected by 5 p.m. That meant she could write to Mum, Doris and Doreen, wash her hair, get that new dress out and look forward to dinner at the Ordnance Club for the last time. Unfortunately things didn't quite work out that way because instead of romantic, farewell dinner dates under a starlit night, or an evening of partying with friends as Madge had planned, every single one of the 250 VADs who caught that train at King's Cross station back in July were confined to barracks on the Sunday night.

The girls were hit with a stark realisation – the party was over.

10

Chittagong, Here We Come

If ever there was a reminder that the good times were over, it came when the Bombay Monday morning rush hour slowed to a crawl and then a halt when a sacred cow ambled into the middle of the road. The 1,500-mile journey across India from Bombay to Chittagong by bus, train, lorry and boat started for Madge with a 7 a.m. breakfast of her favourite scrambled eggs on toast. Roll call followed at 7.45 a.m. in the relative cool of a cloudless September morning at Kirkee Hospital and at 10 a.m. coaches arrived to take the VADs to Bombay.

The nurses disembarked from their ramshackle fleet of coaches along with more than 500 cases and trunks at the magisterial Victoria Terminus. The Gothic station was originally named Bori Bandar in the 1850s but was redesigned, rebuilt, renamed and re-opened in 1887 for Queen Victoria's Golden Jubilee after becoming the most expensive building to be erected in Bombay.

The magnificence of the station took Madge's breath away. It looked unlike any of the stations back home – a splendid, mock-Gothic building complete with gargoyles. Inside, huge volumes of commuters crowded the concourse and platforms. Outside, disabled and deformed beggars bowed constantly as they held out withered arms and hands and homeless vagabonds slept soundly on pavements in the morning sun. The station seemed to epitomise the polarised wealth and poverty that Madge had seen so far in India.

'It's quite a contrast,' Madge said to Vera. 'Look at those poor beggars over there.'

'I was told to expect the two extremes,' replied Vera, 'the haves and have-nots. But it's still something of a shock.'

Madge didn't have long to ponder this, though, as movement control officers soon guided the VADs to the platform where they boarded an ambulance train and by the time the three girls had settled into their carriage they all agreed one thing – it was very hot and very sticky. Little did they know that the next four days it would only get hotter and even stickier. The train had two first-class carriages with air conditioning in the form of a ceiling fan, but the Stoke Mandeville girls, who had sailed in relative luxury on the *Strathnaver*, weren't so lucky this time and they ended up in a compartment with only a window for ventilation. Just as they settled down a familiar head popped round the door and everybody burst out laughing.

'Come in, Sally. Where on earth have you been?' asked Madge. 'We saw hardly anything of you in Kirkee.'

'It's a bit of a long story,' she replied, 'but can you put up with me again? I promise not to be a nuisance.'

'Of course we can, we'd love to have you with us,' said Vera, who slipped her shoes back on and started clearing space for the shy, lonely, but very likeable Sally. She added, 'You're a bit of a mystery, though.'

'Not really,' Sally said with an unhappy smile. The sadness in her eyes stopped Vera from asking any more questions.

The carriage soon settled down again and the girls sat in silence for a little while. It was the first moment of quiet they'd had in weeks and Madge's mind couldn't help but hark back home.

Phyl must have had the same thoughts because she asked, 'Has anybody heard any real news from home? Not just happy family gossip, but how things are going in the push towards Germany?'

'I've heard nothing,' said Vera. 'I wonder if London is still getting hit by rockets?'

No one answered and Madge realised she didn't have a clue what was going on in the UK either. She hadn't seen an English newspaper for weeks, radio news reports were heavily censored and so it was like living in a news blackout. She couldn't imagine it would be any better way out in Chittagong.

There were Mum's letters, of course, and, pulling them out of her handbag, Madge decided to pore over them once again to see if she'd missed anything. Not having much luck, she decided instead to take another look at the advice they had all been given in the original contract from the India Office.

The first thing to catch her eye was a section on 'Train Journeys in India' which warned about the problems that can arise over tipping. The document said: 'If you employ your own coolies to help with your bags, note their numbers otherwise you will get relays of coolies clamouring for pay, and you will never know whether you are paying the correct coolie or not. The usual pay for a coolie is one anna, equivalent to one sixteenth of a rupee, per journey and that figure is printed on their badges.'

The next section made it abundantly clear that to leave a carriage unguarded was simply asking for problems: 'Compartments have a lavatory and a shower or bath and a servants' quarters leading off them. Should you leave the compartment empty at any station make the bearer sit in it to prevent theft or, alternatively, get the guard to lock it.' Madge made a point of getting the girls to agree that whatever happened, be there a party, an invitation to drinks, a game of cards or a jolly little sing-song, at least one of them would be in the carriage at all times.

The India Office also advised them to 'Never use tap water under any circumstances to wash your teeth. Instead use soda water or boiled and chlorinated water, which is available at all station refreshment rooms and dining cars. The purchase of a thermos flask is suggested but never buy soda water from hawkers on station platforms.'

At least the train had corridors so the girls could get some exercise by pacing up and down, but of far more importance was the fact that they had access to the toilets and washrooms. They weren't exactly five-star but at least they could have a strip wash and freshen up for breakfast and dinner.

Unlike many other girls, Madge never really tired of what the British army called 'bully beef' so she was happy enough when it was served on the train. Bully beef was actually corned beef, which her mother used to mix with mashed potato and onions into a corned-beef hash. Madge thought back to the happy days before rationing was brought in when there would be a lightly fried egg on top for each of the Graves sisters as an extra treat.

Madge was more worried about the increasing heat which was becoming quite unbearable and causing real health problems aboard the train. Already there had been a mini-outbreak of miliaria rubra, more commonly known as prickly heat, which caused discomfort, particularly in the afternoons when the humidity seemed to be at its worst in India. Phyl had come out with the most awful rash, and with the sun blazing down from dawn to dusk, she was miserable with the discomfort.

Vera sent a plea down the length of the train and thankfully a bottle of calamine lotion appeared which helped to ease Phyl's blotches and raised spots. Prickly heat was a minor problem, but an early warning that life was about to change in the most drastic of fashions.

Madge and her group had been told in lectures at their stay in Kirkee that they would find many people in India who either spoke or understood English. At best that was wishful thinking. At worst it was untrue because in a country with twenty languages and more than a hundred dialects English didn't even come second. Much emphasis was placed on the need to respect and understand the beliefs, traditions and dietary demands of a number of religions. Hinduism, Madge learned, was the dominant faith, followed by Islam, Sikhism,

Buddhism, Jainism, Parsee, Urdu (taught to the British) and numerous regional creeds. Plus, of course, Christianity.

The Indian caste system and its infinite number of modes and traditions was simply too complex for newcomers to even begin to comprehend. But a delightful Indian nursing sister, who accompanied the group as a liaison officer, informed the girls that there was always one solution to the problem.

'That solution is patience, dears,' she told them. 'The ways of the people out here will seem strange to you, but you must remember that it is their country and you must integrate as best you can. They have what might seem to you very odd beliefs regarding food. For example, you must never ever allow your shadow to fall on food, and be aware that many Hindus do not eat beef as they believe the cow to be a sacred animal and treat it with the utmost respect. Cows are incredibly gentle creatures, and as they produce milk, which can in turn be made into butter, ghee and cheese, you can appreciate why they are so revered. Cow dung is also used as a fertiliser. But, ladies, that is just one of the many ways in which Indians have ideas that are quite different. The best way is to observe and learn and soon you will feel right at home.'

Gertrude Corsar's VADs were urged to practise and preach extreme levels of hygiene and were repeatedly informed before the journey to wash their hands after even the simplest of meals. So when one of the nurses popped her head into Madge's carriage and said that a very large and bold rat had been seen scuttling along the corridor everybody simply burst out laughing, after an initial chorus of 'ooh's and one or two music hall squeals of mock horror. Madge was particularly amused to see that the tea they had been enjoying so much was boiled in a giant urn into which the stewards slopped a grubby old jug to fill the teapots. She couldn't imagine what Miss Corsar would have thought about the way things were washed up.

Throughout the journey nobody was allowed to step off the train even though they stopped at least once a day to refuel the steam-driven engine. The train belched so much smoke and grit over the carriages that to leave a window even slightly ajar meant a cabin full of choking fumes.

Three days into their journey, they thought things couldn't get worse but they were ordered to keep the window blinds drawn for the next thirty-six hours until the train arrived at Howrah Junction railway station in Calcutta. Initially the girls all thought the blackout was simply a way of keeping the heat down in the cabin by stopping the sun blazing in through the windows. When Vera pointed out there wasn't exactly a lot of sunshine when it went dark, the penny dropped. It was a security measure, and a somewhat alarming one at that. Madge knew that since 1942 Calcutta had lived in fear of a full-scale Japanese invasion. They also knew that dagger-carrying 'dacoits' were known to swing into carriages from the roof. This had all sounded rather thrilling from afar but now the danger suddenly felt horribly real.

After a four-day journey, the weary VADs arrived just outside Howrah Junction station at 2 a.m. Madge despaired at just how much further they would have to travel before reaching their allotted hospitals. As they awaited instructions while still aboard the train, Madge decided to take an early morning stroll down the corridor with Sally.

'Just think how lucky we were that every one of us survived the week in London,' said Sally thoughtfully. 'We had a few close escapes, though, didn't we?'

'We definitely did. We were incredibly lucky.' Madge nodded solemnly.

'Did you hear about that group that were in Trafalgar Square,' Sally went on, 'when a doodlebug engine cut out? They hid behind one of the big lions as it crashed to earth just a few hundred yards away towards the Thames. I was over near Leicester Square at that point but even from there I saw huge amounts of debris flying through the air. I could barely believe it when I heard there'd been no injuries . . .' Sally trailed off before holding her tummy and appearing to be in a bit of a hurry to get moving along the corridor.

Surely that was the Sunday morning on our final day in London? Madge said to herself, and remembered just how calm the vicar had been when the grinding, throaty snarl of a doodle-bug suddenly turned to deafening silence.

Before Madge could ask if that frightening incident had been on the same day, Sally excused herself and literally ran to the toilet with an upset tummy.

The train had been stationary for four hours and once it was light again Madge and Vera turned on their charm and the night orderly responded by bringing them cups of tea. But it was not until 9.30 a.m. that the train left the siding and pulled into a platform at one of the busiest junctions in the whole of

India. Madge marvelled at the organised chaos that seemed to be par for the course at every station.

A short while later some of the girls were packed into lorries which would take them to the Grand Hotel in Calcutta. The VADs waved one another off, and the girls laughed about just how long their colleagues were going to soak in the great big baths at this major hotel, but Madge couldn't feel too envious. She knew their postings would range from hospitals in the north of Assam to the banks of the Brahmaputra River, and she couldn't begrudge them even the tiniest of luxuries.

Madge's group had to wait a little longer and they sat on their trunks and cases in a tightly knit circle on the platform. After what seemed like a whole afternoon they were escorted to ambulances sporting giant red crosses and taken straight to the docks at Kidderpore where the SS *Ethiopia* was waiting.

Evidence of the damage inflicted by Japanese air raids in which 350 people had been killed and hundreds more had been injured was still visible from the ship. A deckhand told the girls the Japanese had actually been trying to bomb the bridge across the river and pointed out gaps along the waterfront where warehouses once existed and buildings with blackened, fire-damaged walls stood forlornly. The SS *Ethiopia* eased down the Hooghly River, a tributary of the mighty Ganges, and along the coast on a voyage that would take three days before the VADs finally docked in Chittagong.

Being aboard the SS *Ethiopia* reminded Madge of the good old days aboard the *Strathnaver*. Happily there was no need for destroyer escorts or Sunderland flying boats this time, nor was there the nightmare thump of depth charges in the dead of night. After her exhausting coast-to-coast train journey, Madge was delighted to be awakened the following morning by a knock on the cabin door from a steward who, bless his soul, was standing there with a pot of tea.

But the best was still to come because after a really enjoyable breakfast she went for a stroll on deck without a life jacket or comical pith helmet and then took all the time in the world to indulge in washing her hair for the first time in days. The heat of the afternoon sun and a gentle breeze soon had it dry and Madge spent the rest of the afternoon catching up on letters home, writing an extra-long one to Mum who she knew would be anxiously waiting to hear about India.

The sea was calm and the wind gentle as the SS *Ethiopia* chugged into Chittagong harbour, a frontline port at the mouth of the Karnaphuli River on the Bay of Bengal. Several VAD units headed for the railway station and further journeys, but for Madge, Vera and Phyl it was an overnight stay at the Women's Forces Hostel, which was a short distance from their final destination.

'What a lovely building,' said Madge. 'I reckon this was probably a colonial mansion in the good old days.'

'Shame it's out of town,' said Vera. 'It would have been nice to have a look at Chittagong before we actually start work.'

That night the girls, tired as they were after their endless journey, still had the energy to accept an invitation to attend a dance at the Officers' Club in Chittagong.

A free day the following day turned out to be a godsend.

'Let's make a trip to the shops,' Phyl suggested. 'I don't know about you but I'm after getting myself some trousers. I'm fed up being eaten alive by all these mosquitoes!'

So off the girls headed, all managing to find some suitable trousers and lots of khaki 'drill', which they knew would keep them more comfortable. Tired as they may have been, they still found the energy to attend one more dance at the Officers' Club. They were collected and then driven back to the hostel in time for the 11.30 p.m. curfew.

The girls were up at 8 a.m. to prepare for the journey to 56 Indian General Hospital (combined), which was dedicated to nursing both British and Indian troops. After breakfast all the VADs' luggage was taken away for delivery to the hospital, and later in the day the nurses were called forward and climbed aboard army transport. In the pouring rain, they huddled in the back of the lorries for what became the bumpiest ride they'd ever experienced. At 3.30 p.m. on 20 September 1944 the small convoy finally arrived in the grounds of the Governor General's former residence in the town of Chittagong. Once the nurses had reassembled, a roll call was made, separating those for 56 IGH and other hospitals in the area.

The nurses were greeted and made very welcome with refreshments before being shown to sleeping quarters in the main house. Madge, Vera and Phyl retrieved their luggage, had a quick wash and, as it was getting dark, went into the dining area for supper. They were so tired they decided on a light meal and then an early night.

Their long journey was finally over.

11

56 Indian General Hospital

The following morning the view from the veranda of the Governor General's one-time residence reminded Madge of a beautiful old painting she had seen in a book as a child in one of Miss Radford's history classes at school in Dover. The girls had just finished a delicious breakfast, but they were all keen to get out and explore. The lush green lawn was at its finest after weeks of rain as the monsoon season drew to a close and a multitude of bright red roses added grace and colour. To the left cows grazed happily in the morning sun. To the right a very bumpy pathway led down to a cluster of huts with thatched roofs.

Sister Blossom, home sister of the nurses' mess, had arrived to take them on a tour of the grounds. 'Come on, girls, let's get cracking. There's lots to see!'

The big house had been converted into the hospital's HQ, with offices, sleeping quarters for senior staff, a lounge and dining facilities for all. The area around the house seemed to contain lots of small bamboo huts and the girls struggled to take it all in at first as they walked slowly down a pathway still wet from the morning dew.

Vera pointed out the pretty thatched roofs of the huts. 'How nice it must be for the servants who live there.'

'They are indeed very lovely huts but they are not the servants' quarters. This is where you will be living.' The girls looked at one another and raised their eyebrows. That's not what they had been expecting.

'How lovely,' Vera whispered to Madge, who smiled in agreement.

They made their way over to the huts, which were called bashas. The term, the nurses were told, was used by the British military to describe virtually any sort of living quarters. There were eight bashas split either side of a wide pathway. The bamboo walls supported a thatched roof, but there were no glass windows. Instead there were shutters which could be opened and closed by pulling on a rope.

'Don't forget to put towels on the floor below the shutters when it rains,' Sister Blossom smiled. 'And shake your shoes upside down every morning in case there's some nasty creepy crawly hiding in them!'

Madge shuddered.

Sister Blossom showed each of the girls to their own basha. After so many months of being cooped up together, Madge was secretly quite relieved to see that she would have a narrow hut all to herself. The bashas were surprisingly long with a little chest of drawers alongside the single bed as well as a chair and a narrow wardrobe near the door. Madge noted with amusement that the bed wasn't exactly made with Sister Crowley's 'hospital corners' but it at least had a heavy-duty army mosquito net. She was particularly grateful for the netting because the previous night the mosquitos had made such a noise as they buzzed and bounced off the curtains that they had actually woken her up. Madge looked around with a feeling of contentment. *I think I'm going to be happy here*, she decided.

Once they'd been shown their living quarters, the little group walked away from the bashas and further down the hill to the hospital, which had been built entirely of bamboo with a roof of interwoven palm leaves. Madge turned to look back and was surprised to see that a group of fully-armed Gurkha soldiers had appeared from nowhere. The first thing she noticed was that their khaki bush hats were held in place by a strap under the chin. Their black boots gleamed in the morning sunshine and their khaki shirts and knee-length trousers were ideal for the country's cloying humidity. Over their right shoulders each carried a rifle, but it was their kukris that really caught the eye. Each curved Nepalese knife was almost eighteen inches long, enclosed in a sheath, and attached to the waist belt.

Noticing her expression, Sister Blossom explained, 'They guard the compound and British soldiers guard the hospital. The Gurkhas are the ones who will be guarding you in your bashas at night.' Madge turned to look again, but they had vanished as quickly as they had appeared.

Sister Blossom gave the trio a short summary of what had

happened to the war-weary little town of Chittagong over the past two years. She explained that both the port and the area had suffered heavy bombing raids by the Japanese in April and December 1942, and that many people had fled to the surrounding towns, including Comilla, which was about a hundred miles to the north. Due to its position on the Bay of Bengal, Chittagong was still strategically vital both as a deep-water port and a railway terminus and it had become an increasingly important air base from which supplies were dropped to 14th Army on the constantly changing front line. Sadly the railway workshops, which had employed so many people, had been destroyed to stop them falling under the control of the Japanese in the event that the Allied forces had to retire.

The sister went out of her way to make the new nurses feel welcome and went to great lengths to help them understand some of the idiosyncrasies of the strange new world with which they would be dealing.

'A *dhobi-wallah* does the washing. A *punkah-wallah* pulls the strap on the fans. A *banyan* is a shopkeeper. A dacoit is a robber. A sepoy is a soldier and a *bhisti* will bring you water,' Sister Blossom explained. 'But the most important word of all for you English nurses is *char*. That means tea!'

The walk from the nurses' bashas to the hospital had taken several minutes down a gently winding, gravelled pathway. 'Be careful when it rains because this can be very slippery,' warned Sister Blossom, who showed them the location of various wards and made introductions left, right and centre before they all walked back up the hill to the nurses' mess in the main building.

'It looks impressive even now,' said Vera, after being told the building was once the residence of the last Governor General of Bengal.

'I love the huge veranda with those red roses climbing either side of the main entrance,' said Madge. 'It looks like something out of a storybook.'

Madge was doubly delighted to see that not only had the luggage caught up with them but there was also a neatly tied bundle of letters from home, including several from Mum. A bearer took Madge's trunk and cabin case down to her basha but before she could decide whether to read Mum's news first or unpack, exhaustion took over and she went for an hour's nap.

There was still enough light left when she woke up to make a more thorough inspection of her quarters and Madge found there was no toilet, no electricity and no running water. But the bathrooms in the communal wash house were spotlessly clean and morning, noon or night there was always a delightful aroma of jasmine. *They're an absolute dream in comparison with some of the very smelly places we experienced on the way out,* Madge thought.

Vera was in the next basha down and as the two girls went outside to meet each other Madge spotted the '*bhisti* man', the water-carrier. '*Assalamo aleikum,*' she said, trying to say 'hello' in Urdu.

'*Assalamo aleikum,*' he replied with a grin.

'Glad to see you're learning the language,' said Vera, 'but I'm not so sure about the pronunciation!'

Of all the helpers and servants Madge's favourite was Ahmed, her bearer, who acted much like a butler or personal assistant. He made sure her basha was always clean and tidy, but most importantly, he kept the mosquito nets in first-class order. They were so high off the ground that Madge found them difficult to pull into place. Ahmed made sure she never had to worry about that problem again because he always lowered the curtains at night as well as doing the ironing and keeping the oil lamp in pristine condition.

On the first evening in her basha Madge sat down to write a letter to Mum, Doris and Doreen by the light of her oil lamp, but she soon gave up. *This is no good*, she thought. *It's casting eerie shadows all around the room and the smell is just ghastly!* So she decided to write her letter in daylight the following day and instead tucked herself up in her lovely cool sheets. *We'll be starting work in the hospital tomorrow, so I do hope I sleep well.* She closed her eyes and fell into a deep, restful sleep.

It had rained overnight and after breakfast in the main building Madge, Vera and Phyl took the greatest of care as they walked down the soggy pathway and into the hospital. An orderly guided them along a corridor to a door marked 'Matron' and they were greeted with open arms by Olive Ferguson.

'Good day, girls, am I pleased to see you!'

Madge had become used to the warm welcomes, but the accent caught her off guard. She'd never met a New Zealander before, let alone worked for one. Vera committed the heinous crime of asking if she was Australian and the girls laughed at Matron Ferguson's finger-wagging and mock outrage. Matron Ferguson was a tall and sturdy-looking woman with dark hair and piercing brown eyes, but her quick humour showed Madge that she wouldn't be so hard to work for.

With the introductions completed Madge spent her first shift on the 'British Other Ranks' ward. Officers were placed in different wards, although Madge soon noted that they certainly didn't get better or special treatment from the nurses. All patients were treated the same, regardless of rank or status.

'Good morning, nurse,' said a chatty doctor. 'I understand that this is your first shift. My name is Dr Whittaker,' he said, 'and as you have just arrived in India can you tell me how people are bearing up at home?'

Madge was about to answer when he was called over to examine a poorly patient on the other side of the ward. As he walked away, she heard somebody whispering, 'Nurse, please pop over here,' in a broad Scottish accent.

'Hello,' she said, 'is there a little secret?'

'Not really,' said the Scot, still whispering. 'I just thought, lassie, that you should know that as well as being a doctor the laddie you were just talking to is also the Commander-in-Chief of the hospital. He's the most important man in the whole place! And I canna find my teeth this morning . . .'

Madge was grateful for the fact that the chatty little Scot was trying to be helpful and spotted his name on the chart at the bottom of his bed. As she picked up a mug from a bedside cabinet she said, 'Thank you so much, Hamish. I really appreciate you marking my card. Now, one good turn deserves another and guess what? I've just found your teeth in this mug!'

After helping Hamish retrieve his dentures, Madge turned to see if Dr Whittaker was still busy with a patient and decided that the reality was he probably knew far more up-to-date news than she did, because she hadn't seen or read anything new since leaving London, and he was probably aware of that. *He's just trying to make me feel at home*, she realised. Her mother's letters had been filled with news of the family rather than details of the war effort.

Ten minutes later Dr Whittaker returned and courteously invited Madge to join his 10.30 a.m. rounds so she could see for herself that the majority of the soldiers on this ward were suffering from diseases, not combat wounds. The biggest problems included malaria, dengue fever and dysentery. 'You name it. We do our best to treat it here.' Madge remembered the endlessly repetitive medical lectures on the *Strathnaver* and was going to have a bit of fun by adding sandfly fever, sleeping sickness, typhus and yellow fever, but wisely just nodded.

Chittagong was less than fifty miles from the Burmese border so most of the VADs expected to have to deal with combat injuries. They hadn't heard about the devastation that malaria had caused in the fighting that took place during the Japanese invasion of Malaysia and Burma. In fact, little was ever really heard or written about the heroics of what became known as the 'Forgotten Army'. The truth was that malaria, of all the deadly diseases, came closest to undermining the Allied forces' struggle for victory.

That was until Lieutenant General William Slim, commander of the 14th Army, issued an edict in 1943 that swung the balance of power within a remarkably short time. He reported that for every man evacuated with wounds there were 120 evacuated sick, usually with malaria. He pointed out that the annual rate of malaria was 84 per cent per annum of the total strength of his army and it was even higher amongst the forward troops. 'A simple calculation showed me that in a matter of months at this rate my Army would have melted away.'

Ironically mepacrine, the anti-malaria drug, was first synthesised in 1931 by scientists at Bayer in Nazi Germany. But there were rumours when it was given to troops in Slim's 14th Army that it caused impotence, made teeth fall out and even resulted in baldness. The fact it also had a side effect that turned skin yellow didn't help either and the result was that large numbers of troops did their best not to take the drug.

General Slim brought in a system of random checks and if it was shown that less than 95 per cent of a unit had taken the absolutely foul-tasting mepacrine, he would dismiss the unit's commanding officer. 'I only had to sack three,' he said. That certainly did the trick and infection rates fell dramatically. Another of General Slim's edicts was that troops must not wash or bathe in the open after twilight when mosquitos were so active. Unfortunately he broke his own rules and rued the evening when he had a quick wash-down in the open and ended up in hospital in the spring of 1944 with malaria.

As Madge followed the doctor on his rounds in the BOR ward they stopped at the bed of George, a farmhand with blond hair and a nose he broke after falling off a horse. He had been on the Indian subcontinent for less than six months and after religiously taking his mepacrine went out on his first jungle sortie full of optimism that whatever happened to him he was unlikely to catch malaria, the doctor explained. For just a split second a look of deep concern flickered across the face of the doctor who was doing his level best to lift the young-ster's spirits. George dripped with sweat and looked weary beyond his years. His face was that awful pasty yellow and he had just got over a bout of the shakes.

'Nurse Graves, this looks like your first patient in India,' said the doctor as he nodded to George and left to continue his rounds. It all seemed familiar to Madge, who moved almost instinctively to pick up a cool clean towel and used it to smooth that troubled brow. Her gentle smile had exactly the effect the doctor had hoped for and George seemed to relax and eventually drifted into a fitful, but nevertheless lengthy sleep. She used the time to familiarise herself with the modus operandi of the BOR ward, which she noted with some relief wasn't that different from the system at Stoke Mandeville Hos-pital, but seemed far more relaxed. Despite being busy, she saw that the doctors and nurses smiled and joked with one another.

It was late afternoon and close to the end of Madge's first

shift when she noticed that George seemed more alert than he had in the morning. When she went over to see how he was, he asked what her name was and clearly wanted to talk.

'Please could I have a drink?'

After she helped him sit up and quench his thirst, George poured his heart out. By now Madge should have long been off duty and would have loved to have had a relaxing pot of tea in the nurses' mess, but most of all a shower. Instead she made sure he took his foul-tasting medicine, and was pleased to note that his morning temperature, which at one stage had reached a worrying 105 degrees Fahrenheit, had started to drop. So she listened.

George told her his unit had been on patrol in the Arakan for a fortnight and it had rained almost constantly. Not just showers, but heavy, driving rain that left everybody absolutely soaking wet.

'Instead of easing off, the rain became worse and the swarms of mosquitos became larger,' he said. 'At first I suffered from a minor headache or two. But then the headaches became more severe and I got chills, almost as if I had flu. Then I started being sick and got a dose of the shakes, but because I didn't want to let anybody down I kept it all to myself,' he said to Madge, who again wiped beads of sweat from his forehead.

There was a lengthy pause before he explained how an experienced, older sergeant, who had seen it all before, spotted that there was a problem. And a serious one at that.

In the months before General Slim issued the mepacrine edict the sergeant had been in a unit that had been virtually halved after suffering the same symptoms. He issued orders for the stricken youngster to be taken by stretcher to a casualty clearing station, where malaria was diagnosed.

'I was flown on a DC-3 Dakota to Chittagong and then brought here by ambulance,' he added.

He told Madge that his biggest worry was not about malaria, but instead about not getting back with the boys. He missed his mum and dad, the farm and the dogs. He didn't want to be a problem to anybody. He just wanted to do his duty for England and go home. When would he be able to leave hospital? When could he rejoin his unit? The morning bout of fever had drained his energy and when George once again drifted into a troubled sleep Madge lifted the sheets up over his shoulders and made sure he was securely tucked into bed. She ended her first day at 56 IGH feeling slightly anxious but not sure why.

The calm, professional way she had handled George's problems had been noticed by the doctor and within two weeks Madge was in charge of wards that cared for as many as thirty patients at a time. Her duties included giving the more incapacitated patients bed baths, taking temperatures, making sure medicine was taken, giving injections, administering the dreaded mepacrine, and making sure everybody got breakfast. A multitude of tasks that on the morning shift had to be completed in time for the doctor's rounds, which got underway at 10.30 a.m.

With virtually no nursing assistance available, Madge worried about her ability to help patients turn over to avoid bed sores until she realised that only on the very rarest of occasions would it be a problem. Most active patients did their utmost to help her move them anyway and were also so wracked by illness that they had lost huge amounts of weight.

There was one thing that Madge always checked when she was running wards, either on the day or night shifts, and that was security. After the frightening incident at Stoke Mandeville's kitchen she made sure she knew where help would be if problems developed. At 56 IGH there was always a fellow sister on the next ward, but most comforting of all was the fact that though they were rarely seen, Madge now knew the Gurkhas were always there, even on night shifts. Few were prepared to tangle with the infinitely courteous but utterly fearless little warriors from Nepal.

After she had been at the hospital for ten days Madge was transferred to the dangerously ill (DI) ward to help her become familiar with all the problems that the hospital faced. At the end of one particularly tiring shift, during which the heat and humidity had been especially unpleasant, she bumped into Dr Whittaker who had been so helpful on her first day on duty.

'How have your first couple of weeks at the hospital been?' he asked.

'Fine,' she replied. 'Good. I like the fact that we are getting as much experience as possible by working in all the wards. By the way, how is George, the lad who was struggling with malaria?'

The doctor told her that a few days earlier George had complained about feeling cold in spite of a temperature reading of

105 degrees. That had been followed by a bout of the shakes so severe that the bed frame had banged repeatedly against the bamboo walls of the basha hospital. There were also spells of irrationality.

He had been sick again and wasn't eating, though he did manage to down a few spoonfuls of soup. Other soldiers in the ward had done their best to jolly him along, and repeatedly tried to cajole him into having a drink in an effort to combat the effects of dehydration from that high temperature. Later that night there was another bout of the shakes that became more and more severe.

George became weaker and weaker. He never mentally gave up the fight to recover but sadly passed away. 'For a number of reasons we think that he died from cerebral malaria,' said the doctor.

Madge, feeling sad at the news she had just received, slowly walked up the slope from the hospital to her basha and mulled over what the doctor had said about the fevers, the nausea, the violent shakes, the high temperature but feeling cold, and that young George had died from cerebral malaria. Suddenly it all became clear as she remembered how her dad had suffered from shakes so violent that his metal bed had crashed against the bedroom wall. He'd always had a frighteningly hot forehead, and suffered from nausea, comas and irrationality. He had also served in India in the Great War. It all fell into place. Cerebral malaria had almost certainly killed him as well, not the constant bouts of flu the doctors had diagnosed.

Madge felt a sharp pull in her stomach at the realisation. *I'm too late to help my dad, but maybe being here I'll be able to help others before it's too late for them.*

12

Learning About Indian Life

The first shift on an Indian DI ward opened Madge's eyes to the complications of nursing Hindu and Muslim patients on the same ward. Not only did they have separate kitchens and cooks of their own faith but they also insisted on having servants of the same faith to carry and serve the food, something the VADs were strictly forbidden to do. They had ward-boys to do this, and they also took the plates away. It was a major bonus because as a junior at Stoke Mandeville Madge remembered not only preparing breakfast, but then serving the meal – and collecting the dirty plates into the bargain.

Meal times were probably the most relaxing because the patients were too busy eating to continue their meditation, which often included endless chanting. Normally they fell asleep quite quickly after being fed, especially after dinner. It was the noise late at night that was the problem. At first it was entertaining with some chanting away at the top of their voices, and others happily talking to themselves and humming. In the small hours, however, it could be a worry, especially when the noisy ones were told to be quiet by patients desperate for sleep.

In the main, problems on the ward were few and far between, until patients began to complain to nurses and doctors that they were not being given enough to eat. There were even claims that on some nights they were given nothing at all. When the complaints began to increase Madge went to Matron Ferguson to first inform her of the situation and then ask for advice.

'It's not simply a case of "please, sir, can I have some more",' said Madge. 'From what these patients are saying there are some nights when they are given nothing at all for dinner.'

Matron said how much she appreciated Madge's good sense in bringing the matter into the open, and because it was an unusually quiet day invited her to be her guest for afternoon tea. She explained that the province of Bengal had not long recovered from the effects of a famine 'of Biblical proportions' and food was still a very touchy subject indeed.

'I wasn't suggesting there's a famine,' said Madge, and Matron nodded.

'Depending on which set of figures you believe, an estimated three million people died from starvation and disease after the winter rice crop of 1942 yielded way below what it normally does,' Matron sighed. 'And then the Japanese invaded Malaya before taking control of Burma, and, quite frankly, things just went from bad to worse.'

Between the end of the Great War and the outbreak of war in 1939, she explained, Burma had been one of the biggest exporters of rice in the world and huge amounts went to Bengal and other parts of India. Once Japan controlled Burma it meant exports to India were stopped instantly. Then a cyclone, followed by tidal waves, endless rain and floods damaged more than three thousand square miles of land and harvestable crops.

What started out as food shortages quickly turned into a truly dreadful famine which, in the view of many Indians, was caused by the British, and there was still lingering resentment. Whilst this was just 'a minor hiccup' the last thing needed at 56 IGH were rumours over new food shortages. 'Let's nip this in the bud, Nurse Graves.'

The solution to the potentially tricky little problem virtually fell into Madge's lap when she went for a stroll outside the basha wards just before dinner that evening in the brilliant sunshine. Half a dozen ward-boys had carried canisters of curry and rice from the kitchen and thought they were hidden from view on the unobserved side of the bashas. Instead of ladling the curry and rice onto plates they were happily scoffing handfuls as fast as they could. Madge had caught them literally red-handed, but rather than create a scene she just walked over, nodded and pointed to the wards. They stopped eating and started carrying the food canisters towards the wards as she stood there trying not to laugh at the sight of the boys' right hands covered in bright red curry sauce. Little did she realise, however, that while a potentially troublesome little problem had been laid to rest she had made a mistake that had put everything else in the shade.

Much as she liked the cheery ward-boys Madge had little sympathy over the pilfered food because the soldiers in the DI ward were in need of nutrition to help them recover. She went to bed that night more than a little pleased at sorting things out and looked forward to telling Olive Ferguson all about it.

Madge didn't have long to wait the following morning because rather than starting her shift there was an instruction to report to the Matron's office, where she got a slap on the wrist rather than a pat on the back. She was confronted by a different Miss Ferguson to the woman who had invited her for afternoon tea and talked about the Bengal famine.

'Thank you for solving the mystery of the missing food,' Matron said, but then shook her head. 'How is it that what was a minor problem has now been turned into a far more serious one? What do you have to say for yourself, Graves?'

A somewhat bemused Madge replied that she had caught the ward-boys helping themselves to the rice and curry and indicated that she wanted the food taken straight to the wards, which was what she thought they had done.

'Well, it doesn't look as if they quite did that,' said Matron, whose response left Madge more than a little bewildered.

Far from taking the canisters into the wards, the ward-boys simply carried everything back to the kitchens and told the cooks that they would not be serving anything to the patients because the food had been made inedible.

'There was nothing wrong with the food when they picked up the canisters,' said Madge. 'So I wonder if they carried on eating it?'

She still didn't understand what the problem was, until Matron, with another shake of her head, explained that when she walked over to the ward-boys her shadow had fallen on the canisters. Once the shadow of a non-believer fell on food it was automatically destroyed. 'Instead of the patients getting more last night they got nothing. Nobody got anything to eat at all!' There was, however, the faintest hint of a smile as Matron pointed to the door to indicate that the incident was over.

When Madge met up with Vera later in the day in the nurses' mess she was greeted by a rousing chorus of '*Just me and my shadow all alone and feeling blue*', followed by laughter and applause. The incident had played on Madge's mind throughout the day so the bit of fun and nonsense in the mess cheered her up.

There were more interesting things to talk about anyway because she had been too busy in the past few days to have a good old gossip with Vera, who lowered her voice and said she had been in Chittagong that afternoon and couldn't believe what she had seen. There had been a demonstration calling for home rule for India and it had been very civilised, if somewhat noisy. There were lots of drums being beaten and flags being waved. Some, said Vera, had emblems on them that looked very much like the German swastika and she was worried what the connotations could involve.

As Madge sat listening the ever-present Sister Blossom wandered past and told her not to worry about the 'shadow incident' but sensed there was a bit of a problem and asked if she could help. Because the home sister had been so honest and helpful since the VADs had arrived, Vera told her outright that she was pretty sure she had seen a number of swastikas being waved at the home rule demonstration.

Sister Blossom pulled a chair up to their table and told Vera she was almost certainly right. But the emblem on the flags, far from showing support for Nazi Germany, was a symbol of peace and love and had been so for thousands of years in India. It was sacred to Hinduism, Buddhism and Jainism and was also believed to bring good fortune, said Blossom.

The monsoon season was long over, but the humidity was still extreme with temperatures between 85 and 90 degrees Fahrenheit. In a basha ward that lacked air conditioning and shifts that involved long and very demanding hours Madge found she was becoming increasingly jaded. There also seemed to be a cocktail party, dinner or dance every night as well, which she had been attending regularly, so she decided the best thing to do, for the first time since she had arrived in India, was to have a couple of early nights.

She certainly began to feel more like herself, but that meant that she soon rejoined the others for evenings out again! After one particularly late evening that had begun with a cocktail party and ended with a dance, Madge was looking forward to a lazy morning in her basha as she was not due to work that day. All of a sudden there was a knock on her door. 'Come on, Madge, rise and shine,' said a croaky voice that she just about recognised.

'Have you got a sore throat? You sound terrible,' she asked Vera after escaping from the mosquito netting and opening the door.

'Never mind that,' said Vera. 'I met a rather nice chap from one of the artillery units last night and he says there's a picnic going on this afternoon. He'll take me on one condition,' said Vera.

'So why are you banging on the door so early in the morning? I'm very pleased you've got a date,' laughed Madge. 'Hang on a minute . . . what's this condition?'

'He wants me to bring a friend along for his pal,' laughed Vera.

Just then, as if on cue, a camouflaged three-ton army lorry chugged through the gates with the horn blowing and balloons bobbing from the wing mirrors. 'Surely this can't be them come to pick us up, is it?'

'It certainly is!' smiled Vera.

Nine hours later they were dropped back at the gates after a wonderful time swimming, eating, drinking and singing, and both the girls were on a high.

At breakfast the following morning Madge told Phyl, 'The boys had laid a couple of huge carpets on a riverbank and got a fire going so we had roast chicken with all the trimmings, and the flames kept the mosquitos away. Do you know the best thing about the whole picnic?' she asked, barely taking a breath. 'I didn't get bitten once!'

Later that day, while she was busy on her shift, Matron Ferguson asked Madge whether as a favour she would be happy to help with some catering problems which had developed up at the big house where a conference of bigwigs was taking place. 'You are a brilliant organiser and the staff up there like you,' said Matron. 'It'd be much appreciated if you'd give them a hand.'

Lunch was already running late by the time Madge had walked up the hill from the hospital and changed into a clean, newly ironed uniform. She organised the waiters into two groups and food finally began to arrive from the kitchens, which were in a separate building some ten yards behind the Governor's house, into the dining room.

Even so, it was all still moving far too slowly for her liking so she picked up one of the large oval plates, which was beautifully adorned with cold cuts of chicken and beef. Considerable care had been taken in making sure the plate looked perfect and Madge wasn't at all surprised when she was told it was for the top table.

One of the kitchen staff offered her a cloth to cover the succulent feast and Madge remembered the shadow incident. She decided, however, that because this lunch was almost certainly for Allied officers there would not be a problem this time. Within five yards of leaving the kitchen she wished with all her heart that she had taken that cloth.

As she walked out of the doorway Madge felt something whoosh past her head. She ducked instinctively. A kite hawk swooped from nowhere with claws extended to snatch huge portions of the sliced beef and chicken breast from the plate, which went tumbling onto the lawn. Madge waved her arms and shouted 'shoo!' to try and drive away the greedy black scavenger and as she straightened herself up after picking up the plate the kitchen staff were in hysterics. Her uniform was in a mess and the food ruined. The particularly ugly bird returned for a second helping, leaving Madge with no option. She burst out laughing as well.

13

Madge Goes Dancing

Madge had been at 56 IGH for two months when she walked into the nurses' mess and saw a group so engrossed in conversation that she thought a serious problem had developed. She decided to sit down and join in.

'I can't believe how much I took for granted being able to wash my hair back home,' one of the nurses at the table was saying. 'I wouldn't have been seen dead going out the way I look now!'

Shampoo was virtually unobtainable in Chittagong so soap was the only option for the nurses when it came to washing their hair; Madge herself had got to the stage where virtually every day was a bad hair day. It was coming to something, she thought, when the height of luxury would be washing your hair with shampoo.

The only option was a trip to Calcutta, which by road was hundreds of miles away, and then you ran the risk of being given a large shopping list from the other nurses. A lovely Scottish nurse, Julie Boyle, was a bottle blonde, who asked any friend visiting Calcutta to bring back some bottles of shampoo and peroxide for her.

It seemed everybody missed out one way or another. Girls with curly or wavy locks found that within half an hour of dressing up for a dinner date or a dance the hair on which they had spent so much time and effort became one great big frizzy mess. Girls with naturally straight hair couldn't even wear pigtails because of the hospital's 'above the collar line' rule. Some even found their hair falling out in lumps when it was brushed. Girls like Madge, whose hair was not quite wavy but also not quite straight, found that whatever they did it never looked right, although she had a trick of cutting off the elasticated ends of army-issue stockings and making them into a halo which she would use to keep her hair neatly rolled.

Numerous other worries came to light, but nobody at the table had a solution until a raven-haired Indian sister walked past. The whole table turned to gaze in admiration and it spurred Madge into making a courteous little wave.

'Excuse me,' she said, 'but we're talking about the problems we're having with our hair. Yours is beautiful. Would you be so kind as to tell us your secret?'

The girl was attractive and very charming and said that she had been blessed with beautiful hair, but even she had to take the greatest of care in Chittagong's suffocating humidity. There was almost total silence in the usually noisy nurses' mess when she said that there was, however, a secret, and that secret was coconut oil. The barrage of questions from the table full of VADs stopped only when she held her hands up and laughed as she pleaded for silence.

'While my hair is still damp after being washed I massage coconut oil into it. Many others rinse it off after thirty minutes, but the key is actually leaving it on,' she explained.

'Do you mean not rinsing it off at all?' asked Vera.

'You would have very greasy pillows if you did that,' the sister replied. 'What I mean is leaving it on as long as possible. All evening if possible, or a few hours at least, then rinsing it.'

Madge compared the condition of the shining black locks with her own sadly lacklustre hair and decided there and then that coconut oil was the answer.

As luck would have it, Madge had an afternoon off the following day and she cadged a lift to Chittagong in one of the ubiquitous three-ton army supply trucks that drove in and out of the hospital. She was on a mission to buy coconut oil but wasn't having any success. She turned down a side street that consisted mainly of one-floor shops that included a grocer's, a cafe, a laundry and the inevitable stalls. There was nowhere that sold coconut oil, however, and she was so engrossed in her search that she was more than surprised to find instead what looked like a ladies' hairdressing salon. Madge could hardly believe her luck and all thoughts of coconut oil were forgotten as she peered in through the window. Suddenly the door was opened and an assistant in an intricately embroidered sari confirmed it was a salon and asked whether *memsahib* would like her hair permed? Madge replied that she most certainly would.

The salon was impeccably clean and comfortably furnished,

if a little dark, with the enchanting aroma of jasmine oil. Three double settees were draped in deep red rugs and at the back there was a washroom with stairs leading to an upper floor. There was even a little kitchen and one of the many assistants produced a pot of tea as Madge settled in. When the girls, the same age as their customer, heard that she had been invited to a dance that night they got very excited and promised her a special treat.

There seemed to be a lot of staff, but Madge was told they were needed for later in the day when business picked up. One or two of the girls wanted to practise their English and happily translated every word to their friends who had gathered round. Stools were drawn either side of the carved high chair in which Madge sat, and it turned out the special treat was a manicure on the house.

'This is absolute heaven,' laughed Madge to one of the brown-eyed beauties, who was maybe just a year or two younger than her English customer. 'It is luxury beyond a dream!'

While her hair was being permed Madge took the opportunity to ask if coconut oil was the reason why their hair looked so shiny and healthy. All said they used it but opinion was split on whether to leave the oil on or wash it off. The nicest surprise of all came as she left the salon after tipping and thanking the girls and they gave her a gift of a bottle of coconut oil.

When she returned to her basha the light was fading as Madge made one last check of her new hairdo, had a little twirl to make sure there were no creases in the piqué dress she had bought in Poona, and off she went for a jolly night at the SIB (Special Investigation Branch) mess. After being virtually danced off her feet Madge realised she was beginning to feel a little jaded as she was being whisked round the floor during a Glenn Miller number. That was until her partner said he loved her dress and then asked how on earth she kept her hair in such amazing condition. She felt like the belle of the ball!

Later an RAF pilot won a competition by drinking a pint standing on his head. Another won a bet with his pals when he stood with his back to Madge before he completed a backflip. It left her so open-mouthed in surprise that she simply couldn't refuse when he asked her if he could have the next waltz.

The dancing went on and on and it was only when the master of ceremonies announced that 'the lovely ladies who have graced us with their presence here tonight need a little break' that Madge realised the midnight curfew on returning to her quarters had long since passed. *You're in trouble again, young lady*, she told herself.

Madge's escort drove her back in an open-top jeep from which she enjoyed the sight of a crisp new moon and a million twinkling stars. By the time she got back to 56 IGH it was close to 1 a.m. and it looked for the entire world as if her perfect day was going to end in tears. After she identified herself, the gate was opened by two heavily armed Gurkhas. She was asked to step into the office and introduced to Havildar Bahadur, who checked her pass and looked pointedly at his watch. Just when Madge convinced herself that things couldn't get worse he caught her completely by surprise when he burst out laughing.

'*Memsahib* very late,' Bahadur said. 'Safer if I walk with you to your basha.'

Best of all, as he escorted her down the hill he promised that nobody would know she had arrived back an hour after curfew.

'You remind me of the Welsh missionary lady who taught me to speak English in a little school a day's walk from my village,' he said, and explained that he had grown up in the Himalayas, on the Nepalese side of the Indian border near Darjeeling.

As Madge tried to say thank you he stood to attention and gave her a big smile which was accompanied by an impeccable salute, turned on his heel and marched back to the main gate.

The following morning at breakfast Madge happily told her companions about the salon and what a lovely evening the military police sergeants had staged, but thought it better not to mention just how late she had returned from the dance. She felt as if she was almost floating on air as she strolled down to the hospital wards, but that soon changed when she was told by another of the nurses to be at Matron's office for 10 a.m. She was absolutely certain that Havildar Bahadur had not gone back on his word but try as she might, she couldn't think of the reason for the summons and it worried her. She did not understand either, as she walked in, why there was a giant of a military police sergeant standing by the side of Olive Ferguson's desk.

The MP was far from courteous when he virtually demanded to know, 'Where were you yesterday afternoon, Nurse Graves?'

'I was shopping in Chittagong,' she said, 'and then I had my hair permed in a salon down a side street off the main road.'

There was a prolonged silence during which Madge thought she spotted Matron shaking her head. The strict but always fair New Zealander was sitting leaning on one arm with a hand across her mouth.

'Standards have to be upheld and it's an utter disgrace for a young lady to go into a place like that,' said the increasingly unpleasant MP.

Madge felt herself getting quite hot and before she knew it she said, 'I've worked without a day off for more than a fort-night and I wanted to look nice for a dance. What could possibly be so wrong with that?'

'The salon had been under surveillance for some time and has now been closed down. A repeat of any such behaviour will result in serious consequences,' the red-faced MP splut-tered in response. 'You had your hair permed in a house of ill repute!' With that he thanked Matron for her co-operation, turned on his heel and marched out. Madge turned to Matron expecting another telling-off but instead the Aussie was doubled up laughing.

'Strewth,' she said, 'I can't believe you had your hair permed in a brothel! What was it like?' With tears rolling down her cheeks she just about managed to point to the door and wave Nurse Graves out. As Madge walked smiling down the corri-dor, there, standing on the corner, was the MP, with his peaked hat under his arm. He was well over six feet tall but she noticed that the surety he had displayed in Matron's office had all but disappeared. He half stuttered as he bent towards her.

'Might you be so kind as to join me for dinner tonight?' he asked.

Madge looked up, gave him her sweetest smile, and replied, 'Please excuse me but I have to wash my hair again this evening.'

14

The Gurkhas' Holy Man

Madge wandered out onto the veranda of the BOR ward for a five-minute break. Twilight was approaching and a ferocious autumn storm raged. The wind whistled in from the Bay of Bengal so powerfully that the rain drove in sheets across the grounds of the hospital. With visibility down to less than ten yards it took her time to spot a group of four trudging their way down the hill from the big house.

As they came closer Madge recognised three of the four as Gurkhas who guarded the hospital, one of them being her friend Havildar Bahadur. She waved and got big smiles in return as they finally made it onto the veranda and shook their brollies dry. The fourth man extended his hand and introduced himself as John, but Madge still couldn't work out what could possibly be important enough to make them venture out in such dreadful conditions. Then she noticed that the fourth man wore a dog collar and wondered, after ordering tea for the sodden group, if this was in fact their new chaplain.

Lieutenant Colonel Whittaker, Commander-in-Chief of 56 IGH, had announced weeks earlier that he was optimistic that chaplains would soon be appointed for both 56 and its sister hospital 68. After months of security lectures she had learned never to ask questions about postings, past, present or future but Madge needn't have worried because the visitor thanked her profusely for the tea and introduced himself as the new padre of 56 IGH and 68 IGH. She smiled, pleased that there was religious comfort available for men too badly injured to leave their hospital beds. On a personal note Madge had attended Sunday school and church regularly from her days as a child in Dover and found great comfort in once again being able to continue.

The chaplain quickly added that he was not on official business. 'Not until tomorrow anyway.' John Conway de la Tour Davies also said he was quite used to being called 'the Rev' and asked if it would be convenient to spend a little time with one of the Gurkhas who was suffering from a tummy bug that turned out to be dysentery.

It was well past 9 p.m. and the Padre said he realised it was an unusual request, but he had been in meetings most of the day about his new appointment.

'It's not like England with strict visiting hours,' laughed Madge, guiding the group to the stricken Gurkha who had been drifting in and out of a shallow sleep and must have thought he was dreaming when his three pals and the Reverend appeared at such a time of night. Madge apologised for leaving them but explained that she had to spend time with a new arrival, who had suffered terrible injuries after being caught in a Japanese booby trap.

It wasn't until much later that evening that Bahadur reappeared to thank *memsahib* for allowing them to see their pal so late at night. He said he'd first met the Padre when he was attached to a military hospital in Comilla where he made a policy of dealing with men of all faiths. Because the Rev liked the company of Gurkhas he spent one afternoon a week with a group, which included Havildar Bahadur, who were on a parachute course. The Rev had expressed his sorrow about the death of a twenty-one-year-old when the parachute 'candled'.

'I'm not sure what that means,' interrupted Madge, who was told that the chute had failed to unfold when the young Gurkha had jumped out of a DC-3. The following day, said Bahadur, the company adjutant asked Reverend Davies to conduct the burial service and was told that while it would be a privilege 'perhaps a Hindu holy man may be more appropriate'.

'What happened then?' asked Madge, who found tears begin to well when she was told that a delegation of Gurkha elders approached the adjutant and insisted that 'Rev Davies is our holy man'.

The following day at an open-air service attended by dozens of Ghurkhas the soul of the Nepalese warrior was commended to Jesus by the British padre 'because he gave his life for others'.

Bahadur had to return to duty and Madge made another check on her new patient, who had been seen by the doctors earlier in the afternoon on his arrival before she had cleaned up several still weeping wounds and settled him down for the night. His injuries weren't life threatening but the explosion had left the soldier's face in a terrible state and his hands had also been badly burned. She had seen similar damage when she was a member of Professor Thomas Kilner's plastic surgery team at Stoke Mandeville Hospital and was worried. Very worried indeed.

The following morning, three letters from Mum all arrived at once despite the postmark showing they had been mailed on three separate Fridays. Madge went to the nurses' mess to read them over lunch. Lily wrote:

Things are beginning to look up because for the first time since September 1939, the blackout regulations have eased. There are still restrictions but instead of calling it a blackout it is now officially a 'dim out'; light equivalent to that of the moon is allowed. Goodness knows what that is actually supposed to mean, but it made us all feel better when we read it.

In case this letter is delayed, the 'dim out' was announced in September, and it is wonderful after having lived in the dark for so long. But we still have to follow full blackout regulations if the air-raid sirens sound again.

I just wish that they would also ease up on rationing because I can't get the things I need to make treats for the girls. They love their cakes and keep asking when we are going to have another steak and kidney pudding, but they never moan, bless their souls.

Poor Mum, thought Madge. *Here we all are with fresh eggs every day for breakfast, lovely chicken curry for lunch and even roast beef sometimes for dinner, but then I suppose we do have to go without shampoo.*

Madge read on and was pleased to hear that Ernest Bevin, the Minister for Labour and National Service, had announced plans which would eventually lead to military demobilisation. *If that is true, then I think we really must have the Boche on the run now.*

The letters cheered Madge up no end. It also gave her a lift that just as she put down the last of the letters she looked up to see Phyllis Yearron for the first time in weeks. Different shifts on different wards and a different social life meant their paths hadn't crossed.

'Phyllis! How well you look!'

'Thank you, Madge, and you. How have you been?'

The two chatted for a while, although Madge didn't want to ask if rumours about a failed relationship for Phyllis were true so she changed the subject and told her just how much she had appreciated the gift she had given her of the silver hairbrush.

'It is so beautiful that even Ahmed is impressed and loves to dust and polish the shiny silver surface. You know, one afternoon I actually caught him looking at himself in the mirror side before giving his hair a good brushing!' Phyllis clapped her hands in delight as she laughed her head off at the thought of Madge's bearer posing with the hairbrush.

Just then Vera joined the table.

'Phyllis, I bet you that Madge hasn't mentioned a word about the real story involving her hair?'

'Well, Madge has told me all about the coconut oil,' she

replied, 'and I'm so impressed with the way her hair looks I'm going to try it myself.'

'Yes, but I bet she didn't tell you where she got it from!' Vera said with a wink in Madge's direction. She snorted and then, obviously deciding not to embarrass Madge too much, asked, with a mischievous grin, if the kite hawk incident had been discussed and began to sing '*Pack up all my cares and woe, here I go swinging low, bye bye blackbird.*'

The happy trio wandered back to their bashas and Madge prepared for another night shift with a degree of trepidation because she was worried about the badly burned soldier. He had been under sedation, but as she arrived to begin her shift she discovered he was awake and seemingly alert.

'Oh, hello there,' she said to the soldier. 'How are you feeling this evening?'

'A lot better than yesterday and my hearing is starting to come back,' he said. 'Although apart from a loud bang and a multi-coloured flash I can't remember anything else.'

The incident that had left him dreadfully disfigured had also rendered him almost completely deaf for more than forty-eight hours. All he could recollect was advancing, very carefully, through a thickly forested area of jungle and following instructions from his sergeant to stay ten paces away from the next man in case a mine was triggered. That advice almost certainly saved his life because when the explosion came, whether it was from a mine or a booby trap, the soldier to his left took the full blast and was killed instantly.

Madge listened without passing comment as she changed

the dressing on his hands as well as wiping away sweat that had formed on his brow. The facial disfigurement, appalling as it appeared to be, would heal in some form or another, although it would take months, or even years. In Professor Tommy Kilner's plastic surgery unit Madge had been taught to try and make an assessment of the emotional condition as well as the physical damage when someone had been injured in this way. The services section of Stoke Mandeville hadn't exactly been overstaffed and there were times when Madge had run four and five wards at night on her own, but in comparison with the number of nurses at 56 IGH it was light years ahead. She wanted desperately to stay with the corporal, but others needed attention as well so she had little option but to move on after doing her best to make sure he was as comfortable as possible.

There was no such thing as a 'front line' in the brutal confrontation in the jungles of northern Burma, but there had been a notable change in the type of patients arriving at the hospital, who were increasingly suffering from combat injuries rather than disease. The success of the 14th Army in pushing the Japanese back, deeper and deeper into Burma, was remarkable but it was being accomplished at a cost that included massive extra pressure on hospitals and already overstretched nursing staff in particular.

Madge fervently wished there was more help available on that very busy night and her wishes were answered almost within an hour when the Padre made his first official evening visit to the hospital and dropped by to say hello, and then have a chat with the dysentery-riddled Gurkha.

'I'm so sorry for turning up after visiting hours again,' said Rev Davies, who had been at 68 IGH since early that morning. He made it clear he wanted to be a hands-on padre and was well aware of the unique pressures nurses faced at night. 'Is there anything I can do to help?' he asked.

From the moment she had seen him standing on the veranda soaked to the skin after marching through that raging storm Madge had instantly liked the caring and courteous new padre. 'Actually, we do have a new arrival who has terrible facial injuries after having been caught in an explosion. I'm worried about him. The soldier he was with was killed instantly and he's beginning to show signs of stress. Do you think you could spend some time with him?'

'Of course I can. Just point me in the right direction.'

Madge showed him where the soldier's bed was and then left the Padre to do her rounds.

When the ward finally began to settle for the night, Madge decided to take a fifteen-minute break and walked over to join the Rev, who had been encouraging the young soldier to relax and take things day by day until he was back on the road to recovery. Reverend Davies' words seemed to strike a chord with the corporal because Madge could instantly tell from the expression on his face that the depression in which he had sunk had already begun to ease.

'I hope you don't mind me asking, sir,' he suddenly said to

the Padre, 'but where did you get those tattoos and how did you end up in Chittagong?'

Madge followed the corporal's gaze and spotted some very prominent tattoos on the Reverend's forearms.

Madge had brought three cups of tea with her in the hope that the corporal would take a few sips as well so she handed one to each of the men and began to drink her own as she listened to the Padre's extraordinary reply.

'In answer to your first question,' replied the Padre, 'when I was working with troops in Orkney I wanted to show I was a missionary of the church and one of them, not a superior officer, and that was why I decided to have both arms tattooed. There was a slight problem, however, because there was no tattooist in Orkney!'

Madge thought she had detected the faintest hint of a smile from the corporal, who was listening intently. For the first time since arriving at 56 IGH his mind was focused away from his terrible injuries.

The memory of the time and trouble he went to in trying to find a tattooist on Orkney made Rev Davies smile and he added that it wasn't until he arrived in Bombay on a troopship after a six-week journey from Liverpool that he eventually found a tattooist.

'I drew the designs on a piece of paper before having "God with us" put on one arm and "Who loved me and gave himself for me" on the other. There are also images of Jesus on the cross and with his mother Mary. It took two hours to complete and it was terribly painful, but definitely worth it,' he said.

The Reverend then went on to tell the corporal more of his story. 'On the voyage over to India I had to conduct a burial at sea, but unfortunately there was a submarine around so the troop carrier had to continue at full speed. That was tricky to say the least!' he said, chuckling slightly. 'I wanted to get to know the troops I was with better so I joined in with a bit of sparring one day with a group of keep-fit fanatics, but one caught me with a punch that sent me spinning onto the metal deck. That's why I'm slightly deaf in one ear,' he said.

His determined effort to communicate with the troops had paid off, however, because he conducted two baptisms, but the naval tradition of using the ship's bell as a font had to be ignored this time because it couldn't be removed.

'We used a pie dish, disguised with a silk scarf, to hold the baptism water instead,' he said with a smile.

From Bombay he travelled by train to Calcutta where the Rolex he was given as a twenty-first birthday present was pickpocketed. He had placed it in his breast pocket after the strap broke and the corporal actually smiled when the chaplain added, 'The watch cost £50 but I got £70 in the insurance payout!'

Madge's break was over and the Rev had put in another long day so they left the bedside of the sleepy corporal and discussed his chances of recovery.

'Time will be the greatest healer,' said the Padre. Madge agreed but knew from her experience on Professor Kilner's team that long-term pastoral care would be even more important once the physical damage healed.

In the early hours of the morning shift Madge found the corporal wide awake and filled with utter despair so she told him about the wonderful things that she had seen accomplished with plastic surgery patients, in particular RAF pilots, who had been taken to Stoke Mandeville after suffering facial damage when their aircraft had burst into flames.

'One of his specialities was rebuilding noses through skin grafts,' she said, 'and once the grafts settled down it changed their lives. With a bit of luck you will be back in England soon and I'm sure you'll be able to have similar treatment.' But even that failed to cheer him up.

'I know it must be getting towards midnight,' he told Madge, 'but is there any possibility of having an omelette? My mother always made me an omelette when I was poorly as a little boy. It's just what I fancy now.'

'I'll see what can be done,' promised Madge, who was only too aware that the corporal had hardly eaten since his arrival. The problem was that as the only nurse on duty she was worried about leaving the ward even for a few minutes. There were no ward-boys around at that time of night and the kitchens wouldn't be staffed, but as she wracked her brain for a solution Big Arthur, one of the night guards from the RASC (Royal Army Service Corps), strolled past, said hello and asked if everything was OK.

When Madge explained the omelette problem the giant Yorkshireman simply nodded and said, 'Right, love, leave it to me.' Just fifteen minutes later he reappeared with his rifle over his shoulder and a very tasty and fluffy-looking omelette ringed with sliced tomatoes. He had even brought a knife and fork. 'Couldn't find bread,' he said, 'but them there tomatoes make everything look right luverly.'

It looked so good Madge could have eaten the whole lot there and then. Instead she thanked the guard. 'Where on earth did you manage to perform this little miracle at this time of night?'

Arthur said that as there was no reply when he knocked on the kitchen door he gave it a little kick and it just sort of burst open. 'There was nobody in the kitchens so I made it myself, love,' he added, before resuming his lonely patrol. The corporal was staring at the ceiling when Madge walked in with the omelette and because his hands were still so painful she fed him a forkful at a time. After eating what was his biggest meal since arriving from the casualty clearing station Madge thought he would soon fall back to sleep.

Instead he talked, with a wistful look on those painfully distorted features, about his 'sweet and beautiful girlfriend' back home and how she had given up the chance of a place at university to become a nurse. She had even tried to get a posting to India to be near him, but had been turned down because she was just nineteen.

'What will she think if she sees me like this?' he asked.

Madge didn't even need to think about what to say in response because the answer came straight from her heart.

'If she's a nurse, then she will love you even more.'

15

Letters From Home

The hours were awful, the heat and humidity were suffocating and the mosquitos were lethal, but Madge was happy because she felt needed and appreciated at 56 IGH. Yet one autumn Monday morning she woke up feeling down in the dumps and couldn't work out what the problem was.

Depression could be a side effect of mepacrine but she had been taking it religiously for months so that wasn't to blame. There was no food rationing or blackouts or doodlebugs or depth charges to worry about and the team spirit at the hospital was first class, but, Madge realised with a tug at her chest, there was no dear Mum, no Doris and no Doreen. For the first time since walking out of her twenty-first birthday in tears on the troopship *Strathnaver* Madge was homesick.

That day everything reminded Madge of home. The smell of newly baked bread wafted down from the kitchens of the big house and made her think of happy days as a child in Dover. The deep red roses on the veranda brought to mind the beautiful blooms in the back garden of the house in High Wycombe, and the sound of laughter in the nurses' mess triggered images of her sisters Doreen and Doris joking together. *Mum's advice would be to put your shoulders back and get on with it*, she told herself, and she tried.

There had been no letters from home, or indeed any mail at all, for weeks and Madge was so blue she certainly didn't expect any that morning. However, Sister Blossom, who handed out the mail, had a little treasure trove for her that included a card from her cousin Ruby in Anerley and a big envelope from Auntie Bea in Dover, who had enclosed several pages from the *Dover Express*.

By far the pick of the bunch was a lengthy and funny letter from Mum saying how proud she was that Doris had joined the Women's Land Army and was working on a farm near East Grinstead in Sussex. Madge could almost see the twinkle in Mum's eye as she'd written about it.

Can you believe that one of the first things she learned to do was drive a tractor? My little Doris, driving a tractor! Although I told her that driving a tractor was better than driving me mad by coming home late from all those dances.

Mum also said that she'd caught Doreen dancing in front of the lounge mirror with the wireless on full blast as Vera Lynn sang 'There'll be bluebirds over the white cliffs of Dover'.

Doreen looked so graceful and beautiful that I joined in and we had a lovely time. We just wished you could have been with us.

Lily's words helped lift Madge's spirits and she put the bundle of mail into her little bag and walked into the dining room for breakfast. Vera waved her over and couldn't wait to say that she had a bit of gossip.

'That's very unusual for you,' smiled Madge.

Vera blurted out, 'Guess who's coming to see us today?' Without waiting for an answer Vera said she had been told that Gertrude Corsar would be visiting 56 IGH. 'Apparently she wants to see all two hundred and fifty of us to make sure we've settled into our "arduous and testing new lives". But I'm not sure what that means exactly,' said Vera.

'All it means,' said Madge, 'is that she's trying to make sure that we are all OK and I take my hat off to her for that. She really is a good old stick.'

Madge went to her next shift feeling much cheerier than she had that morning. One of her patients, Adam, who had been very poorly with amoebic dysentery, was due to be released and returned to his unit, which he said was involved in heavy fighting in the Arakan.

Adam had told Madge that he sold flowers at Columbia Road market in the East End of London and the other lads in the ward nicknamed him 'L.O. Flower' because that's what he always said to nurses who came to clean him up. He was the only patient she had nursed who survived on custard and cans of British army tinned fruit for a number of days before eventually returning to a normal diet.

'I hate that bully beef stuff and my stomach is so upset I can't eat nuffink else,' he insisted in his Cockney twang.

Madge liked 'L.O.' and when he started to recover he helped out in the ward, happily fluffing up pillows, lending a hand to turn some of the bigger patients over to stop them getting bed sores and writing letters home for one soldier, whose right arm was heavily bandaged and in a sling. The nursing sepoys loved him because he spent time helping them with their English and taught them some very funny and naughty words.

L.O. was a jolly soul who cheered everybody up and teased Madge mercilessly. A few weeks after he'd been admitted he appeared just before her lunch break dressed in his army khakis, looking a different man to the weary and dispirited character who had been carried in on a stretcher.

'Thank you, thank you, thank you for saving me, *memsahib*,' he said in his Cockney accent as he bowed his head. Then from behind his back he handed Madge a beautiful bouquet of deep red roses wrapped in brown paper before picking up his few possessions and walking up the hill.

Madge felt a lump in her throat as she watched him go. She put the roses in a jug of water and later took them with her to lunch in the nurses' mess where she had arranged to meet Vera.

After listening intently to Madge recounting what had happened, Vera gave a mock swoon and said, 'Ooh, it sounds to me just like an episode straight from Mills and Boon.'

Madge ignored the interruption and picked up the deep red blooms. 'What a kind and thoughtful gesture. He must have walked all the way in to Chittagong to buy them for me,' she said.

By this time Vera was laughing uncontrollably and pointed to the bush on the veranda. 'Your cheeky chappy has only gone and pinched them from here!' she said.

At the end of her busy day shift, Madge returned to the

nurses' mess to discover that Miss Corsar had arrived. The VAD liaison officer kindly poured Madge a cup of tea and then offered a plate of biscuits. She was holding a meeting in a room away from the main dining area and within twenty minutes everybody was in place. The esteem in which Miss Corsar was held was underlined by the attendance of Lieutenant Colonel Whittaker, who asked politely if it would be in order for him to listen in.

Gertrude, a very different figure in khaki from the Red Cross uniform she had worn on the *Strathnaver*, told the hospital chief he would be most welcome, walked over to the door and locked it. 'Security purposes,' she said after receiving one or two inquisitive glances, then started by outlining how the group had been split once they got off the ambulance train in Calcutta.

'Quite a few,' she said, 'are working with the 14th Army and all of you are divided between eleven very busy hospitals, where the matrons have been highly impressed with the enthusiasm and professionalism that has been shown under conditions which are often little better than primitive. The turnover of patients in the eight forward area hospitals is particularly high, as the figures here at 56 IGH have shown. Nobody knows just how busy this hospital has become better than you girls, of course,' said Gertrude, in a comment that was greeted with numerous nods and smiles. 'The other three hospitals to which VADs have been posted are further west in Ranchi and Dacca.

'I have been shown the bashas in which you are living here

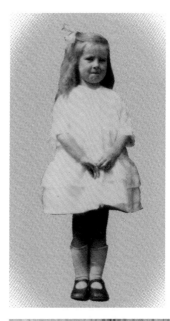

Left Madge Graves in 1930, aged seven.

Doris, Mum, Doreen and Madge
in High Wycombe in 1941.

Madge as a trainee Voluntary
Aid Detachment nurse at
Stoke Mandeville Hospital, 1941.

Madge with Vera Clark,
her fellow VAD.

Madge with Phyl
Irvine in 1942.

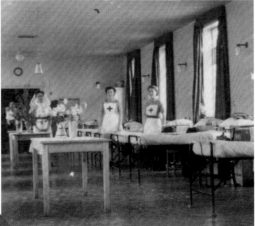

Ward 11, Stoke Mandeville
Hospital, May 1943.

Madge in London,
July 1944, as she
waited to depart
for India.

Arriving in Poona and
enjoying a banana.

With the girls at
the mess at Poona.

Vera outside
a basha ward.

56 Indian General Hospital,
view from the mess.

Above The Lamberts on parade. From left to right: Bill, Buster, Beryl, Basil, Brian and Bob.

Left Basil at the Officers' Training Centre in Mhow in 1943.

OPPOSITE PAGE
Top From left to right: Basil, Jock, Jim and Tom in Chittagong, March 1944.

Middle An entry in Lieutenant Colonel Whittaker's war diary, mentioning the Japanese woman with a gunshot wound.

Bottom Patients and staff at Christmas, 1944.

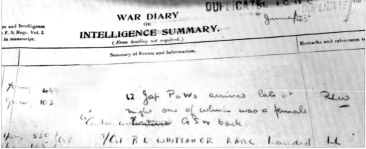

DUPLICATE

WAR DIARY
OR
INTELLIGENCE SUMMARY.
(Erase heading not required.)

es and Intelligence
F. S. Regs. Vol. I.
in manuscript.

Summary of Events and Information.

Remarks and references to

62 Jap PoWs arrived late ô
night one of which was a female
Captain with GSW back.
S/Col R L WHITTAKER RAMC Landed

A beautiful bridesmaid in a dress made from a sari.

On holiday in Calcutta with Basil, April 1945.

Saying goodbye. A picnic on the beach at Patanga, May 1945.

Madge and the girls on the MV *Georgic* as they began their journey home.

Vera, Phyl and Madge on Regent Street, London, 1947.

Basil came back to the coldest winter of the twentieth century, February 1947.

Madge and Basil on their wedding day, 16 October 1948.

Madge and Basil meeting Dame Vera Lynn on Horse Guards Parade on the 60th anniversary of VE and VJ Day, July 2005.

Madge meeting Prince Harry at Buckingham Palace Garden Party in 2017.

at 56 IGH and seventy-five per cent of all VADs are in similar accommodation. Many have to use hurricane lamps because there is no electricity available and few have running water. One unit is sleeping in tents,' she said, 'whereas the lucky few are in more substantial buildings.

'Of far more importance,' Miss Corsar underlined, 'is the question of safety on night duty and the strain that it places on you nurses, who at various points are looking after more than a hundred patients at a time.

'One girl even has three hundred patients in three separate blocks, with just a night sister on duty with her apart from the nursing sepoys, who are prone to fall asleep themselves.' There were a few giggles at this point.

'Please talk to me later,' she said, 'if any of you are worried about safety on night shifts and don't hesitate to write if you run into any other problems.'

'Security is the least of our worries at 56 IGH,' Madge whispered to Vera, because she had become fond of the Gurkhas who guarded the complex, and British army soldiers maintained a high profile outside the basha wards.

After twenty minutes there was a short break in which Miss Corsar again made sure everybody had tea and happily walked round with plates of biscuits. Madge thought she came across as the mother hen of her widely spread flock. 'I really like her,' whispered Vera and Madge nodded in agreement as the second session got underway.

Miss Corsar began with a compliment about how impressed a number of matrons were with the way in which Indian soldiers had been nursed. 'My overall view is that you are doing a magnificent job under the most testing of conditions. I am visiting as many hospitals as possible to reassure you nurses that far from being forgotten, your sheer enthusiasm has ensured a warm welcome and the number who have volunteered to work closer to the battle zone is also very impressive indeed,' she added.

She thanked them all for attending and being so attentive and said she was pleased to hear that their social life in Chittagong was such a lot of fun. As one last word of advice, she added, 'But please don't worry about turning down invitations. Everybody knows just how hard you have to work in the basha wards, which are not air conditioned, and lots of late nights on top of that can lead to tiredness. If you get run down in this heat, it can also lead to illness. So just learn to say no!'

Laughter and applause followed as Miss Corsar walked across to unlock the door and the VADs went slowly through to the dining room, many of them by now desperate for more food as they had been up and on the go since early that morning.

'What did you think of the meeting?' asked Madge.

'Impressive. Very impressive indeed,' said Vera, who also admired the Commandant's courage in travelling so many hundreds of miles on the notoriously dangerous Indian railway system on her own.

'I agree, and it is really nice to know there is somebody looking after our interests and we haven't been forgotten,' said Madge.

As the duo walked towards the door, a familiar figure suddenly appeared and asked if they had time for a pot of tea in the nurses' mess.

'Sally! Where have you suddenly sprung from?' smiled Vera.

'The last time I saw you was in Calcutta,' said Madge. 'Where have you been?'

'It's a long story,' replied Sally, as they walked through to the mess.

She insisted on getting the tea and cakes and sat down opposite Madge and Vera. 'I feel terrible as I wasn't even able to say a simple thanks for your kindness to a very lonely and unhappy me. One minute we were all together at the station in Calcutta. The next minute you had gone.'

'Bonnie lass, you've become a real mystery to us,' said Vera. 'I know I'm being nosy, but let's start at the very beginning. I can't even work out your accent.'

'That's good coming from you,' laughed Madge, 'and you are being very nosy.'

'I don't mind,' said Sally. 'I owe you an explanation. As a teenager I dreamed of becoming a doctor, but then war broke out and my elder brother JP – that's short for John Patrick – packed in his job, made his way to Cape Town and caught a boat to England to join up.'

'Slow down,' said Madge. 'Made his way to Cape Town from where?'

'Sorry, I thought I'd told you I come from Southern Rhodesia,' said Sally. 'We had only been there for a few years after emigrating from Edinburgh because Dad had health problems

179

and needed to be in a warmer climate. Two years after my brother joined up Dad gave me the money and suggested that instead of knitting socks and sweaters for the war effort like my mum, I got a boat back to the old country as well and became a nurse.

'To cut a long story short, Dad has since died, my brother was taken by the Japanese as a prisoner of war in Singapore, I haven't seen Mum for five years and the last we heard about JP was a message that he may be working on the Death Railway somewhere in Thailand near the Burmese border. I answered Lord Mountbatten's plea for nurses because I thought it might help me get closer to my brother.'

'Goodness me,' said Madge. 'That's some story.'

'Keep going,' said Vera. 'How have you ended up in Chittagong?'

'I actually asked to be transferred from a hospital much further north to be closer to the front line,' said Sally, 'and have been nursing at 68 IGH.' She had been totally calm in revealing details of the way in which her life had started to fall apart. Now, however, tears began to trickle down her freckled face as she broke down and sobbed. 'I just want to feel needed.'

'That's what we all want, love,' said Madge, placing her hand tenderly on Sally's arm. 'That's what we all want.'

16

Captain Basil Lambert

As the battle to drive the Japanese from the north of Burma intensified there was a huge increase in the turnover of patients at 56 IGH, with dozens of sick and wounded men coming and going, and for the nurses it was all work and no play. Every day they had to remake dozens of beds as patients left and others arrived after being transported to Chittagong by trains and DC-3s. Mattresses had to be turned as well as sheets changed and that was an exhausting task in the heat. This was before administering even basic medication and the all-important TLC.

Madge was more than grateful when she was given an unexpected afternoon off, which meant she could write an overdue letter to Mum while there was still natural light rather than by the dull glow of the hurricane lamp in her basha. In spite of the cheery letters she received from High Wycombe, she wondered how Mum was coping on a widow's pension of just ten shillings a week, plus the ten shillings a week she received from the Dover flour mill where dad Charles had worked before he died. It really wasn't very much on which to clothe and feed Doris and Doreen.

Madge kept her return letter deliberately cheery as well, addressed the envelope and opened the little chest of drawers in the basha to get a stamp, but couldn't find one and realised she had run out. That was a problem because if the letter missed the 5 p.m. collection, it wouldn't be on the boat that was due out of Chittagong first thing in the morning and Mum would start imagining that all sorts of things had happened to her eldest daughter.

Madge went straight to the nurses' mess to ask if anyone there had stamps she could buy, but it was unusually quiet and there was no response. That was until an Anglo-Indian officer, who had been visiting the hospital, waved and introduced himself as Mac. As Madge reached into her purse for some rupees, he told her not to worry about money. 'I haven't got the stamps with me; they're back in my room and my living quarters are only ten minutes' walk away.'

Madge was in somewhat of a quandary. Her initial reaction was to be wary of the man's intentions, but there was nowhere else to buy stamps and time was fast running out. 'How kind of you,' she said, and off they went.

It was getting dark and Madge began to feel nervous as the pair walked further from the hospital grounds. Eventually they arrived at his room near the officers' mess and stepped inside. 'Would you like a gin and tonic?' Mac asked.

Madge was about to tell him that she wasn't the sort of girl to drink alone in men's rooms but relaxed when Mac introduced her to his room mate, who was concentrating on a file of papers.

'Madge, this is Basil Lambert, 10th Baluch Regiment; Basil, this is Madge, a nurse at the hospital.'

'Hello there,' said Madge, feeling slightly shy all of a sudden.

'Pleased to meet you,' Basil replied with a brief smile, before turning back to his papers. The sleeves of his khaki shirt were rolled up to the elbows and even though it was late on what had been a sticky, humid day he still looked neat and tidy with barely a hair out of place. Madge also noticed a natty, Clark Gable-style moustache. All very impressive, in fact, except for one thing.

He didn't even rise to greet me, the cheeky so-and-so, Madge thought. She collected her stamp, declined Mac's offer of a drink once again and hurried off to post her letter.

Madge was so busy that she barely thought anything of the encounter until a week later when she went to collect her mail and discovered a letter without a stamp. *What on earth is this?* she wondered.

Captain Lambert had written a charming apology and invited her to join him for dinner. Madge considered it. *He was incredibly rude when we met, but then he wasn't bad looking, and I don't have anything better to do so I might as well.*

She wrote a short note accepting his invitation and asked Ahmed, her bearer, if he would be so kind as to deliver it to the small brick hut which Captain Lambert shared with Mac. There was also a letter for Mac, thanking him for being such a gentleman. Not only had he refused to accept any payment for the stamp, but because it was such a dark night he had also insisted on escorting her back to the hospital.

Vera once laughingly told Madge that she had broken hearts from the moment she boarded the *Strathnaver* on the Forth of Clyde to the time she arrived in Chittagong. Along the way, in the mad social whirl that was Poona, she had been invited virtually every day to the grandest afternoon teas, sophisticated cocktail parties and glamorous, moonlit dinners. There were dates by the dozen, but the flirtations, however enjoyable, had been entirely fleeting.

The upcoming date with Captain Lambert, however, was different. The coconut oil was left on for an inordinate length of time when she washed her hair the night before. The piqué dress from Poona was taken from the wardrobe and checked time and again and Ahmed was asked to make sure her favourite shoes were free of creepy crawlies and the mould that gathered with such monotonous regularity in the humidity of Chittagong. She was even tempted to borrow some of Vera's bright red Coty lipstick, then remembered the advice from that splendid old lady at the Governor General's Welcome Ball about not wearing too much make-up in this heat.

The growl of an approaching jeep alerted Madge to Basil's arrival as she waited just inside the hospital gates and within seconds he stood alongside her looking rather handsome in his neatly pressed khaki trousers and long-sleeved shirt, his short light-brown hair swept to the side.

He had previously warned her that, weather permitting, they would be dining on the veranda of a little cafe in

Chittagong so long sleeves were important in keeping the mosquitos at bay.

'Good evening, madam,' he said with a bow that instantly made her laugh. 'My name is Lambert. Basil Lambert,' he continued, a cheeky grin lighting up his face. 'Please step this way.'

He helped her into the jeep and within minutes they were sitting in a secluded little cafe off the main road in Chittagong having drinks.

'I'm so sorry about the other night,' he said, 'but by the time I got to my feet it seemed you were walking out of the door.'

Madge realised very quickly that this was not just another moonlit date because within minutes they were chatting away like old friends. Even though they wanted to know about each other, it was their first date and both had been repeatedly warned about the infinite importance of security, so it simply wasn't the time or place to ask how long they had each been in India, where their next postings would be and which units they were with.

She decided to steer clear of anything on the military side and told him a little bit about her life at home instead.

'So, I was brought up in Dover but after Dad died and war broke out I moved with my mum and my two younger sisters to High Wycombe, and that's when I decided to become a VAD. With Christmas on the way I really miss Mum and the girls,' she said. 'What about you?' she asked. 'How did you come to be here?'

'Well, in July 1941 my brother Brian and I got the train from our home in Woking to Surbiton, where we went to the local recruitment office and volunteered for active service. I signed up and was earmarked for the Middlesex Regiment, but Brian was rejected because he was only just seventeen.'

'So what did you do then?' asked Madge, who was full of admiration for the patriotism of a boy who had tried to join up straight from school.

She was told that the brothers immediately took a bus to nearby Richmond where there was another recruiting centre.

'Brian told them he had celebrated his eighteenth birthday in April and he was asked to sign on the dotted line straight away,' said Basil.

There were dozens of questions that could have been asked by a young couple under normal circumstances. However, with Burma some fifty miles away and vicious hand-to-hand combat taking place across the border the circumstances were far from normal.

There was even a problem arranging a second liaison because Madge was due to start another spell of night duty and Basil, who told her he was in Troop Movements, was endlessly busy throughout the day, and often at night as well.

'This evening just seems to be flying by,' said Basil, 'and it would be so wonderful if we could arrange to have dinner again.'

'Of course we will,' said Madge. 'But I've told you lots about me. Are you going to tell me more about yourself? Or is it a secret!'

Basil, who was due to turn twenty-two in a few weeks' time, on 1 January 1945, was, in fact, part of an experienced group of administrators involved in the massive movement of troops and equipment that was taking place in the battle to drive the Japanese back south out of Burma. Because of the strategic importance of Chittagong thousands of troops and huge volumes of supplies were channelled through the most important railway junction in Bengal and for Basil's unit the work went on round the clock. Madge listened attentively to the few details he was able to tell her, enjoying every moment of getting to know him better.

Madge was normally asleep within minutes of her head hitting the pillow but that night she stayed awake into the small hours recalling the events of what she decided was one of the loveliest nights of her life. *By the end of the evening,* she mused, *we were chatting away as if we had known each other forever!* She had been far from impressed on their first, brief meeting but had soon realised that he was, in fact, a perfect gentleman. On her return to the table after a visit to the ladies' powder room he had stood and eased her chair back in when she sat down. He had walked on the outside on pavements and always stood back to let ladies go first. *Little things,* Madge told herself, but they meant a lot and she remembered what her mum had told her – 'You can always judge a man by his manners.'

Most of all she played the scene at the hospital gates at the end of an enchanting evening over and over in her mind. Basil had bent in the moonlight to give her the sweetest of goodnight kisses that had left her saying with a wildly beating heart, 'Your apology is accepted.'

The following afternoon as Madge relaxed in the mess at the end of her shift she was called to the phone and it was Basil asking if she fancied a drive along the Bay of Bengal to a vantage point ten or so miles away where they would see 'a rather splendid sunset'.

'The only problem is,' said Basil, 'would you be able to bring one of your friends along to make it a foursome?'

'Why, who is he?' asked Madge.

'Jim, an officer I know from our Movements unit,' said Basil. 'He's a very pleasant person.'

'I'll see what I can do,' promised Madge, after arranging a 6 p.m. rendezvous with Basil at the hospital gates.

As Madge walked down to her basha Phyl suddenly appeared. She ummed and aahed when Madge asked her to join them on their evening drive.

'Come on, Madge,' she said, 'I need a bit more information. Is he going to be dashingly handsome?'

'I've never even heard of him before, let alone met him,' laughed Madge. 'I honestly don't know.'

On the dot of 6 p.m. Basil neatly parked a station wagon with eye-catching wooden panelling so that it wouldn't block the main gates and alighted to introduce Jim, who was his commanding officer. Madge then introduced Phyl to the two men.

'Lovely night for a drive,' said Basil, 'but the road will be greasy in places after that heavy rain early today.'

He was ultra careful as he manoeuvred his way round a sacred cow that was happily wandering down the middle of the road and wisely pulled over and stopped as a convoy of army supplies thundered past heading south in the direction of Cox's Bazaar, a key port in the confrontation with the Japanese.

After thirty minutes he pulled off the potholed highway and onto a tranquil section of beach that was slowly turning from yellow to rose pink as the sun began to set. 'For my next trick,' said Basil . . .' pulling a hamper from the back of the vehicle. Within minutes he and Jim had placed a rug on the sand, set up a makeshift picnic and passed around gin and tonics that looked so inviting in tall-stemmed glasses.

'This really is gorgeous,' said Madge an hour later as the rose-pink horizon flickered into a red haze when the sun set with remarkable speed. 'Sadly it looks as if that is it for the night,' she added and it became so dark that Basil switched on the headlights so they could see to pack the picnic debris away.

'Thanks for that, boys, it was a really nice surprise,' said Phyl.

Madge looked over to see that Jim had got behind the wheel and was insisting on driving home in spite of Basil asking if he was sure it would be OK. 'If you don't mind me saying so, I haven't seen your name on the list of authorised drivers,' he added.

'Never mind about that,' said Jim. 'I'll be fine! I think it's time to go so let's head off, shall we?'

The clutch screeched in protest as he put the station wagon into gear. By now it was almost pitch black on a moonless night and patches of moisture glittered on the road in the headlights. One minute the girls were chattering happily in the back as the vehicle eased into what looked like the most uncomplicated of bends a couple of miles from Chittagong. Then all of a sudden there was utter chaos as it skidded on a patch of greasy road. Jim jammed the brakes on but that made the station wagon slither sideways. A front wheel caught a pothole and almost in slow motion the vehicle turned on its side and then rolled upside down.

Madge's heart seemed to stop momentarily. As soon as the car came to a standstill she looked across at Phyl, who seemed to be fine, but they were both trapped.

'Are you OK?' Phyl asked her.

'I'm fine. Are you?'

'I'm OK. But I can't seem to get out.'

Just then Basil appeared and somehow or other pulled both girls free. Madge realised then that there was a nasty smell of petrol and she was far from impressed when she looked over and saw that Jim was lighting a cigarette.

'You surely aren't intending to smoke when there's such a strong smell of petrol, are you?'

'That's definitely not wise, sir,' Basil said, then, turning to the girls, he asked, 'Are either of you hurt?'

'No, we're both fine – just a few bruises,' Madge answered.

'Jim got a bit of a bump when his head hit the windscreen,' Basil said, 'but it was a minor miracle that we all escaped in one piece.'

They set off walking towards Chittagong but had not gone far when they were rescued by two RMP sergeants on a routine patrol. As soon as they heard about the crash, the sergeants said they would organise to have the damage to the vehicle taken care of, after which it would be returned. They then offered to take everyone back to their billets. A chorus of grateful thanks was their reward.

When Madge, who had finally got to bed in the wee small hours, explained over breakfast what had happened the night before, Vera said, 'You are so very lucky. That's another of your nine lives gone.'

Sister Blossom, who had been let in on the secret that there was a new man in Madge's life, could hardly wait a few days later to hand her the single item of mail addressed to 'Miss M. L. Graves'. Madge saw that the envelope had 'HQ Movements, Chittagong Area' on the back but with Sister Blossom hovering on one side of the table and Vera snooping on the other she swiftly slipped it into her bag. Vera, however, couldn't bear the suspense.

'According to mess rules all invitations are supposed to be put on the noticeboard but if you show us what it is, we promise not to tell a soul about the new love in your life,' she said.

Madge just snorted at the very thought of Vera keeping a secret, but relented when they pleaded and told her she was 'just being a meany and a killjoy'. With Vera and Sister Blossom on tenterhooks she delved into her bag, lifted out the embossed envelope and feigned indecision about whether or not she would open it.

'It's from HQ Movements, Chittagong Area, and it says this

information is not for the attention of nosy parkers,' joked Madge, who added that the invitation was from the Movements officers requesting the pleasure of the company of Miss Graves at a dance to be held at their mess. 'Transport will be arranged on request.'

'Sounds serious to me,' said Vera as she leaned over to take the invitation to read for herself before handing it to Sister Blossom.

'I'm thrilled that everything is pointing to a very happy Christmas for my favourite VAD,' Sister Blossom smiled. But she was nowhere near as clearly delighted as Madge.

'Calm down, young lady. You look like the cat that got the cream,' said Vera.

Madge had to keep her mind on the job, though, and when she reported for her morning shift she was invited by Matron Ferguson to take part in a briefing about a problem that was beginning to get out of hand. There were several other nurses in attendance. Madge looked around nervously.

'A month previously Lieutenant Colonel Whittaker expressed concern at the alarming increase in numbers of Indian troops arriving at 56 IGH with venereal disease,' Matron Ferguson said. She went on to explain that he had written to medical authorities in New Delhi asking if a specialist could be sent and the military police had done their best to help locally by closing several brothels in Chittagong, but there was still no reduction in the number of cases arriving at the hospital.

'There have been major advances in the treatment of gonorrhoea in particular, with the treatment period being reduced from thirty days to just five. But as you know, we are still faced with problems in caring for them because as non-believers you nurses are not allowed to step foot in the VD ward to inject the infected patients.' Matron did her best not to laugh when she added that further discussions had resulted in an agreement which involved a nurse standing, syringe in hand, at the entrance to the basha ward and completing the injection from there. In the dark!

Madge was one of the first nurses to be rostered on this new system when it was introduced the following week. There were twenty-eight patients who needed to be injected with penicillin, the new wonder drug, so she waited until twilight and prepared the syringes and needles. Out of the blue there was a short, sharp rainstorm and by the time she got to the ward it was very dark indeed and a swirling wind was gathering in strength. The nursing sepoy who helped her carry the large volume of syringes and needles was also in charge of the one hurricane lamp.

Madge had to hold back her giggles as the pair stood on the basha ward veranda, barely sheltered from the rain, as the stricken Indian soldiers came one by one to the door with their trousers hanging down. After being injected they returned to the ward. The wind became so intense it extinguished the hurricane lamp, whose pallid light had been far from perfect in the first place, but Madge stoically continued to administer the injections. Things went from bad to worse when she ran out of syringes and clean needles and they had to make a mad dash back for supplies. Madge cursed herself. She was sure that she'd counted out the right number.

A few days later Basil managed to get away from HQ Movements for a few moments with Madge over lunch, during which she explained the scene. She told him how bad the weather had been, how awful the sepoy's complaining had become and that she had actually run out of syringes and needles.

'The strange thing was,' she said, 'that the other nurses who were rostered before me also ran out of needles. It seems that however carefully the syringes are counted, there never seem to be enough.'

'Perhaps I can help,' said Basil. 'The least I can do is check the number of patients and try to shed some light on this problem once and for all.'

He could see that Madge was concerned, so that night he held the hurricane light as she carried out the injections. Everything was carefully checked and counted, but while greater love hath no man than one who holds a hurricane lamp as his beloved injects the bottoms of VD-infected soldiers, the number mix-up continued.

'The only thing I can think,' said Basil to Madge, 'is that some of the earlier patients went back into the queue for another jab!'

At the end of her stint on nights Madge was carpeted once again by Matron Ferguson and asked to explain the needle shortage.

'I simply don't know,' said Madge, 'unless some of the men were injected twice. But that doesn't make sense either.'

'It's not as silly as you think,' said Matron. 'We got one of the nursing sepoys to pretend he was preparing medicine in the ward when the injections were actually taking place and he spotted what they were doing. It turned out there was a group of soldiers who made sure they were always at the head of the queue and once they had been injected they would run to the back and line up again. They thought that by having double the dose of penicillin they would recover in half the normal time!'

Not for the first time Matron Olive Ferguson was smiling as she pointed to the door to dismiss a laughing Nurse Graves, who held up her hands, pleaded guilty and asked for these mitigating circumstances to be taken into account. 'I'm afraid I find it impossible to identify bums in the dark.'

17

Christmas in Chittagong

Matron Ferguson had made it clear from the start that all her VAD and QA (Queen Alexandra's Royal Army Nursing Corps) sisters would be working on Christmas Day. The boys in the wards had to come first in all circumstances. Madge didn't mind; the girls had been planning a good old-fashioned British Christmas since November. In a strange way Matron's edict was comforting for Madge and Vera, who had looked at each other in amusement when they had heard that Christmas for nurses had again been cancelled. It reminded them of their time as trainees at Stoke Mandeville when Sister Crowley terrified even the doctors into making an appearance on the big day.

We're in a different hospital in a different country and on a different continent but it is still the same for us nurses, Madge thought, when she had a closer look at the rotas pinned up in the mess hall. But she was so surprised that she had to look again. Her night duty had been due to begin the day before 25 December, but she had been put on the early shift from the morning of Christmas Day.

'You know what that means?' she said to Vera. 'I can see Basil in the evening after all, and the way the days fall, we'll also be able to go out for dinner on New Year's Day for his twenty-second birthday.'

'Forget his birthday, you still haven't told us how you got on at the dance he invited you to at the Movements mess,' said Vera, who was shushed as the Christmas planning meeting started. A little present for each and every patient was suggested, but ruled out because the number of troops arriving and those leaving varied enormously from week to week. A Christmas card each was vetoed for the same reason and Vera's idea of having 'a hamper or two sent over from Fortnum and Mason' got the response it deserved. Eventually they agreed that Phyl's suggestion of an English roast for Christmas lunch would be a treat above all else. They decided that the menu would be discussed with the kitchen staff to guarantee a meal that would remind one and all of home.

Roast beef was vetoed because of the upset that would be caused if a sacred cow suddenly disappeared, and nobody had even seen a turkey since they arrived in Chittagong. Madge pointed out that there seemed to be large numbers of scraggy-looking chickens scratching around the grounds. 'What about roast chicken with bread sauce, roast potatoes and plenty of veg and gravy?' she suggested.

56 IGH treated all nationalities and religions together but there were concerns that Hindus and Muslims might be upset by the celebration of a Christian religious festival in the wards. However, Sister Blossom pointed out that there had not been

a problem over Christmas when she had worked in similar hospitals. 'The main thing is to make sure all the patients have a good time,' she said.

With the next nurses' shift approaching rapidly the mini-meeting broke up. On their way down to the basha wards, two of the hens that had been earmarked for Christmas dinner wandered across the path in front of Madge and Vera, which made them both chuckle.

'They can cluck, cluck, cluck all they like,' said Vera, 'but they will still be ending up in the pot. Now come on, Madge, how did that dance go?'

That was as far as the conversation went, however, because as they approached the main entrance there, larger than life, was Matron Ferguson talking to one of the doctors, so the two young nurses just smiled and went their separate ways.

'Sorry for the delay over telling you about the dance, Miss Nosy Parker,' smiled Madge when she sat down with Vera for a quick lunch later in the day, 'but I'm sure you will be delighted to hear that it was a wonderful evening with really nice food, lots of dancing and some first-class singing.' Madge described how the men looked very dashing and the ladies had made a special effort as well.

'The singing, at first, was quite low key,' said Madge, 'but then a table of very happy gentlemen set the tone with a rousing rendition of "Rule Britannia" and everybody got to their feet to join in the chorus. Then there was "Land of Hope Glory" which, oh Vera, it was so moving; there was a lady soprano who wouldn't have been out of place at the Royal

Opera House who sang a verse on her own, and then came "Jerusalem". I just felt so . . . patriotic. And Basil loved every minute too,' she added, with a sparkle in her eye.

'We had a nightcap by the bar and one of the senior officers told us that he had been waiting at Alipore airport for a flight back to Chittagong when he met an RAF ground crew who were determined to make the most of being stuck overnight in Calcutta, and one of them joined him for a drink – a delightful West Country character called John Giddins.' Madge told Vera how the previous evening Giddins, an electronics and radio specialist, had been turned out of his bed along with other NCOs (non-commissioned officers) of each trade and told to be ready with small kit, minimum spares and toolkits for a 6.30 a.m. start, because the squadron was relocating from Ceylon to a strip near Imphal, northeast of Calcutta. The gear was duly loaded onto a Dakota, which had arrived at twilight the day before, and with minutes left to take off the pilot ordered one last check of the aircraft. Everything got the thumbs up until the pilot, who was bursting for a pee, opened the toilet door on the plane only to be confronted by a snarling beast, which was far from amused at having been locked in the loo rather than being taken for his usual early morning walk. The shocked pilot was even less amused, slammed the door and ran down the plane yelling that there was a leopard hiding in the thunder box and he wanted the animal shot.

But Giddins calmed things down by explaining that the months-old cub was the mascot of No. 17 Squadron and was a much revered and very well-behaved young chap, who simply loved having his ears and tummy tickled as well as being given a bottle of milk and a cuddle before bedtime. The official version was that the leopard would die if it was left behind when the squadron relocated from Ceylon. Unofficially the shocked pilot was told 'There is no way this f***** plane is taking off without him.'

'It's quite true, Vera! I saw a photo!' Madge said as she saw Vera looking at her in disbelief. She went on to tell the rest of the story.

The cub had been adopted as a mascot by the No. 17 Spitfire Squadron when they were based in the north of Ceylon after he was found yowling for his mother by a lake. When she failed to appear the off-duty pilots took him back to the aerodrome and, after lengthy discussions involving many beers, agreement was finally reached to name him Bagheera, after the leopard in Rudyard Kipling's *The Jungle Book*. In spite of chewing a very large hole in the arm of the CO's favourite chair and bursting the one leather football on the base, the leopard became a pampered addition to the squadron.

'There is a happy ending to this story,' said Madge, 'because once the flight landed, dear little Baghi was chauffeur-driven straight to Calcutta Zoo. They neglected to mention that Baghi got overexcited in the mess and had a little nibble at the leg of a *punka-wallah*, who had to have ten stitches,' she laughed.

'It was such a funny end to an amazing evening,' continued Madge, 'and all the singing earlier gave me an idea. I think that once everybody has been fed on Christmas Day we should get as many of the patients as we can out into the sunshine and sing a few carols for them. The boys will surely want to join in and it will cheer them up no end.'

Madge at times felt frustrated that the nurses knew so little and were officially told even less about how the Allied effort to chase the Japanese out of Burma was progressing. There were rumours and eye-witness claims that Lieutenant General William Slim was flying in and out of Chittagong to see the front line for himself, and even suggestions that Lord Louis Mountbatten had been spotted.

It wasn't until a Royal Engineers sapper, Samuel Laughton, was brought in with a nasty, smelly thigh wound that Madge heard first-hand news. Experienced as she was with combat injuries, Madge still grimaced at the putrid odour of the pus as it began to ooze from the wound and knew instantly that it had all the hallmarks of full-blown gangrene. Fortunately a doctor was on hand and, after confirming the diagnosis, told Madge, 'This looks like another one for the new drug.'

'Will I lose my leg?' Samuel asked when Madge returned from the pharmacy with a syringe and the medicine.

'Your recovery could take some time but hopefully not,' she answered with a smile. 'This new drug, penicillin, has been working wonders for similar injuries.'

After a series of injections the sapper, as Madge had hoped, began to recover and he was delighted to be told that because the infection had been caught in the early stages surgery had been avoided.

He then started talking about returning to his unit because

he had been near Maungdaw in the Arakan when Lord Louis Mountbatten had 'appeared out of the blue'.

'I'll never forget the way Lord Louis cheered everybody up,' said Samuel, who, Madge noticed, had very precise diction and sounded almost as if he was reading a BBC newscast.

It was part of a tour of the front line that the Supreme Commander of SEAC was undertaking. 'He told us that the major difference between Allied troops and the Japanese is that the Japs wished to be killed in battle because it is the highest honour they can achieve. Lord Louis told us, "I hope you give them that pleasure." He also said that we shouldn't think of ourselves as the Forgotten Army because the real truth is, nobody even knows we're here!'

Madge always admired patients who were keen to return to their units and hearing that the Allies were relentlessly driving the Japanese south also gave her a boost. *All the more reason*, she thought, *to make sure that the boys in the wards are treated to the best Christmas Day we can put together.* The odds were on the weather being sunny but slightly windy, so there was no reason why the patients couldn't be brought out onto the ward verandas.

The forecast was certainly accurate, thought Madge, as she woke on the first Christmas Day morning she would be spending without Mum, Doris and Doreen. The good thing was that there wasn't a cloud in the sky, but she was slightly worried about the wind because squalls could blow up in next to no time from the notoriously fickle Bay of Bengal and that would be the last thing they needed on today of all days. *It's going to be strange enough spending Christmas in this heat for the first time,* Madge told herself.

At home the family tradition had been for everybody to open their Christmas presents after breakfast, until Mum and the girls moved from Dover to High Wycombe and Madge started at Stoke Mandeville as a trainee nurse. Then Mum ruled that presents would only be opened once her eldest daughter had arrived home from the hospital, whether she was on days or nights. Just thinking of the fun of unwrapping beautifully parcelled gifts made Madge feel a little weepy. That there had been no mail from home since the first week of the month didn't help either.

Madge's early morning gloom was instantly lifted, however, when the sound of footsteps thumping on the veranda of her basha was followed by a tuneless version of 'We Wish You a Merry Christmas' that came bellowing through the doorway. It was Vera, of course, as full of vim and vigour as ever as she issued a simple instruction, 'Time for us to go for breakfast, bonnie lass!'

Sister Blossom was already on duty in the nurses' mess when they arrived, but waited until they sat down before she smiled at them. 'A little surprise for you both.' Madge and Vera couldn't believe it when Blossom lifted a cloth off the tray she had brought over to them to reveal two bundles of letters from home tied in beautiful pink bows.

'Please forgive me,' she said, 'but I have been keeping your letters as a special surprise for you to open on Christmas Day.'

Both girls were so moved at Blossom's thoughtfulness, as

well as relieved that their families were OK, that they stood up and gave her a great big hug.

Vera had insisted on an early breakfast rather than the usual last minute hurry-scurry for tea and a slice of toast and a race down the hill so they both had time to open their Christmas letters. Madge was touched to discover that in addition to three from Mum, there was a card from Auntie Beatrice in Dover and another from all the girls on Tommy Kilner's plastic surgery team at Stoke Mandeville. Of the three letters Madge received from home it was the one telling her what was going to happen at the family home in High Wycombe on Christmas Day that interested her most.

'You'll never guess what Mum and the girls are having for Christmas dinner,' she said to Vera. 'Roast chicken, just like we will be here.' Mum said that the special treat was all down to Doris, who was getting on really well at the farm in East Grinstead where she was now working for the Women's Land Army. The chicken as well as a dozen fresh eggs were her Christmas bonus and she was planning on carefully bringing the lot back to High Wycombe. Madge's mouth watered as she imagined what Mum would cook up for pudding. A Victoria sponge, gingerbread or maybe a fruit crumble!

She heard that Doris had been boasting that the man who owned the farm was very pleased with the way she had fitted in and said that she had green fingers.

I told her there was a simple answer to that one: Try washing your hands more often.

The gentle family humour made Madge wistful and she

wondered if she should tell Mum and her sisters about Basil, but decided it was all a little too early. *There'll be plenty of time for that in the new year*, she decided.

The first thing Madge noticed as she walked down the hill after breakfast was a great big 'Happy Christmas' sign in front of one of the basha wards. She wondered where on earth it had appeared from. Big Arthur, one of the hospital guards, soon answered that question as he marched past on his rounds, gave her a cheery wave, and said, 'All the best, Madge. Do you like the greeting that me and the lads have been working on?'

'Nice, very nice,' replied Madge, although she saw that it had been placed outside one of the Indian wards where she would be nursing through the day and she worried about what the patients might think. She soon saw that there was nothing to worry about; they were also looking forward to the day and wanted to know all about it. *I know just the man to answer all those questions*, Madge thought to herself.

Reverend John Davies arrived just before lunch, having visited other patients earlier in the morning and following that with a morning church service. Behind the scenes he had also been working to ensure that everybody, regardless of race, creed or colour, had a special day and happily helped out in the BOR ward where a special Christmas Day curry was to be served alongside the roast. He had also managed to acquire a few tins of Christmas pudding that were particularly appreciated.

There was a short but moving service after lunch which, as part of Reverend Davies' policy of involving as many people as possible, included the reading by a lance corporal from the

BOR ward of 'A Christmas Prayer From the Trenches'. The first verse ensured instant attention:

> *Not for us may Christmas bring*
> *Goodwill to all men and peace;*
> *In our dark sky no angels sing,*
> *Not yet for the great release*
> *For men, when war shall cease*

The little group of VAD nurses had put considerable effort into ensuring that everything would go smoothly and Madge was so pleased to see just how many patients sat on the veranda of the basha wards to listen to a carol concert in which the girls would, with the help of the Rev, get everyone singing. The nurses had been told by Matron, in the most diplomatic manner possible, to enjoy the day but not to let things overrun 'because there is a war on and there are a lot of very poorly patients who need your help'. They were nervous enough anyway until they looked up towards the big house and smiled when they saw Big Arthur, officially on guard duty, pushing the sapper with the damaged thigh towards the gathering in a rickety old wheelbarrow.

'He said he had never been in a governor's residence before and wanted to see that big 'ouse for himself,' explained Arthur as he picked the soldier out of the wheelbarrow like a baby and placed him gently into a chair on the veranda.

The schedule took another hit after a heavily bandaged Sikh told the Reverend how he had stood outside a church as a little boy and heard the congregation sing a hymn about 'Onward Christian Soldiers' and did he know the words.

'I think I may actually do so,' nodded the smiling Padre and he was soon leading everybody in a rousing version of the English classic.

The girls were in their full VAD uniforms. One had a smear of blood on her apron. Another had done a remarkable job in camouflaging the after-effects of a soldier who had vomited his breakfast, but they still looked as striking as they had at the Governor's Welcome Ball in Bombay back in August. To get everybody in the mood they started with 'Jingle Bells' and then followed that with 'Hark the Herald Angels Sing' and 'Come All Ye Faithful'.

In between hymns Madge leaned towards Vera and whispered, 'This all seems to be working quite well.' As she turned to look at her friend she was surprised to see a little tear rolling down her cheek.

'Yes it is,' said Vera, smiling through her tears. 'It makes me feel so very proud just to be part of all this.'

The temperature was still pushing towards 80 degrees Fahrenheit even though it was almost the end of December, but in spite of dripping with perspiration the nurses sang on and on and were boosted by the wonderful choral response of some very poorly patients. What they didn't know was that the Reverend Davies, who had become accepted as a 'holy man' to Gurkhas of the Hindu and Buddhist faiths as well as Christians, had been secretly working hard behind the scenes to help make sure that everyone enjoyed the day. The result was that he delivered the most entertaining little surprise that in reality was a master stroke of religious diplomacy.

The nurses had been enjoying cold drinks during a short break when the Rev mischievously asked, 'Does anybody know what all that noise is about up at the big house?'

'I hope there's not a problem on a day like this,' Madge said to the Padre.

'Not sure about that,' he replied with a twinkle in his eye.

Suddenly a group of Gurkhas came marching down the hill in flamboyant style with the one-time Governor General's residence providing a spectacular background and three ladies in traditional Nepalese dress adding colour and elegance. Whistles blew, drums were beaten and kukris flashed in the evening sun as the ferocious little charmers and their graceful companions whirled and twirled their way towards the wards. The smiling faces and enthusiastic applause from all wards underlined what a success the Gurkhas had been.

Reverend Davies had sworn Havildar Bahadur to secrecy before asking if his Gurkhas could 'put on a bit of a show' for the hospital patients. Agreement had been reached with the British troops who guarded the hospital complex that they would keep an eye on the nurses' bashas while the Gurkhas 'were otherwise engaged'.

The Rev had one more task to complete as the concert continued. 'It is my great privilege,' he said, addressing all the patients, nurses and Gurkhas, 'to introduce Victoria, a lady who I am sure will conjure visions of a green and pleasant land that many of us here today call home.'

Victoria was the seventy-year-old widow of a one-time British colonial civil servant who was on an extended visit to old friends who once ran a tea plantation. In her younger days back in England she was a much admired soprano in Cheshire operatic society circles.

'I am told she has the voice of an angel,' smiled Reverend Davies, 'so judge for yourself!'

The wind had eased to a whisper and only the gentle rustle of leaves accompanied Victoria's hauntingly beautiful version of 'Silent Night' as she stood shoulder to shoulder with the nurses, whose timing when they joined in to sing 'sleep in heavenly peace' was so perfect it could have been rehearsed.

The grand old lady from the days of the Raj sang non-stop for almost forty minutes. Eventually she appeared to be tiring so said, 'I think it's high time these lovely girls in my chorus had something cold to drink.' Cheers broke out instantly from the boys in the wards for their beloved nurses.

'Now then,' said Victoria, 'I have promised to end the concert with the three most popular requests so let's get on with it!'

First came a rousing version of 'Land of Hope and Glory', which was followed by 'Jerusalem', in which she expertly and generously conceded centre stage to the nurses for the last two lines:

> '*Till we have built Jerusalem*
> *In England's green and pleasant land*'

Victoria joined the applause for the nurses and then announced that there would be one more song.

'I'm not sure if you boys will have heard this one,' she smiled, 'and please forgive me for not being Vera Lynn, but here we go . . .'

As she began to sing 'We'll Meet Again' the boys in the wards roared their approval and happily joined in to provide an emotional, if somewhat out-of-tune, end to a thoroughly memorable Christmas concert that left Madge and the girls hot and sticky, but delighted that the patients were so happy.

'Only one thing went wrong,' Madge told a heavily perspiring Vera.

'What on earth are you talking about?' Vera replied. 'It couldn't have gone any better!'

'Basil couldn't get the time off to be here and it's such a shame because Victoria was the lady who sang so beautifully at that Movements mess dance I told you about. He's so patriotic and loves "Land of Hope and Glory" and "Jerusalem",' said Madge.

'It certainly was a shame,' said Reverend Davies, 'because he was the man who did all the work in arranging for Victoria to sing here. He even organised her transport.'

'Basil? You mean my Basil?' asked Madge.

'Yes, Captain Lambert,' said the Padre. 'When he heard about your Christmas concert for the troops at 56 IGH he found out that Victoria was still in Chittagong and asked her if she would be so kind as to spend an hour or so entertaining the patients. She agreed without the slightest hesitation. He did a splendid job and certainly knows how to keep a secret,' added Reverend Davies with a wink.

'He didn't drop even the slightest hint about what he was up to,' said a very proud Madge to Vera and the other girls as they walked over to the wards and started moving the boys from the verandas.

The soldiers, who had clearly enjoyed the afternoon fun, were full of smiles and jokey banter. It was no mean task to help the boys back into bed and Madge was more than a little relieved when her long but thoroughly rewarding shift came to an end. More to the point, it meant she could stroll back up to her basha, clean up and change from her nurse's uniform into that piqué dress she had bought in Poona, and see Basil for dinner.

First of all, she wanted to thank him for the lovely surprise in arranging for Victoria to sing at the carol concert. But she hadn't seen him for two whole days and she also wanted to tell him about a surprise invitation they had received. What's more, he had said that he had something special to discuss with her on Christmas Day. Try as she might, she couldn't work out what it could be, but her heart sang at the thought of seeing him and she couldn't imagine being anywhere else on this special day.

18

Auld Lang Syne

'It was such a shame you couldn't get away for the carol concert,' Madge told Basil as they sat having a drink on Christmas
night at the end of a day that had left them both so tired they
decided to postpone their festive celebrations until New Year's
Eve.

'The patients all loved the carols and the Gurkhas and Victoria's beautiful singing in particular,' said Madge. 'Thank you,
Basil, for that wonderful surprise. Funnily enough, it wasn't
the last surprise of the night because Sally has asked me to be
a bridesmaid at her wedding!'

'Sally? I don't recognise the name.'

Madge nodded in agreement. 'It did come as something of
a shock. She was the fourth girl in our cabin on the *Strathnaver*,
and a bit of a mystery really. The truth is, I don't know her all
that well, but the good thing is that the actual marriage will be
at a church in Chittagong and the reception will be in the hall
of the old Governor's residence overlooking 56 IGH, which
means no travelling. I haven't even met her fiancé yet, but Sally
really is lovely so I'm sure he will be too.'

'You kept that one up your sleeve,' said Basil.

'Not really,' replied Madge, 'I've only just found out myself because when I had a quick cup of tea with Vera at the end of today's shift there was a letter for me from Sally saying that she was getting married and asking if I would do her the honour of being a bridesmaid. She's such a nice girl and has had such a sad couple of years I couldn't refuse. Sally has also asked Vera to be her other bridesmaid. You will come, won't you?'

'Of course. But you must be careful about when the wedding is,' Basil said with a twinkle in his eye. 'We've worked for months without a break and I couldn't help but wonder if you might enjoy a holiday in Calcutta in the New Year.'

'A holiday!' Madge marvelled at the idea. 'Do you think we could?' Madge knew that they were allowed time off but most of the girls spent it shopping or going out for meals. A trip to Calcutta with Basil would be such a treat.

A few days later they met again when they went to see a pantomime, *IGH & LOW*, at a local theatre, which was a joint effort between the two hospitals. Madge was particularly keen to see it because the only two women in the cast were both VADs. The couple joined in enthusiastically with the boos and cheers and were still laughing as they left the theatre.

They then went on to attend a six-course feast on New Year's Eve at the United Services Club in Chittagong. Fittingly, at a traditional Scottish celebration, several officers were wearing kilts and the evening got underway with a choice of several rather fiery cocktails. The meal started with grapefruit and was followed by a good thick Scotch broth. The third course was fried fish with game crisps and the main course of the evening was roast stuffed goose with apple sauce, new potatoes, cauliflower and green peas. Plum pudding came with lively brandy sauce and finally they were served a savoury Scotch woodcock (scrambled eggs on toast spread with anchovy paste).

'That was lovely,' Madge told Basil. 'I can't say I'd ever tried Scotch woodcock before tonight and I thought the anchovy added the most delicious bite. I have to tell you, this feels like pure luxury. I can't remember the last time I ate so well. I'm not actually sure I ever have!'

There was a choice of French or Italian wines and sherry and port were also available, along with curaçao and crème de menthe. Basil had even arranged for the pair to have Christmas crackers on the table – a real luxury.

As they waited for the port to be served Madge looked around at couples determined to enjoy themselves on what, for all the world, could have been a most enjoyable New Year's Eve celebration dinner in one of the Home Counties, Edinburgh or Belfast. Madge allowed her mind to wander, and began dreaming of the kind of future she hoped for. She wanted an end to the suffering of the boys on the wards, and she wanted to be with Mum, Doris and Doreen. But most of all, she found as she gazed across at Basil, she wanted a future that included the kind and charming man who was sitting opposite her. *Oh, stop daydreaming, Madge*, she admonished herself. *You don't even know if he feels the same way so it's pointless getting carried away with yourself – especially as the war isn't over yet!*

'A penny for your thoughts?' She looked up at a smiling and inquisitive Basil, and she smiled back at him.

'Sorry,' she replied, 'I was miles away.' But she was saved from having to explain any further as six proud Scots, with their arms aloft and their kilts gently swaying, encouraged people onto the dance floor to join an emotional and increasingly rousing version of 'Auld Lang Syne'.

Basil put his arm round her waist and looked deep into her eyes as they joined in the last verse.

> *'And there's a hand my trusty friend*
> *And give me a hand of thine!*
> *And we'll take a right good-will draught,*
> *For Auld Lang Syne.'*

The 11 p.m. curfew had been put back to 1 a.m. for the nurses at 56 IGH yet it irritated Madge that such a wonderful evening had to draw to a close when there were still so many things to say to Basil.

As the ancient taxi bumped and growled its way back to the hospital complex she ended the evening with a little story that made Basil laugh out loud.

'I wrote to Mum to tell her that there had been a lot of moans and groans from the nurses about the hospital curfew but added that I did realise it was for our own safety,' said Madge. 'When she wrote back she said, "You may be twenty-one now, my girl, but it will still do you the world of good to get to bed at a reasonable time instead of being out gallivanting at all hours of the night!"'

'I haven't even met your mum yet,' smiled Basil, 'but I like her already!'

Madge's heart leapt at Basil's reply. *He's intending to meet my mum. He must see us having a future then.* For the first time she was 100 per cent sure that this wasn't a romance that had bloomed because of the heat of India and the intensity of war. *That must mean that he feels the same way I do.* She felt a warm glow spread through her as she allowed herself to begin daydreaming all over again.

19

A Moonlight Serenade

While Madge had been genuinely surprised at the invitation from Sally the truth was she had only been a bridesmaid once before and she was very much looking forward to the event as the weeks counted down to the nuptials. Everything seemed to be going smoothly enough because she had been promised the day off by Matron Ferguson; the boys on the wards had been teasing her since the news had got out.

'Always the bridesmaid, Madge, never the bride. You're getting past it at twenty-one, old girl.' It was exactly the sort of leg-pulling that would have gone on with the soldiers' adored younger sisters had they been at home and, far from worrying her, the jibes made Madge laugh. Her one concern, as the wedding approached, was that there were hardly any clothes shops in Chittagong. Vera didn't bat an eyelid about the teasing in the wards because she was more than capable of giving as good as she got but, like Madge, she was flummoxed over what to wear as a bridesmaid for the wedding.

One afternoon she and Vera were discussing their problem in the nurses' mess. Sister Blossom overheard and suggested that maybe they should buy matching saris and have them customised. 'All you have to do is to show one of our local seamstresses a picture of what you would like and she will copy it,' said Blossom. The hunt was on!

Madge and Vera, after trying for days to arrange an afternoon when they had downtime from the hospital, finally pencilled in their shopping trip. Lunch, of course, was mandatory and it gave them a chance to discuss the latest twist in the complex life of the very likeable, but very mysterious, Sally Mallins.

'We don't even know how she met her fiancé!' said Vera. 'The last time we saw her she was heartbreakingly lonely. Now she's all set to get married.'

'It's certainly a huge change,' said Madge, 'but after all the turmoil she's been through she deserves some happiness.'

'Oh, she does,' said Vera. 'I can't imagine being so swept off my feet I would marry a man I'd just met, but perhaps she's known him a while.'

'We'll find out soon enough,' said Madge, 'and I reckon it's time we got going or we're never going to find anything to wear.'

There were just two weeks until the wedding, but try as they might, the girls couldn't find what they wanted. After hours of poring over fabrics in hot, stuffy shops, they decided to try one last store, which from the wooden front door looked as if it had once been a little house. The moment they walked in Madge saw a gorgeous heliotrope pink-purple sari hanging on the wall. She noticed Vera looking at it too but, miracle of miracles, at the back of the musty old store there was another. They both tried them on, bought one each and took them back to show Sister Blossom, who offered to arrange an appointment with a seamstress.

'What would we do without you, Blossom!' Madge exclaimed.

Vera had her nose buried in a 'borrowed' copy of the *Coronet* magazine that had been left unattended at one of the posh cocktail parties she frequented. She showed Madge various pictures and, after lengthy discussions, the bridesmaids decided to ask if an elegant Ginger Rogers-style gown could be copied.

They made an appointment to see Zynah, the seamstress, and were taken to a dingy little room at the back of a grocery store where she had a small workshop. Vera looked at Madge pointedly, and she could tell they were both wondering if they had done the right thing.

'Not sure about this place,' whispered Madge.

'It's a bit dusty and I think from the smell there's a hint of mould,' said Vera. 'Not the best place to get dresses made for a wedding.'

The girls were well aware that while the material and the colour of the sari was exactly what they wanted, the cut of it was very different to the design to be copied from *Coronet* magazine. So they began to feel rather nervous when nothing was measured as they stood in the saris after changing from their khaki uniforms. No chalk marks were made. Everything was 'nipped and tucked' with a multitude of pins.

'Please, *memsahibs*,' said Zynah, 'be very careful removing your dresses in case the pins fall off.'

Two days later Sister Blossom told them that Zynah had sent a message to ask if they would be so kind as to return to her workshop for a fitting. The girls were worried about what would be waiting for them so they went over as soon as their shift came to an end. The first thing Madge noticed when she tried on her new gown was the beautiful, hand-made buttons that ran from the base of the neck down the spine. All thirty-six of them.

'This is absolutely stunning,' Madge whispered over the curtain. 'And have you seen the buttons?' The cherry-sized buttons, fastened by loops, were covered with the same material as the girls' dresses. The box of pins came out again, but only minor alterations were necessary before the gowns were ready to take away.

'*Memsahibs*,' said Zynah, 'you look very beautiful in your gowns, but I have a suggestion that I hope will bring great pleasure.' Vera looked at Madge and gave an almost imperceptible shrug of her shoulders as two lengths of yellow silk sashes suddenly appeared as if by magic. 'Please lift your arms,' said the seamstress, as she walked behind Madge and proceeded to wrap a hand-stitched sash around her waist.

Madge looked at herself in the dusty full-length mirror. The yellow contrasted perfectly with the heliotrope and the sash was ever so flattering for the figure.

'Very slimming,' smiled Madge.

Vera grinned at her and Madge knew she had the seal of

approval. *I wonder what Basil will think*, she thought. *That is, if he can get the day off.*

Zynah carefully wrapped the gowns in brown paper. They paid the bill, making sure to include a sizeable tip and a big hug for the seamstress who had put in an enormous amount of work to turn the saris into excellent copies of the Ginger Rogers gown.

'Zynah, you're a miracle worker,' Madge said. 'Perhaps, with enough coconut oil, we won't look half bad at all!'

As the pair strolled happily back to the hospital complex, they considered their next problem: footwear. Vera was worried that if she wore high heels they might catch the back of the full-length gown. Madge knew she would be shouted down for her suggestion, but said it anyway.

'There's going to be a lot of standing around in the church and then at the reception,' she pointed out. 'Our dresses are full length so nobody will be able to see what sort of shoes we'll be wearing. I wonder if our nurses' lace-ups would be best . . .'

'Feel free, darling!' laughed Vera as they finally reached their bashas.

With the three girls on different work patterns there was no wedding rehearsal or indeed any detailed discussion about how the day would go. Even more frustrating for the bridesmaids was that they still didn't have a clue how the whirlwind romance had got underway.

Reassurance came, however, from Reverend Davies who told Madge and Vera as he passed through the wards on his hospital visits not to worry in the slightest because everything would just flow smoothly once the ceremony got underway. 'That's the way it goes with weddings.'

There was one thing, however, that was too awful to even consider: what if another of the demonstrations telling the British to get out and demanding home rule for India took place on the day? The campaign was becoming increasingly violent but they decided that a Gurkha guard of honour would be based outside the church and would escort the congregation back to the hospital complex for the reception in the main hall.

A few days before the wedding Basil took Madge to see *This is the Life*. On the way to the cinema he told her that he would be able to accompany her to the wedding because he had been assured of getting the day off from Movements HQ. One by one, a solution was found to each problem and by the time the big day came around, Madge could hardly wait.

The arrival of two camouflaged army three-tonners carrying friends of the bridegroom from their base heralded the start of the wedding day. Madge and Vera watched as the troops clambered off the vehicles and transformed them within minutes from dust and grime-coated old bangers into truly glorious wedding transport. The boys simply draped great big Union Jack flags over the lorries and somehow attached massive bunches of roses to the vehicles.

As Madge changed into her bridesmaid outfit she made two important decisions about the wedding. First, she was going to wear next to no make-up. The advice of the splendid old lady at the Welcome Ball in Bombay had proved 100 per cent right on numerous occasions and on what was already a sticky and humid day she mentally thanked her for the umpteenth time. The second decision had taken a lot more time and thought. On the one hand, high heels were always a plus because they added height. On the other, she knew they would play havoc with her feet and scrunch her toes if she had to stand for any great length of time. Then there was that walk from her basha up and down the hill that could be tricky even on a good day.

What would Mum say? Madge asked herself, and the answer came like a bolt from the blue. Madge was taking her favourite handbag anyway and both the nurses' lace-ups and her high heels just about fitted in. So for the walk back to the big house and the first part of the day she would wear the lace-ups and then she would change into her high heels for the reception.

As luck would have it, Madge was more than happy with the shoe arrangement because there was a mix-up with transport to the church and the girls had to cadge a lift in one of the flag-covered army lorries. Madge watched as Vera tried to climb into the cabin in her high heels. She laughed as the men almost fell over themselves scrambling to help her up.

The little church in Chittagong was already filling up as they waited in the vestibule for the bride to arrive. Madge smiled as she looked to her left to see a group of soldiers that included handsome bridegroom Charles nervously puffing away on his last cigarette as a single man.

'What a lovely old church this is,' said Madge to Vera. 'I didn't even know it was here. That design with those lovely white spires makes me wonder if it was built by the Portuguese.'

Basil then arrived and couldn't help but laugh when Madge walked over and asked him to look after her handbag, which by then contained her nurses' lace-up shoes. She gave him a gentle but loving hug, followed by a welcome kiss and smiled sweetly. 'Take my word for it, Basil, the bag matches your outfit!'

Just then the most magnificent maroon Humber Super Snipe driven by an Indian chauffeur with a black peaked cap came around the bend. The six-cylinder engine growled gently and the car sported a spare wheel alongside the bonnet. A spectacular chrome-plated emblem of a bird with a long silver beak gleamed in the afternoon sun and white-trimmed tyres made it even more special. It looked like something straight from a Pinewood Studios film. Madge almost laughed out loud when Vera whispered, 'Where on earth did they get their hands on a car like that in a place like Chittagong?'

As Madge and Vera moved to help the bride alight, the aroma of expensive leather drifted from inside the vehicle. The girls embraced.

'You look so beautiful, Sally,' Madge said, standing back and admiring her long-sleeved, high-necked cream cotton gown and the full, silk veil that swept down to her waist.

'Thank you,' she replied, smiling, 'but I'm feeling *very* nervous right now!'

If the car was impressive, the inside of the church was breathtaking in its beauty with lotus flowers everywhere. The sacred lotus is for Hindus a symbol of beauty, fertility and eternity; to the Buddhists of Burma the exquisite bloom represents purity and tranquillity. Sally had told Madge she had chosen lotus flowers in the hope they would finally bring her some good fortune.

The nervousness that both Madge and Vera felt as they waited in the vestibule was calmed in the gentlest of ways by the Reverend Davies, who greeted them as old friends and said how colourful and stylish their gowns were. He then proceeded to conduct a service of such tenderness that the congregation, who lived day to day on the fringe of infinite savagery, floated in a sea of very welcome tranquillity.

She glanced over to the bride. *She really does look stunning*, Madge thought to herself. A ray of light shone through a window high on the church wall to act almost as a spotlight to accentuate the delicate little freckles on the bride's face that beamed with happiness.

Madge wondered what was coming when Reverend Davies said that they would take a moment to forget the turmoil through which they were living and think instead of three simple things that feature in Corinthians 13:13. When he began to read the passage from the New Testament she was so profoundly moved that she wished she had been sitting alongside Basil to share the moment.

> *'If I speak in the tongue of men or of angels, but do not have*
> *love, I am only a resounding gong or a clanging cymbal.*
> *'If I have the gift of prophecy and can fathom all mysteries*

and all knowledge, and if I have a faith that can move
mountains, but do not have love, I am nothing.

'*Love is patient, love is kind. It does not envy, it does not*
boast, it is not proud.

'*Love does not delight in evil but rejoices with the truth. It*
always protects, always trusts, always hopes, always
perseveres.

'*Love never fails. But where there are prophecies, they will*
cease; where there are tongues, they will be stilled; where
there is knowledge, it will pass away.

'*And now these three remain: faith, hope and love. But the*
greatest of these is love.'

The silence at the end of the reading was palpable and even the square-jawed troops from Comilla had to swallow hard.

There was one last hymn, which, quite suitably, was 'Love Divine, All Love Excelling', and marriage vows complete, the congregation filed out.

Madge had told Basil in their brief conversation before the ceremony about the transport hiccup and he had a car ready to take the two bridesmaids 'and that handbag' back to the reception in the main hall. Jeeps containing the Gurkha guard of honour were at the front and back of the convoy.

After a few cocktails on the veranda the two bridesmaids strolled back to find that the multitude of lotus flowers that had graced the church had already been transferred to the main hall, along with roses, frangipani, jasmine, hibiscus, giant sunflowers and the most incredible orchids. Waiters walked round with a tray of exquisitely displayed hors d'oeuvres that had been brought over from the kitchens. One of the servers recognised Madge as 'the brave *memsahib* who fought with the devil bird' and gave her a mischievous smile when he explained that he was so worried about being attacked like she was that he had put a big cloth over the food.

'You cheeky boy,' she said with a big grin.

Within an hour or so one of the two army lorries loaded up its passengers and was on its way back to Comilla, with the intention of arriving before darkness fell. It meant they missed the speeches, which were short but witty, and the fun and games that went on later with a drinking competition between visiting soldiers and the Chittagong-based boys as the reception became entertainingly raucous.

'Watch this,' Vera told Madge, as they stood chatting at the reception, and she smiled at the handsome best man, who burst out laughing when she gave him the most outrageous wink before slowly turning her back on him. Within seconds he was at her side!

'Good evening, beautiful bridesmaids. My name is Robert Adam,' he said.

'Robert Adam what?' asked Vera in her cheekiest manner.

'Just Robert Adam,' he replied. 'It's been a wonderful evening, hasn't it? I would like to thank you both for having always been so kind to Sally. She told me and Charles all about you two,' he said.

'When did you meet her?' asked Madge.

'When she was nursing Charles at your sister hospital over

the past weeks. We thought he was going to die, but she spent her every waking hour on the ward and helped bring him back from the brink.'

'What was the problem?' asked Madge.

'Malaria,' answered the best man, who then invited Vera to partner him once the first dance was over.

'My pleasure,' she said, before half turning to Madge and whispering, 'I think that finally solves the mystery of Sally!'

The dancing began with the bride and groom leading a tribute to Glenn Miller. 'What else could we start with here in Chittagong other than "Indian Summer"?' said the master of ceremonies. Madge and Vera were standing talking about how moving the Padre's reading at the wedding had been and overheard a couple saying what a terrible shame it was about the American.

'I'm not sure I heard that right,' said Madge, 'but I get the impression that something has happened to Glenn Miller.'

A wedding guest chipped in to confirm that there had been reports before Christmas that a flight taking him from an airport somewhere near Bedford to Paris had gone missing over the English Channel. 'That was some time ago and nothing has been heard of him since,' the guest added.

Basil rejoined the group and eased Madge away by saying that the next record was going to be 'Moonlight Serenade'.

'I know it's one of your favourites,' he said, 'so could I have the pleasure of the next dance?' The overwhelming sadness that Madge felt over the singer's death in the very waters she had seen every day as a child growing up in Dover was tempered by the warmth and security that came from being held in Basil's loving arms and she thought how lucky she was to have found him.

Basil guided her gently from the throng on the dance floor out to the veranda to look up at stars twinkling and a new moon glimmering over an impossibly romantic scenario. Then they looked down to the flickering lights of the wards of 56 IGH where brave young men were fighting so valiantly to recover from disease and combat wounds. As the dulcet tones of the Glenn Miller classic drifted away on the evening breeze, Madge realised just how strictly her life, at just twenty-one years of age, was being governed by love and war.

20

Nursing the Japanese

Since she had arrived in Chittagong Madge had relied on the *South East Asia Command* for news about the war. This forty-thousand-circulation daily newspaper, which was published in Calcutta with the intention of keeping Allied forces in touch with events back in Europe, was understandably circumspect about progress in the Burma Campaign. It was always a treat to see the occasional copy of *SEAC*, but as the weeks passed, Madge had the sense that there was much more going on behind the scenes than any of them were aware of.

By the start of 1945, however, it was obvious that the tide had turned in favour of the Allies and early in the year the Japanese were being chased remorselessly back through Burma. They suffered unsustainable losses and ran out of ammunition, fuel and food as the Allies ruptured their supply lines beyond repair. As a result, Japanese POWs were being captured, some in need of hospitalisation, but treating them was not straightforward, as Madge would soon discover.

Atrocities by Japanese troops against hospital patients and Allied medical staff in Hong Kong began shortly before the crown colony's surrender on Christmas Day 1941, when nurses were raped and murdered, doctors slaughtered, St John's Ambulance men bayoneted and wounded soldiers tortured. Japanese forces had started their attack on the crown colony within hours of the 7 December raid on Pearl Harbor, which led to the US declaring war against Japan.

The garrison held out for seventeen days against overwhelming odds before the Governor General of Hong Kong, Sir Mark Aitchison Young, along with a group of colonial officials, formally surrendered. But the violence didn't stop. The number of casualties on the morning of the surrender was impossible to confirm but of the nurses who were raped and murdered two were reported to be VADs. In addition, there were claims that more than fifty wounded Allied soldiers were executed as they lay in bed.

Then on 13 February, patients were murdered on operating tables and hundreds of injured troops and medical staff were executed at a British military hospital in Singapore. It was just after 1 p.m. when heavily armed Japanese soldiers were spotted advancing towards Alexander Hospital, where a British army captain held up his arms, clearly marked with red crosses, in surrender. A shot was fired at him and a grenade was thrown, but he escaped by jumping over a wall. A white flag waved from a window was met with an outbreak of rifle fire. By then the Japanese had marched into the hospital. The staff of a surgical unit, standing with their arms aloft in surrender, were bayoneted and a patient under anaesthetic was mutilated and murdered on the operating table.

By late afternoon the Japanese had trained their rifles and machine guns on a group of more than two hundred staff and soldiers whose arms were tied behind their backs. They marched their hostages to tiny huts, where they were held through the night without water or food. The wounded who failed to keep up or fell over on the short march were hacked to death where they lay.

The next day half the group were taken from the huts after being promised water and fresh air, but were systematically butchered. While the morning slaughter was taking place a stray shell loosened a door of one of the huts and several men escaped. The remaining prisoners were murdered before the Japanese accepted the surrender on St Valentine's Day of Allied forces that totalled almost eighty thousand.

Details of the outrages that had taken place in Hong Kong and Singapore slowly began to emerge within the close-knit medical community that served throughout the Burma Campaign. Nothing official was ever revealed, but anger expressed by the boys on the wards over the beheadings and bayoneting in Singapore and Hong Kong left little to the imagination.

On a swelteringly humid morning in February 1945, the nursing staff were gathered and told that a casualty ward for Japanese prisoners of war was to be opened at 56 IGH. By lunchtime the new ward had become the focal point of heated and often tearful arguments that went on in the nurses' mess for days as fierce debate raged over the rights and wrongs of British nurses being told to care for an enemy who beheaded and disembowelled our boys as a matter of course.

'That came out of the blue. I wonder when the ward will be opened,' said Madge.

'I'm not sure what I think about it,' said Phyl. 'I know it's our job to care for anyone who needs medical attention. But you have to ask if it's right after the way our boys have been treated by the Japanese.'

'What I would like to know,' said Vera, 'is what the powers-that-be in New Delhi really think.' She was referring specifically to Jane Patterson, Chief Principal Matron and Director of Medical Services, and, of course, Gertrude Corsar.

'I suppose the truth is that they have to do what they're told like the rest of us,' said Madge.

Rather than precipitating confrontation by arbitrarily listing everybody on the Japanese POW ward rotas, Matron Ferguson spoke to nurses individually but at the same time made it clear they would be expected to follow orders if they were assigned to duty there. Judging by the response in the mess, Madge thought that was a wise move. One of the nurses refused point blank to have anything to do with the Japanese because she had a brother who had been taken prisoner during the defence of Singapore. The family simply didn't know whether he was still alive. 'I won't nurse a single one of those people,' she said.

One of the hardest-working and most dedicated nurses at the hospital had a first cousin who had died in the Battle of Kohima and said that she thought it totally unacceptable that the latest drugs, like penicillin, would be used to save the lives of people who tortured and mutilated Allied soldiers. Madge felt overwhelming sympathy for girls who had suffered such grievous and heartbreaking personal losses, but as a nurse she simply felt morally bound to help those in need and made her position known to Matron Ferguson.

'I'm willing to do whatever's required of me, Matron,' she told her.

Matron Olive Ferguson eventually announced to a group of her nurses that Japanese prisoners of war were expected to arrive at the hospital early in March 1945. 'Rest assured that security has been discussed in great detail,' she said. 'The POWs will be guarded day and night, with responsibility shared between British troops and Gurkhas.'

To ensure maximum security the guards would work four hours on duty and four hours off. Nurses would be accompanied at all times by two riflemen on guard duty as they treated the Japanese POWs. The Gurkhas, of course, much preferred their trusted kukri knives. Madge was surprised to hear that the ward would not be surrounded by barbed wire or by specially built security fencing. 'From what I've been told our "guests" aren't exactly going to be in good enough condition to go hopping over the main fence,' said Matron.

Some of the nurses began to feel scared at the prospect of treating the POWs.

'What if people come in to attack the Japanese and they attack us as well?' asked one VAD during another intense debate in the mess one afternoon.

Madge pointed out that they had volunteered to serve in the Burma Campaign as nurses in the first place, knowing there would be risks involved. 'There's no point in being scared. In reality, it's just another job and we're going to be put on the rosters whether we like it or not. And they've put strict measures in place to make sure we and the patients are kept safe.'

Later that evening Basil warned her not to expect the same gratitude from the Japanese for trying to save their lives as nurses got from Allied soldiers. 'You must remember,' he said, 'that they feel enormous shame at being taken prisoners of war and would prefer death before the dishonour of being treated by the enemy.'

Nurses were briefed about the arrival of the Japanese POWs and told what to do in the case of any emergency. It was made very clear that should an incident occur on the ward, the most important thing was personal safety. 'Don't think about being a hero. If you are attacked, get out of the way as quick as you can and let the guards step in. The greater the distance you can put between you and any attacker, the safer it will be, but if necessary, hit them as hard and as fast as you can with anything you can get your hands on,' they were told by a security expert.

'It is highly unlikely,' he went on, 'that one of the Japanese will escape, but in the event of that happening, remember the old motto that there is safety in numbers. The more of you there are together, the less likely it will be for one of you to be taken hostage.' He ended by saying just how much he admired the nurses for the task they were undertaking. 'You may think that these prisoners are seriously ill, but it is absolutely vital that you be on your guard at all times,' he added.

As they left the briefing, Madge said to Vera and Phyl, 'Well, at least he told it to us straight so we know how to deal with anything that might happen. I suppose we'll just have to expect the unexpected,' to which the other girls nodded in agreement.

The first two Japanese POWs were carried in on stretchers to 56 IGH on 3 March 1945. Within days the ward was full of demoralised Japanese soldiers suffering, in the main, from malaria, dysentery, dehydration and malnutrition. For those with combat injuries the length of time they spent at the hospital could vary, but the others were soon moved to purpose-built POW camps.

Despite the evidence that the push against the Japanese was working to plan, the boys on the BOR ward, where Nurse Graves was on duty, were outraged and bewildered over what they described as 'an un-bloody believable decision to mollycoddle the Japanese'. If debates in the nurses' mess were heated, the arguments on the wards became increasingly fierce. One particular Lancastrian lance corporal insisted that it didn't mean the Japanese POWs were being mollycoddled just because they were being treated as human beings. 'We are a civilised nation and must not lower ourselves to their level,' he insisted, but he was met with some even fiercer responses.

In typical British fashion, however, they maintained their sense of humour. David, a patient from Cardiff who was recovering from a nasty shrapnel wound in his left shoulder, called Madge over and told her in a stage whisper that he knew the key to dealing with the Japanese. 'Madge, my little lovely, even if one of these people has a sword hidden in the bed, remember you must keep your 'ead at all times!' As the rest of the ward burst out laughing the cheeky Taff chuckled so much that his laughter turned into a yelp of pain.

'Serves you right,' Madge grinned, before walking on down the ward to check on another of the soldiers who had been brought in two days earlier with a very unpleasant bout of dysentery. He had a cast in his right eye and a rugged, danger-ous look about him. He had said virtually nothing since arriving and she was worried he might also be suffering from shock. Out of the blue he told her, in a clipped accent, that he had something that would solve the chronic constipation from which the Japanese were said to suffer. Without further ado, he produced a hand grenade from under his pillow.

Madge hadn't been sure about this new patient but the utter shock, brilliantly acted as it was, on those scarred features as he dropped the grenade certainly didn't fool the unflappable Nurse Graves. 'Boys and their silly toys,' she said with a shake of her head and a whimsical smile as she calmly placed it back under his pillow.

He apologised profusely for the jape with the grenade which he said he'd won in a little wager with two gentlemen from the Land of the Rising Sun. 'It has, of course, been defused,' he added. 'I just thought the boys on the ward needed a little fun in their lives.' He turned serious for a moment and said, 'You know, Nurse Graves, in a strange way I understand why this casualty ward for the Japanese prisoners has been opened. We're British and it's the right thing to do, isn't it?' he added.

Several men on the ward were on the edge of serious illness, but their laughter reminded Madge of the indomitable spirit shown by the wounded boys from the D-Day landings, when she was in Stoke Mandeville. They all knew that Madge would be in the Japanese POW ward the following morning so when she left at the end of her shift she gave them a huge smile and a few words from a Gracie Fields classic: 'Wish me luck as you wave me goodbye . . .' The laughter and applause, along with shouts of 'be careful', rang in her ears as she headed towards her basha.

Madge was going to be amongst the first on duty in the new ward. She had never actually set eyes on a Japanese soldier before, let alone nursed one, and she was interested to see what they looked like. She was still smiling over the day's mischief that had taken place in the BOR ward when she met up with Vera for a late afternoon pot of tea on the eve of the big day.

'Those boys,' she told Vera, 'are always up to monkey business, but they're a lot of fun!'

'I know, they are cheeky,' Vera replied. 'But they make what we do worthwhile, don't they?'

'They most definitely do,' Madge agreed.

That night Madge washed her hair and checked that her uniform for the following day had been ironed. She gave her lace-up shoes one last polish and thought about spelling out her thoughts in a letter home to Mum and her sisters, but decided instead to write after her first day on the POW ward. Normally one of the last things she would do before bedding down for the night was to scribble a few notes in the diary that she had restarted in Kirkee after disembarking from the *Strathnaver* in Bombay, but the security briefing she had attended about the arrival of the Japanese made her wonder if it was sensible to continue.

Madge read back over some of her entries and decided that there wasn't a single thing that would be of interest to anybody other than her sisters and Mum. There was a bit about a dog that she knew the family would enjoy, but couldn't possibly be interpreted as a security risk. Sapper was a loveable, mischievous Alsatian with one blue and one brown eye and a floppy right ear. He was owned by the Mess Secretary of HQ Movements, known to all as Flossie Dirkin. Sapper's greatest joy in life came after a dinner or dance at the mess because he always got a doggy bag full of juicy, meaty treats that he wolfed down within seconds. *How could that cause problems?* Madge asked herself. Nevertheless, she decided that with the enemy just a few hundred yards away she should discontinue her diary keeping. She'd just have to remember every detail so she could tell Doris, Doreen and Mum all about her adventures when she got home, whenever that might be.

The following morning Madge was determined to look as pristine and efficient as possible for her first day with the Japanese so she checked her uniform and hair one last time before heading over to have breakfast with Vera, who had been earmarked for service in another ward that day. They discussed the order that these POWs must be listed as numbers only.

'It seems almost inhuman,' said Vera.

'But there's really nothing else we can do,' Madge pointed out. 'Nearly all of them are refusing to give their names.'

After breakfast Vera and Madge walked together to their shift but were stopped in their tracks by a scene that was unfolding at the bottom of the hill around the POW wards. To the right, a squad of British soldiers, rifles glistening in the early morning sun, marched in unison towards the troop of Gurkhas, who had been on duty through the night guarding the Japanese. The nurses were still a considerable distance away, but because he was so tall Madge instantly recognised Big Arthur in the British contingent, and she found comfort in the giant Yorkshireman's presence. As they got closer they overheard the last few words of the troop's briefing. Though they had gathered in a rugby-style huddle, Madge distinctly heard the term 'court martial' being repeated and knew that if the guards laid so much as a finger on the prisoners they could be in for the high jump.

Vera attempted to relieve the pressure as they headed towards the ward by announcing that she had learned to speak Japanese and when Madge challenged her to say something in the alien tongue she indignantly replied 'Tokyo!' It was an awful joke, but both girls laughed before going their separate ways.

'Eyup, Madge.' Big Arthur, who was assigned to accompany Nurse Graves on her rounds, introduced her to his fellow guard, Joseph, a particularly tough-looking Scouser from Liverpool. Madge looked at her heavily armed bodyguards and felt reassured by their presence. *Right, let's do this*, Madge said to herself. They stepped into the ward together.

Already the temperature was over 85 degrees Fahrenheit and a thoroughly unpleasant smell was permeating from within the ward. The odour was so awful Madge initially thought it might be gangrene. Then it dawned on her that the smell was nothing to do with gangrene, it was just the stench of so many men stuck in the heat with the shutters closed.

The ward was surprisingly quiet and she was keenly aware that twenty-eight sets of enemy eyes were monitoring her every step and movement. Big Arthur, hand resting lightly on the Lee Enfield rifle that was slung across his shoulders, stayed close to Madge as she got her bearings in a ward full of tiny and very emaciated Japanese prisoners of war. She found it difficult to associate the atrocities carried out by forces of the Japanese Empire with soldiers in such dreadful physical condition. Several appeared closer to death than life, but their eyes seemed to gleam with such pure hatred that Madge was glad that Big Arthur was never more than a few feet away from her at any time.

Sets of medication had been laid out in the shade of the veranda and a quick check of the contents confirmed that the majority of the patients were suffering from malaria, dysentery, combat wounds, malnutrition or a combination of the afflictions. A doctor had spent considerable time on the ward over the past two days and diagnosed most of the illnesses, but even without his notes Madge would have identified the fact that patient number one was seriously ill with malaria. He was sweating profusely and shaking so much that she was reminded of the scenes with her father back in Dover.

Inevitably she didn't receive even a nod of the head in thanks after giving him treatment, but rather strangely she thought she saw a flicker of gratitude in his eyes.

Madge moved on to the next bed whose occupant seemed to be little more than a human skeleton. The doctor's notes said that he was suffering from dysentery and malnutrition and his little arms looked like sparrow's legs. The noise of the guards clumping up in their British army beetle crushers woke him from what was the deepest of sleeps and for a moment it looked as if he was going to make a protest, but he simply didn't have the energy. Instead he lay stricken as Madge administered large doses of medication.

It had been the most glorious, sun-drenched start to the day when Madge walked down from breakfast with Vera from the nurses' mess, but within an hour clouds had begun to gather, the wind had started to shriek and another downpour was threatening. The humidity was unbearable and as she continued her rounds the odour within the ward became so extreme it was a relief when the rain actually started.

Madge's next patient had an amputated arm in addition to a number of shrapnel wounds and a respiratory infection. He didn't speak English and she didn't speak Japanese, but Madge's smile seemed to calm the somewhat agitated young man. Because beads of perspiration were standing out on his forehead she gently mopped his brow and helped him drink a glass of water. Next she prepared to administer a penicillin injection. When the inside of his one arm was swabbed and the needle was about to be inserted he turned his head away before flicking it back to very carefully spit in Madge's face.

All hell broke loose as the lethargic morning calm turned within seconds to a bear pit. Rain splattered on the roof of the basha and the shutters creaked and groaned in the howling wind. Madge stepped back and turned to the guards with green phlegm dripping from her eyebrow, across her nose and onto the white apron of her uniform. All the noise from outside failed to drown out the roar of anger that could be heard from inside the ward.

'Disgusting! Utterly disgusting!' roared Big Arthur.

He had moved to protect Madge from any second assault and he let loose a stream of obscenities that could be heard the length of the hospital. Joe, a veteran of the Saturday night action that took place at throwing-out time in the pubs on Scotland Road, stood with his back against a wall, waving his Lee Enfield in a 180-degree arc to dissuade the rest of the POWs from getting involved. He had made an extravagant display of pretending to remove the safety catch.

Both British guards had been warned that morning that they would face a court martial if unnecessary violence was inflicted on the prisoners and Big Arthur took exceptional care not to lay so much as a finger on the one-armed 'little ****', who had responded to Madge's compassion in such a foul way. Instead, he kicked the underside of the bed with his size 12 British army boots with such enormous power that the bottom two legs became momentarily airborne. The patient squealed with fright. That started the other POWs shouting and yelling and there was bedlam. Only when a group of Gurkhas walked through, hands casually on their kukris, did it all calm down. Big Arthur was mortified that he had let the incident take place and apologised time and time again to Madge 'for using such bad language in front of a lady'.

'Nobody could have seen that coming and you are absolutely not to blame,' she told him.

Instead of retreating from the fray, Madge took a thirty-minute break to clean up and went back to the ward to nurse other POWs who had been committed to her care. Unfortunately it happened again and again but there was little that could be done to stop the practice, other than to be very watchful when attending her patients. *It's not much fun, basically being used as a spittoon*, she thought.

After such an awful day, Madge decided to have an early night and sat down to write a lengthy letter to Mum and the girls. She decided not to include a single word about the spitting so as not to worry the family. Instead the letter told how fond she was becoming of Basil and the fun they had at dances and dinners. *Doris and Doreen would love him and I just wish you could meet him, Mum*, she wrote.

The following day Madge was called to a meeting with Matron Ferguson and other hospital officials to talk about the best way of dealing with the Japanese patients, who had again been spitting at nurses. It was generally agreed that Madge's idea of wearing surgical face masks and tight-fitting caps was worth trying.

That evening Madge met Basil in Chittagong for an early

drink and she told him about the difficulties she and the other nurses had been having. He gave her hand a reassuring squeeze. 'The truth is, there's no easy answer to the problem. For the Japanese it's death before dishonour and they feel they've already let their country down by being taken prisoner. I don't want to sound unsympathetic but the reality is that they don't want to be kept alive, and I suspect that's the reason for their behaviour. I'm afraid they'll probably just carry on doing it for as long as they're there. But don't worry, we'll be off on our holiday soon enough and then you can try and forget them temporarily.'

Madge smiled. 'Perhaps we'll be able to forget that there's a war going on at all.'

Basil had to return to work, but escorted Madge back to the main gate of the hospital where she bumped into Havildar Bahadur, who said there had been more problems with spitting on the POW ward and a nurse had gone off in tears.

'There's a lot more to cry about in the Burma Campaign than the Japanese spitting in your face,' she calmly replied.

But the POWs, and the war as a whole, seemed to slip from her mind as she wandered back to her basha thinking only of Basil and hoping that time would pass quickly until they could see each other again.

21

Holiday in Calcutta

Madge, who was in charge of the couple's accreditation documents for the holiday in Calcutta, spotted that Basil's primary cholera immunisation was out of date. Thankfully they had driven less than a mile so she asked the driver if he would be so kind as to divert the short distance to 68 IGH, their sister hospital. As luck would have it, the first person they saw was a QA sister who also helped out at 56 IGH and they quickly explained the problem and how pressed they were for time. The QA smiled. 'What else would you expect from a man?' she joked, telling Basil to follow her.

'Would you prefer it in your bum or arm, sir?'

Basil laughed. 'I'll take it like a man in the arm.'

Within minutes they were back en route to the Patanga airfield, some ten miles from Chittagong. The casual, laid-back charm of the American security officer belied the hawk-eyed efficiency with which their accreditation documents were scrutinised before access was granted. The official spotted that Basil had received a cholera booster that morning. 'I hope it didn't hurt too much but it sure is wise, buddy, with the way things are in Calcutta.'

Madge thought the official was just being friendly and told him how much she was looking forward to the trip. 'Neither of us have ever flown before,' she said, the excitement clear on her face.

'Well, I'm sure you'll have a ball then, miss.'

With that they were escorted to a jeep and driven across the PSP (pierced-steel planking) runway to a DC-3 that was being loaded with crates, parcels and all sorts. It was their first surprise on what would be a very interesting trip.

'Have a nice day, youse guys,' said the driver as he dropped them off by the plane, which was a hive of activity. By the looks of things Madge and Basil would be the only English passengers because the others were casually dressed with badges on their shoulders featuring two yellow eagles over a white star. Everybody mixed happily together and Madge noticed a marked difference from the 'them and us' divide that separated the ranks in the British military.

Not only had Madge never flown before, she had never really spent time in the company of Americans and she found that she loved their courtesy and their accents. Basil had to smile when the pilot, wearing knee-high boots, a leather flying jacket wrapped over his shoulders and Hollywood sunglasses, gave them a casual salute as he walked past with a cigarette dangling from his lips and a soft drink in his left hand.

The temperature was rising rapidly even though it was still early in the day and Madge was dressed in her nursing khaki, which she found quite comfortable as she and Basil stood talking by the side of the plane alongside their two lightly packed cases. The handsome young American turned back and said the weather forecast was predicting swirling cross-winds from the Bay of Bengal and because of that the flight could be quite entertaining.

'We may go a little higher than normal to get above the winds,' he added, 'but this here old crate is a stripped-out Dakota DC-3 and just about the safest taxi you'll ever get to fly in.'

What a nice man, thought Madge as they began to board the flight that would take around an hour and a half before they reached Calcutta's Dum Dum airport. Madge was surprised at the steep incline passengers were forced to make once they boarded at the side of the plane.

'That's because the tail wheel is so low when the plane is on the ground,' one of the crew explained.

If the slope surprised her, then the inside of the plane was a real eye-opener. Instead of a passenger flight they were on a narrow freight carrier. Parcels were everywhere with some US personnel sitting on packages that were strapped to the floor in the central gangway that ran the length of the interior. Madge and Basil had been allocated so-called seats, which meant sitting on a long length of strong rope, woven like a fishing net, which was secured to the fuselage. Madge's dreams of enjoying a gin and tonic above the clouds like Betty Grable in those Hollywood movies very quickly evaporated.

They were, of course, grateful for their 'seats' but conversation became difficult when the plane began to vibrate as the twin engines coughed into life and the old warrior of the skies rumbled down the runway. Madge looked around once the plane was airborne to see signs either side of the pilot's cabin stating, in big red capital letters, NO SMOKING. Underneath both signs were guys happily puffing away on their cigarettes and downing beers hidden in brown paper bags. *Why on earth shouldn't they?* thought Madge. *They're putting their lives on the line to support the Allies on an alien continent. Let them have some relaxation!*

One soldier shuffled across the aircraft on his backside and courteously offered both Madge and Basil a swig from a bottle of Jack Daniel's, but took no offence at their refusal.

'I've never been to Calcutta before,' he told them, 'and me and the boys are sure as hell going to party round the clock when we get there! Listen, buddy,' he said, looking at Basil, 'can you tell me, is the airport we're flying to really called Dum Dum? I thought that was the name of a bullet!'

Basil had to shout over the noise of the engines when he replied that Dum Dum was actually an airport, but he could understand the American's confusion as the word dumdum had become associated with a controversial soft or hollow-nosed bullet that expanded on impact and caused extensive damage. This bullet had been developed at a British military installation in the area known as Dum Dum Arsenal.

Apart from a couple of minutes of bouncing about and one blast of turbulence that made the aircraft feel as if it was actually flying sideways the rest of the journey was calm enough and the pilot landed the DC-3 as smoothly as he had handled the take-off from Patanga. They were cleared through US security at Dum Dum at remarkable speed. The American soldiers accompanied them and after their flight Madge and Basil were invited to become honorary Americans. The only stipulation was they had to promise not to say a word 'in case that limey accent gives the game away'.

The DC-3 boys invited Madge and Basil to ride into Calcutta on their waiting US Forces truck and even diverted the vehicle to Chowringhee, where Basil had booked a week in the Grand Hotel. The young English couple's luggage was handed straight to the bearer at the front entrance of the fabled hotel and with much whooping and waving and lots of voices hollering 'Have a nice day, you guys' the happy group of Americans drove off to paint the town redder than red.

'There's certainly plenty of staff here,' said Madge as they were escorted into the lavishly appointed lobby where a magnificent chandelier and carved stone fountain vied for attention along with dignified, teak-panelled walls. It was little wonder that the Grand had become a byword for luxury and was normally so busy that it was very difficult to book even the most insignificant of rooms. Before Madge could even sit in one of the almost regal mahogany armchairs she was handed an iced flannel. 'It's like being in a palace,' she said to Basil, not realising he was deep in conversation with the concierge.

'I'm surprised the hotel is so quiet,' Basil said.

'Well, sir, I'm afraid there's been something of a problem with an outbreak of cholera in the building!'

Madge could hardly believe her ears! Calcutta was in the grip of a full-blown cholera epidemic with a hundred cases and upwards of thirty deaths being reported daily. A dozen of the British troops billeted in the Grand had also caught the deadly disease and had been taken to an isolation hospital. The rest of the British contingent had left. When news of the outbreak had emerged, close to 140 American servicemen had also moved to other accommodation and the finest hotel in town was decreed to be off limits to the rest of the US forces.

As the conversation between Basil and the concierge continued Madge suddenly remembered the security officer at Chittagong airport.

'It seems,' she said to Basil, 'that just about everybody knew about cholera in Calcutta except us!'

Suresh, who was standing in for the main concierge, explained that because of the number of people who caught cholera on the premises every room was being fumigated. 'As soon as that is complete, madam, the Grand will once again be the finest and the safest hotel in the whole of Calcutta,' he said with a beaming smile and a lot more positivity than Madge and Basil themselves felt. 'The kitchens are, however, to be fumigated later this week so it is better you have breakfast somewhere else,' he added.

Much to Madge's amusement Suresh, a happy soul who let slip that he loved a glass of Chivas Regal to start the day, wanted to turn the conversation to cricket rather than cholera.

What should have been a joyful and relaxed week was on the verge of becoming a holiday from hell. The immediate problem the couple faced was where to go next if they checked out of the Grand. There was certainly no guarantee that a new hotel would be any safer. As Suresh lavished praise on Douglas Jardine, a controversial former England cricket captain 'who gave those Aussies what for', Basil asked how busy other hotels were in the city.

'Well, I should imagine they are in a similar situation,' Suresh replied, 'but I can assure you that fumigation of the majority of the hotel will have been completed in just a day or so.'

'When you think it through,' said Basil, turning to Madge, 'if we move, we could be jumping from the frying pan straight into the fire so it's probably better to stay put.'

'Good idea,' she replied, 'because this hotel certainly looks rather splendid. The situation's not ideal but I think I'd rather be here than anywhere else.'

Only after the check-in formalities were completed did they find that their separate rooms, beautifully decorated and luxuriously furnished, were actually at totally opposite ends of the hotel, but they decided not to make a fuss. Instead they opted for an early lunch at a nearby restaurant that was the haunt of kings and queens, governor generals, maharajas, film stars and touring cricket teams.

Impressive as the list of celebrities who frequented the fabled Firpo's restaurant may have been, there was one thing that attracted Madge far more than the autographed pictures of the likes of the Aga Khan.

'I can't believe what they've got on the menu,' she said with a delighted smile.

Basil looked across the table as Madge waved the menu at him and said, 'First place goes to . . .' She handed the menu over so he could read for himself. 'Yes, steak and kidney pudding!' she said, choking up a little at the thought of Dad and his second helpings at Friday lunch. The smell of steak and kidney pudding always took her straight back to her gloriously happy childhood in Dover.

'Oh, that sounds delicious,' agreed Basil. 'I haven't had one of those in such a long time! But my goodness, there are some treats on this menu . . .'

Madge hadn't eaten since her 7 a.m. breakfast of two slices of toast and a cup of tea in the nurses' mess and she had no hesitation in choosing the steak and kidney pud with new potatoes and green peas. Basil decided on roast sirloin of beef followed by gateau mille-feuille, which he said was 'a posh way of describing a vanilla slice in flaky pastry'.

Madge hadn't realised just how much of a relief it would be to be away from Chittagong. Basil seemed to feel the same way. The barriers melted away and they were finally able to talk heart to heart.

'Well, I know a bit about you, like the fact that you were brought up in Woking and you have four brothers and one sister, but there's still so much I don't know. Like how on earth did you finally end up in the 10th Baluch Regiment of the Indian army?'

'Well, you know how my brother Brian and I enrolled and we were accepted and joined the Middlesex Regiment there and then. My regimental number was 6216153,' said Basil, 'and I have never forgotten it.'

He said that the most interesting time during his many months of training in Chester was being taught to operate the water-cooled Vickers machine guns, which he had to dismantle and reassemble wearing a blindfold during sessions in the battalion camp at The Dale. When it was announced that a war office selection board was being held at a military centre in Kent, Basil and Brian decided it was worth trying and both were recommended for commissions into the Indian army. They sailed on the one-time cruise liner RMS *Strathaird* from Gourock to Bombay in February 1943.

'And can you remember your commission number?' Madge teasingly asked.

'EC11754,' Basil replied instantly.

Madge was interested to hear details of the brothers' sea voyage, because the threat from German submarines was so perilous in the Mediterranean in 1943 that Allied troopships, often carrying personnel in excess of four thousand, went down the coast of west Africa and round the Cape instead of through the Strait of Gibraltar and the Suez Canal. However, time was running on and Basil promised faithfully to compare his sea journey with her own another time.

Once the bill was paid they made their way to the door, but

stopped outside Firpo's green shutters wondering what the sudden noise was all about. There was banging and shouting and a banner emblazoned with the slogan '*Jai Hind*' was waved by a group of protestors.

'Back inside, quickly,' said Basil and they watched from Firpo's upstairs windows as the demonstration demanding 'Home Rule for India' marched past. '*Jai Hind* means victory to India,' he told Madge, who expressed surprise at the size of the demonstration.

Once the protest had passed, they decided to walk to a local cinema and got caught in such a torrential downpour that their clothes squelched as they sat down to watch Ginger Rogers and Ray Milland star in *The Major and the Minor*. Their clothes were still soggy when they got back to the Grand Hotel, where they were given flasks of freshly boiled water for drinking and brushing their teeth.

'The hotel is completely deserted,' said Madge. 'It actually feels quite eerie, don't you think?'

'Yes,' agreed Basil. 'It's certainly not what I had in mind, that's for sure! Let me walk you to your room.'

At the door to Madge's hotel room, Basil took her hand before kissing her lightly on the lips and wishing her goodnight, then making the surprisingly long walk to his room at the very other end.

At the end of the first full day she had spent in Basil's company Madge had an overwhelming feeling of happiness and within minutes of her head hitting the soft pillow, she was fast asleep.

★

They thought they had escaped the attention of stand-in concierge Suresh the following morning as they strolled hand in hand through the lobby but were a little too slow.

'Good morning, good morning,' he called out, and although the door was in sight, they politely turned back. After asking how they had slept, he said how sorry he was that the hotel was so quiet because it used to be a lot of fun many years ago. 'The best time of all was New Year's Eve when there was iced champagne for everyone and at the stroke of midnight twelve little piglets were released. Anybody who caught one could keep it,' said Suresh.

'Well, thank you for telling us that,' chuckled Madge, and they beat a hasty retreat from the lobby and the very chatty concierge to make an early start exploring a city that had once been the capital of India. They planned to have a leisurely breakfast, enjoy reading a daily newspaper for the first time in months and then slowly make their way across town to see the Victoria Memorial. Traffic was heavy as cycles, rickshaws, motorbikes, cars and several lorries emblazoned with 'Jai Hind' banners drove past while they waited to cross the road to pick up a copy of The Statesman, an English-language newspaper.

'I don't believe it,' said Basil, as he glanced at the front page. 'President Roosevelt has died. He was only sixty-three. Apparently it was a stroke!'

'Oh my goodness, that's terrible,' said Madge, just as shocked as Basil.

Their plans were put on hold as the pair discussed the news at length over a good old fry-up in Firpo's.

'I wonder what those American boys who were so kind to us on the flight from Chittagong must be thinking,' said Madge. 'They must be wondering what the future holds for US forces in the Burma Campaign.'

'They won't be the only ones wondering that,' replied Basil.

Elsewhere on the front page of *The Statesman* it was reported that the Allies were closing in on Berlin. A Reuters story said that 'the collapse of the entire German central position was imminent' and that Allied entry into Berlin was just days away at the most. British paratroopers had been dropped fifteen miles from the German capital and total victory in Europe seemed in sight, but there wasn't a single word about progress in the Burma Campaign. Frustrating as that was, Madge and Basil were well aware that strict censorship was the reason. Their security training kicked in and they decided not to discuss that situation in Firpo's.

Madge had a spring in her step as they walked out to wait for a rickshaw in the shade of the green shutters outside Firpo's because the wonderful news from London meant Mum and the girls would hopefully soon be able to move back from High Wycombe to the family home in Dover. *Although it will be a while before the house is fit to live in again*, she remembered with a pang. All thoughts of home took second place, however, at the first sighting of the Victoria Memorial set in sixty-four acres of lawned splendour on the banks of the Hooghly River.

A guide approached and instantly started telling the couple in almost perfect English about the history of the building. He wore a traditional flowing white cotton kurta top and dhoti, sandals and a faded brown trilby hat that had seen better days. He was one of those characters who had an irresistibly cheeky charm. He explained that after the death of Queen Victoria in 1901 George Nathaniel Curzon, First Marquess Curzon of Kedleston and Viceroy of India, suggested the building of a stately, spacious and grand monument in her memory. 'This magnificent creation in white Makrana marble from Rajasthan that stands before us is the result,' he said.

'It certainly is beautiful,' Madge agreed, 'but it doesn't look like white marble?'

'*Memsahib*, you are right,' the guide replied. 'The Japanese were bombing us and the British said the building had to be camouflaged to prevent it being damaged. I think they painted it black so the Japanese pilots could not use it as a landmark. It used to gleam white in the moonlight and I hope it will do so again once this terrible war is over.'

'For just a few annas it has to be worthwhile to have a guide like this,' whispered Madge to Basil, as they walked towards the magnificent structure. The guide told them that construction of the building had begun in 1906 but by the time the Victoria Memorial was completed in 1921, New Delhi had already been earmarked to replace Calcutta as the nation's capital.

'The official reason,' he explained, 'was that a more centrally located capital city would be in the country's best interests.' He looked at them with an apologetic, almost sardonic, smile. 'The British couldn't wait to relocate the capital from Calcutta after a spate of bombings and political assassinations.'

Without saying another word, he doffed his hat and simply walked away.

'He left very abruptly,' Madge said, slightly confused.

'He did indeed!' laughed Basil. 'Well, while we're here let's have a wander round the grounds and then make our way back into the city centre to do some exploring.'

When they arrived in the centre of the vibrant but troubled city, the pair were shocked when they saw for themselves the huge divide that separated the haves from the have-nots. The Victoria Memorial had been overwhelmingly impressive yet just a taxi ride away poverty-stricken families lived on the edge of rubbish dumps and pavements where they begged for money to buy food to feed their starving children.

They came across one family who were living under a large cotton sheet that was attached to the top of a shoulder-high wall and two wooden poles driven into the ground. Underneath, three little children were playing on the unpaved surface that also served as their bed. The mother looked so weary and downcast that even when Basil dropped a generous handful of coins into her begging bowl she barely had the energy to acknowledge his kindness.

'That was really kind of you,' said Madge. 'Imagine living like that. That poor woman looks so weary. It really is very sad.'

As they walked away, Basil turned to take a photograph as proof of just how truly dreadful the conditions were. Within seconds the calm of the sultry afternoon was brought to an arm-waving, shouting end when a bare-footed man in a badly stained dhoti appeared from under the cotton sheet and started marching towards them. Madge and Basil took the hint and beat a hasty retreat.

All in all it had been a thought-provoking day in extreme heat and debilitating humidity and Madge was happy to return to the Grand Hotel to freshen up before strolling over to Firpo's for cakes and a pot of tea.

As the week wore on they explored as much of Calcutta as they could, strolling the streets and soaking up the atmosphere. On their last evening in the city they decided to try the Great Eastern Hotel for dinner, which in the glory days of the Raj was known as the Jewel of the Far East. The hotel was above a department store so Madge took the opportunity to purchase the six bottles of peroxide that nurses at 56 IGH had begged her to bring back to Chittagong. In spite of closing time approaching she also had a wander around the ladies' shoe section before time, much to Basil's amusement, ran out.

Madge consoled herself by joining Basil in ordering a gin and tonic in the bar of the Great Eastern. As she sipped it in the sultry heat she couldn't remember having had a more refreshing drink in her life.

The couple then went through to the dining room where a prominent notice stated: 'Owing to Rationing – NO A LA CARTE. Under the Bengal Meat Control Rules 3 Items Only Allowed Each Person.' Madge chose the hot buffet which started with a thick French vegetable soup, followed by a very tasty steak and kidney pie and vermicelli pudding. Basil opted for the cold buffet with chicken pâté, sirloin of beef and the vermicelli.

'This has been both a rather lovely and a very interesting day,' he told Madge over dinner that night. 'But most of all today has made me realise just how lucky I have been to meet you in Chittagong.

'When I volunteered at the recruitment office in Surbiton I would never have dreamed that I would be posted to India, and never in a month of Sundays would I have imagined meeting someone like you out here. Madge, I can honestly say this holiday has been the most wonderful week of my life.'

As Madge hung on his every word Basil reached for the wine, made sure both their glasses were full and added that he would like to make a very special toast.

'Here's to us. Whatever the future may hold.'

22

A Painful Goodbye

The peace and calm of the holiday was soon broken once Madge and Basil returned to base. When Madge joined Vera for breakfast in the nurses' mess Vera said that she had been to a cocktail party thrown by one of the US Air Force squadrons the night before and everybody was talking about a German radio report which claimed Adolf Hitler had committed suicide on 30 April, along with his wife, Eva Braun.

'To begin with everybody was really sceptical,' Vera told Madge. 'We all thought it sounded more like wishful thinking than reality.' However, Vera explained, as the evening drew to a close a pilot and his crew, who had just flown one of the giant US transport planes in from Calcutta, arrived at the party for a beer. He had the latest copy of *Stars and Stripes*, the American military newspaper, which confirmed the story on its front page. 'Unfortunately,' added Vera, 'it was made very clear in the paper that in spite of Hitler's suicide there's still no end in sight for this blasted war.'

Vera was then asked by another of the nurses if there were any more details about Hitler's death.

'Surely it could just be an elaborate hoax?' the nurse suggested.

'No. Apparently he shot himself,' Vera replied. 'But it was difficult to find out too many details as everyone was desperate to read the article so I had to try to read it over somebody's shoulder.'

During the first week of May whispers began to circulate that Allied troops were on the fringe of liberating Rangoon from the Japanese, who had been in control since March 1942. The key, according to the widely repeated rumours, was to get it all sorted out before the start of the monsoon, which they did with just hours to spare. The rains began late on the afternoon of 2 May but the city had been secured by then and the official announcement of the liberation of Rangoon was made the following day.

Back at HQ Movements, Chittagong, it had been so frantically busy that it was a couple of days before Basil was able to get away to celebrate the 14th Army's triumph with Madge, who was delighted to see him again.

'It seems like forever since we last met,' said Madge as she gave him a welcome kiss and a big smile. 'Thank you again for that wonderful week in Calcutta. I've already started wondering where we can go next,' she added with excitement.

However, there was no response from Basil to her enthusiasm and Madge was concerned that something was wrong, but put it down to the fact that he had been so busy and working virtually round the clock. *He must just be tired*, she thought.

'On our next leave perhaps we could go up to Darjeeling,'

she suggested. 'I've been told that you can even see Mount Everest from there and that the views of the tea plantations are out of this world.' But still there was virtually no response and Madge's tummy turned in despair. *What on earth has gone wrong?* she thought.

Then Basil sighed deeply before gently putting an arm round Madge's shoulders and telling her he had been included in a Movements unit that was being transferred to Rangoon. 'I leave by sea in forty-eight hours,' he said, 'but I've been given tomorrow off to get my things in order.'

A long and loving hug that seemed to go on forever said more than words could ever express as it suddenly dawned on Madge that it was highly unlikely that she would ever see Basil again in the Far East. She turned away and shook her head so he couldn't see the tears that were slowly trickling down her cheeks.

The heartbreaking thought of such a lengthy, or potentially even permanent, separation made her all the more determined to ensure their last day together in Chittagong was one to remember. She suggested they spend the precious hours on a secluded beach.

What Basil didn't know as they parted company at the end of lunch was that Madge didn't even have the following day off, but when Vera heard about the dilemma she instantly agreed to swap shifts. The kitchen staff loved the little *memsahib* for her good humour after her brave battle with the kite hawk and when Madge explained why she wanted a picnic to take to the beach the following day they were only too keen to help the blossoming romance along.

When she went to bed that night she thought about how her world that just the previous day had been full of love and enchantment had been turned upside down. Most of all she worried about what would happen to Basil. She worried about his sea voyage down the Bay of Bengal to Rangoon. She worried about the chaos and blood-letting still taking place in the Burmese capital. She worried about the Japanese fighting on the outskirts of the city. She worried about him catching malaria. Eventually she worried herself to sleep as sheer exhaustion brought a merciful end to the emotional turmoil.

The following morning Madge went straight to the kitchens and could hardly believe the feast that had been produced. She was told with great pride that among the contents of the two huge, flower-decked baskets were freshly baked bread, cold pureed vegetable soup, tomatoes, spring onions, samosas, pakoras, spiced potatoes, curry sauces, chicken breasts, roast beef, and enough cakes, Indian kheer (rice pudding) and fresh fruit 'to feed the 14th Army'. Hidden away in the bottom of one of the baskets was an expensive bottle of bubbly the girls in the nurses' mess at 56 IGH had clubbed together to buy. *That's so kind and thoughtful of the girls. I must remember to thank each and every one of them*, she said to herself. The sadness of the previous evening had eased and she suddenly started to laugh. *This hospital is no different to any other*, she mused. *Any news here travels at the speed of light.*

The weather forecast predicted a cloudless, sunny day with light winds and at 10 a.m. on the dot Basil arrived in a chauffeured jeep for the drive to Patanga beach, about an hour north of Chittagong on the Bay of Bengal. The traffic on the way down was mainly military in one form or another.

A virtually deserted golden beach was bathed in sunlight and the gentlest of breezes wafted through the few palm trees. Just weeks previously there had been numerous freighters and naval vessels off the coast, but many had already moved south so the view out into the placid sea was unblemished. Madge and Basil quickly changed into their swimming costumes, politely and bashfully looking away from each other. They ran into the sea together holding hands and floated on their backs looking at the sky. The water was so warm it felt like they were swimming in a warm bath. Madge knew this was a day she'd never forget.

They stayed in the water for an age before emerging to enjoy the picnic that had been so superbly prepared by her friends from the kitchen staff at 56 IGH it seemed almost a shame to eat it. The chicken was delicately spiced with masala and there was even horseradish to go with the cold beef.

'You never got to the end of that tale you started on our last night in Calcutta. If you have a moment after your second portion of that delicious rice pudding,' she teased with a cheeky grin, 'perhaps you would be so kind as to continue.'

'Well, Nurse Graves,' he said, 'as you have asked so nicely I will do so – with great pleasure.'

He had been telling Madge about how he and his brother Brian fared on the *Strathaird*, the troopship that took them from Gourock to Bombay on a journey that ended for him in Chittagong.

'We didn't exactly travel first class like you ladies,' he said with a smile as they lazed on a rug after lunch.

The temperature at Patanga was almost 90 degrees Fahrenheit so they went back into the sea to cool down and as they swam Basil continued his story.

'Brian and I were six decks down and on a mess deck with fixed tables. Every night forty or fifty of us cadets would hang our hammocks and swing back and forth together with the ship as it zigzagged in the Atlantic. We had to change course constantly to avoid the German Wolfpacks so the ship was always pitching and rolling. We slept remarkably well,' he laughed. 'The main problem was that the heads were always in use as so many of the cadets were seasick!'

Basil went on to tell Madge how eventually the troopships pulled in to Freetown to take on fresh supplies and remained there for three days. The locals came alongside in their bum boats and sold lots of local produce to the troops by throwing up ropes attached to baskets.

'Children would swim out to our boat and beg for money, but would only dive for silver coins so we covered the copper coins with silver paper and it worked for a while but they soon cottoned on to that,' Basil said. 'On the third day we rejoined the naval escorts and continued zigzagging down the Atlantic coast of Africa, past Cape Town and on to Durban, where the beef was even better than what I had in Calcutta!'

Virtually all the ship's passengers came on deck as the *Strathaird* pulled out of Durban harbour to listen to the much-loved Lady in White, a retired opera singer called Perla Siedle

Gibson, who sang to all Allied ships 'There'll always be an England', 'Land of Hope and Glory' and other favourites through a loudspeaker as she stood on the harbour wall.

'She gave us and, no doubt, thousands of others a huge boost as we steamed out to sea again. I don't think I've ever heard such applause and cheering, and she waved to us until we were out of sight.'

Basil explained that his ship eventually left the convoy and sailed to Port Suez, where the Argyll and Sutherland Highlanders disembarked to fight in the North African campaign. The troopship then proceeded on the last leg of its long journey to India. Madge interrupted to ask Basil if he wanted yet another helping of rice pudding, but he laughed her off and instead began to tell her about his first memory of Bombay. He said that when the *Strathaird* arrived there in May the Indian navy had gone on strike, which had escalated into a full-scale mutiny by June. The rebellion had started as a protest over food, living conditions and complaints about racist behaviour by the British and spread to almost eighty boats and shore establishments involving twenty thousand sailors.

'Within four months of arriving in India and after an intensive course at the Officers' Training Centre in Mhow, 350 miles from Bombay, my brother and I were awarded emergency commissions in the Indian Army, 10th Baluch regiment. We were immediately seconded to Movements and Transportation for operations with the 14th Army in Burma. We then returned to Bombay for more in-depth Movement tuition and while we were living in the Colaba district there was another little incident involving a certain Mr Gandhi that may interest you,' he told Madge.

'I assure you that I've heard so much about Gandhi that anything about him really interests me,' said Madge.

Basil held his hands in the air and jokingly asked for permission to continue and when Madge nodded he added that Mahatma Gandhi had not long been released from the Aga Khan's palace where he had been in custody on hunger strike in protest against British rule.

'A group of us who had been swimming at a pool on Malabar Hill saw him as he walked at the front of a large group of people. It wasn't a demonstration, just a group following the great man, so I filmed it all on my cine-camera. I was so thrilled to have seen him. After handing the film in to be developed I returned a few days later to find the footage was a complete blank. I'm absolutely certain it was censored because other things had also been removed on the film as well. I was so disappointed to have lost such an interesting piece of history,' he added.

The day at Patanga beach just seemed to fly by as Basil continued to tell Madge about his time in India before they met. He told her about how after Bombay he was sent to New Delhi to pick up his own Movements unit complete with staff, office stores, cabinets and a 15-cwt lorry – all of which was transported to Chittagong in time for his arrival before Christmas.

'During the following year I suffered from malaria, then diphtheria a few months later, so I got to know 68 IGH, your sister hospital, quite well. The best thing about the move to Chittagong was it meant I had the lasting pleasure of meeting you,' he told Madge.

'That's very kind of you to say so,' she replied, feeling ever so shy all of a sudden. 'And it's important that you know the feeling is mutual. Absolutely mutual.'

Basil had thought long and hard about what to discuss and what to say on that final day together. He knew already that he was head over heels in love with Madge and under normal circumstances a picnic on a deserted golden beach with the sun beaming through palm trees and a balmy breeze wafting in from the Bay of Bengal would have been an ideal setting in which to ask for her hand in marriage.

He also thought long and hard about the potential consequences of missing the perfect opportunity in the perfect location. A beautiful English nurse among thousands of lonely, homesick soldiers would never be short of company. It was a community that lived day to day under intolerable pressure. What would happen if through sheer loneliness she fell for another? What if one of those absurdly handsome and infinitely charming American airmen whisked her off to the USA?

Logically this was the day. This was the hour. But much as he wanted to follow his heart his head told him otherwise. In the end there was a heartbreakingly honourable reason why he decided not to go down on one knee and ask Madge to marry him. He simply couldn't bear the possibility of this caring, compassionate and very loveable young lady becoming a war widow at the tender age of twenty-one.

I just hope with all my heart that everything will fall into place if we ever get back to England and we are able to meet again, thought Basil.

After another dip to cool down and a short nap they spent the rest of the afternoon letting the cares and worries of the past and future drift on the tide. They talked and talked and Madge made sure that Basil still had her mum's addresses in both High Wycombe and Dover. He, in turn, double-checked that Madge had the address of his parents Alys and Herbert in Surrey. The question of marriage was never brought up. No promises of undying love were made, but without spelling it out, an unbreakable bond had been formed and Madge dreamed that somewhere, sometime, they would meet again. Even the normally insufferable humidity was the lowest it had been for weeks and Madge thought things were so perfect it was almost too good to be true.

She was right. An hour later they had both turned bright pink and were on the verge of sunstroke. They'd thought that if they stayed in the sea they wouldn't be burned by the sun's rays, but it didn't quite work out like that as the salt in the water helped to blister their bodies.

'Look at us! We're red as lobsters,' said Madge.

'Apart from one place,' said Basil. Madge looked a little closer at him. The sun had intensified their already yellowish faces into sallow masks.

'If there's one thing I won't miss, it's mepacrine,' Madge said, covering her own face with embarrassment.

Basil gently prised her hands from her face. 'You're

271

beautiful, no matter what,' he said as he leaned in for their final, agonising kiss on the beach that day.

'There's one thing we cannot do,' he said, as they got ready to leave. 'We cannot report to the doctor, as putting ourselves out of active duty is a courts martial offence.'

The sun that had been so seductively brutal was slowly setting as they began the drive back from Patanga to Chittagong. By the time they arrived at the gates to the hospital the sky had turned a vivid and very romantic red. As they sat chatting in the jeep that had picked them up, the sun disappeared at speed to be replaced by a crescent-shaped moon and a multitude of stars.

The setting was almost perfect for a Mills and Boon farewell – except for two things. The first was that the Gurkha guards were scrutinising their every move from the other side of the barrier. The second was that the shoulders and backs of both Madge and Basil were as red as the sunset had been, and infinitely painful.

The farewell on the eve of Basil's seaborne departure to Rangoon was always going to be emotionally painful, but combined with the burning agony of sunburn, their final, loving embrace was overwhelmingly tender, to say the least. Basil was in such severe pain that he almost forgot to give Madge the elegant jade bracelet that he had bought her as a farewell present.

'My greatest worry,' said Madge, 'is that I'll never see you again.'

'Don't think that way,' said Basil. 'This war will end sometime, hopefully sooner rather than later, and then we'll be able to pick up just where we left off.'

Madge could only hope with all her heart that he was right.

The following morning Madge was in such pain that she took a roll of lint and cut two holes for her arms to go through, fashioning herself a kind of soft bodice that marginally eased the pain of those sunburned shoulders and back rubbing against her nurse's uniform.

The emotional pain of her separation from Basil, however, was simply unbearable and she yearned to be back with the man she knew was equally heartbroken.

In fact, Basil had been so severely sunburned that on the first day of the three-day journey by sea he was bed-bound. On the second day there was a knock at the door and he was told that the captain of the rust-bucket of an old freighter that was carrying the Movements unit down the coast of Burma had a very important announcement to make and wanted everybody on deck without delay. For the life of him, Basil couldn't think what it would be as he gingerly pulled a shirt on over his blistered shoulders before going up. The captain stood in the middle of a large group and spoke through a loudhailer when he said that the information he had received in a radio transmission had been verified by two other sources. The announcement was short, sharp and greeted with an enormous cheer.

'The Germans have surrendered!'

Within seconds the deck was alive with men jumping up, yelling question after question, shaking hands and slapping one another on the back. When Basil got a full-blooded smack on his shoulders, the pain almost took his breath away but he wasn't going to miss this for the world and joined in a somewhat off-key version of 'God Save the King' with enormous gusto.

At the celebration party on board in the afternoon Basil put on the bravest of faces, but the pain of his blistered shoulders became so intense he left the fray after an hour and retired to his cabin. Later that evening when things began to calm down he wished fervently that he had been with Madge when the wonderful news was announced.

The converted freighter carrying Basil and the Movements units finally sailed up the Irrawaddy River, which had been heavily mined by the Japanese but swept clear within days of the Allies taking over. Enormous numbers of troops with tons of food and supplies were arriving into Rangoon docks. Lieutenant General Hyotaro Kimura, the Japanese Commander-in-Chief in Rangoon, having been instructed to defend the headquarters of the Imperial Japanese army to the death, simply abandoned Burma's capital. Before they fled the Japanese systematically demolished a convent that they were using as a hospital, resulting in the death of almost four hundred of their own soldiers. In addition, Rangoon's main jail was burned to the ground. Once the Japanese left, Rangoon suffered widespread looting and vigilantes ran amok while heavily armed robbers caused terror in the suburbs. Units of the 26th Indian Division along with British troops were seconded to police the city.

The Japanese were being systematically driven back towards

the Thai border supply lines. Basil's next few months would be a furiously busy period. Every day he would make a round journey of almost a hundred miles from Rangoon to Pegu in his army jeep to a barren area of land with only a pebble track leading to the vital trans-shipment zone. It was from Pegu that Basil and the Troop Movement unit organised the transfer of thousands of tons of equipment, ammunition, food and troops to the front line.

The big worry is not the Japanese, Basil wrote in a letter to Madge, *it's the thought of letting the troops down if things go wrong. That is what plays on all our minds every moment of every day.*

Madge felt tears come into her eyes at the thought of the weight of responsibility on other Allied unit's shoulders, and gave a silent prayer that he would return safely to her.

23

The Casualty Clearing Station

Back in Chittagong, 56 IGH heard about the end of the war in Europe a day after Basil. Madge celebrated in a very crowded nurses' mess where Matron Olive Ferguson had gathered doctors and medical staff to raise a toast to victory. Sister Blossom was doing a sterling job of making sure every glass was full of good cheer. Unfortunately it was nothing stronger than fresh orange juice and not the pints of Newcastle Brown Ale that Vera had demanded because it was such a special occasion. Madge's first thought when she heard the news was to hope Basil's blistered shoulders were on the way to recovery so he would be well enough to join in the celebrations.

She wondered exactly when Mum and her sisters would finally be able to return to Dover, and kept her fingers crossed that in spite of all the reassurances this was not just another groundless rumour. Happily, radio reports that had previously been heavily censored began to reveal details of the unconditional surrender. Apparently, London had celebrated through the night and Prime Minister Winston Churchill said that there was 'no greater day in the history of our country'. The royal family had made no fewer than five appearances on the balcony of Buckingham Palace in response to huge crowds gathered in the Mall. The report drew to a close by saying that for the first time in six years searchlights illuminated St Paul's Cathedral.

In spite of VE Day, vicious fighting was still taking place in Burma and the nursing staff at 56 IGH were warned to be extra careful in Chittagong where another '*Jai Hind*' rally in support of home rule for India was scheduled. For Madge, however, there was a more immediate problem because she was due back for duty on the Japanese POW casualty ward and had been made aware that the atmosphere had become increasingly unpleasant. She was told that many of the POWs were squabbling among themselves.

The surgical masks and tight-fitting caps the girls wore made spitting at the nurses harder for the Japanese, but they continued nonetheless. In spite of trying to block all medical treatment they still continued to eat and drink, however. Not a single case of a POW going on hunger strike was recorded in the war diary of 56 IGH. The British guards were starting to lose patience, despite the threat of a court martial, and began to make their feelings known. The key was to follow orders and not physically touch the POWs so, as had happened on Madge's first shift with the Japanese prisoners, bed legs were kicked when they misbehaved. A senior Japanese officer became so disgusted by the POWs' behaviour that he held talks with the worst offenders in a bid to end the continuing abuse of the nurses. Fortunately, guards were on hand to save him from serious injury when a furious row broke out and several POWs trapped the officer in a corner.

The day after VE Day, Madge had a fractious and somewhat tiring shift. The humidity was particularly unpleasant and as she sterilised wounds and administered injections, she could only wish that the Allied POWs were being treated the same way by the enemy.

The Japanese officer hobbled over and surprised her when he said, in passable English, that he had told the soldiers they should appreciate the nurses instead of behaving the way they were doing, but his mission had failed. It was the first conversation Madge had had with any of the Japanese POWs and while there clearly was no apology forthcoming, the sentiment reassured her that her work was necessary and right.

A few days later, there was a call for nurses to staff a casualty clearing station (CCS) that was to be set up in the hills east of the port of Maungdaw near the Arakan area just south of Chittagong. Madge was one of six who volunteered. The Arakan was one of the most bitterly fought over areas in the Burma Campaign and for medical staff it was a very dangerous place indeed. The previous year during the Battle of the Admin Box a field hospital operated by the Royal Medical Corps and the Indian Medical Service had been overrun by Japanese, who were looking for medical supplies. During that search they bayoneted bed-bound patients and shot a Red Cross doctor, all in their quest to steal morphine and quinine, and even cotton wool. Indian soldiers who survived being shot were told that the Japanese aim was to be in control of Chittagong within two months. The slaughter of doctors and helpless patients continued and when the Japanese were finally forced out of the hospital complex the bayoneted patients and thirty other bodies were discovered.

Madge was told, along with five other VADs including Vera and Phyl, that they would spend more than a month in the Arakan jungle during which time they would be living in tents. It was unlikely there would be running water and the nurses would be expected to be on duty from the moment they awoke to the time they fell asleep. There certainly wasn't much sleep on the journey by road and track down the coast from Chittagong to Cox's Bazar, a strategically vital port on the Bay of Bengal. *At least this will be good preparation for when we arrive*, thought Madge on the arduous journey.

On the day before the group were due to leave Madge had a wonderful surprise when a letter from Basil arrived. The letter was deliberately upbeat, filled with stories designed to make her smile. It was obvious from the way he signed the note 'your loving Basil' that he still felt just as strongly about her as she did about him, and just that knowledge helped to lift her from the sadness she felt at being apart from him.

The distance from Chittagong to Cox's Bazar was little more than a hundred miles but for the nurses travelling in the rear of the battered old green army ambulance it turned into a bone-shaking nightmare that seemed to take hours. The constant rainstorms turned the roads to quagmires and Madge was grateful for the kindness of the Ghanaian driver, who went out of his way to make the trip as bearable as possible.

Awooner was a member of the Royal West Africa Frontier Force that fought with such distinction in the Burma Campaign and he was an expert at manoeuvring the rickety old vehicle through floods and round deep and dangerous potholes.

'Don't you ladies worry yourselves,' he told them as they each gripped their seats as hard as they could. 'Back in Ghana the roads are always like this when the rains come. It's no problem to me!'

He always had a smile and went out of his way to make things as comfortable as possible for the girls, which helped to put them all at ease.

If they thought that leg of the journey was bad, the drive into the hills after a two-day stopover in Cox's Bazar was terrifying. They spent several hours driving on what were little more than jungle tracks before they reached the CCS. Once the group had settled in to the tented accommodation that would be home for several weeks a very welcome late evening meal was served.

'I thought we would at least have our own tents,' said Madge. 'But I suppose it's quite nice to be back together again under one roof. Even if it is only canvas!'

The nurses were all so dog-tired when they eventually got into their camp beds that they slept like logs, but they got a big surprise when they woke just before dawn. There had been another heavy and prolonged rainstorm during the night and a bubbling, gurgling stream was flowing right through the middle of their tent!

'Oh look, we have running water!' joked Madge.

Luckily, due to the tarantulas, poisonous spiders, leaches and other creepy crawlies that were inclined to pop into the CCS tents, the camp beds were high off the ground so nothing of importance was damaged.

Later that morning their tent was moved away from the stream that was still happily flowing from a crevice further up the hill. What really surprised the newly arrived group of VADs was the size of the camp that was camouflaged and neatly tucked away at the bottom of a lush green valley. Birds fluttered in and out of the trees that grew on the slopes and pretty little flowers sprouted alongside thick, spiked bushes that surrounded the camp.

A main tent acted as an operating theatre and makeshift casualty ward, and then there was a kitchen, a separate toilet and a makeshift shower hidden behind a tarpaulin that the soldiers had rigged up. That was about it, so far as Madge could see. She was told that there were always troops on guard, but those boys must have slept elsewhere because there were no more tents in sight.

The staff at the camp more than welcomed the young nurses because the first thing that Phyl did when she saw the kitchen facilities and sacks of potatoes was to teach the cooks how to make 'very passable' chips.

Wisps of mist rose as the morning sun broke through to turn the valley into a scene of such beauty that it came as quite a shock when the peace was shattered by the rumble of thunder.

'Does this thunder mean we're in for another of those heavy downpours?' Madge asked a guard after another loud and prolonged burst.

He shook his head and smiled gently. 'That noise wasn't thunder, miss. It's our artillery giving the Japanese their early morning wake-up call,' he said.

That will teach you to ask silly questions, Madge said to herself, and try as she might, she found it difficult to balance the Arakan's forested glory with the utter brutality that was taking place just a few miles away.

Madge had spent the early part of the day in the operating theatre, where it had been a surprisingly quiet start. Most of the 'repair work' took place on men who had been brought in overnight with shrapnel damage suffered in a twilight confrontation with a Japanese raiding party. Casualty clearing meant exactly what it said. Doctors had to decide whether the injured soldiers could be patched up and returned to their units, or if they needed specialised treatment, in which case they would then be stretchered to the nearest air strip and flown to Chittagong or Calcutta. Only rarely did wounded troops stay for more than a couple of days and if that did happen, it was usually to get them fit enough to travel on to more sophisticated medical facilities. Thankfully, there was no shortage of medicine at this stage of the war because everything was supplied by air. The team were free to carry out blood transfusions, minor operations, stitch wounds and treat soldiers for everything from malaria to typhoid as well as dysentery and beriberi. They even had to sort out one poor young lad who had been bitten by a snake.

His pal who had brought him in to the station kept on teasing him that he was going to die in minutes.

'Just you leave him alone,' Madge said jokingly, aware that in a bizarre way his friend was trying to keep his spirits up. 'Don't you worry,' she said, turning to the lad who had been bitten, 'it wasn't one of those really poisonous ones they have around here so I'd say you're actually pretty lucky. You'll be fine in no time.'

The state of some of the boys when they first came in was often very worrying because they arrived with literally nothing and Madge had to clean the soldiers up, find out what the injury was and get them to theatre as quickly as possible. As warned, the nurses worked round the clock until they were told to get some sleep. It wasn't unusual to be called to deal with the wounded at 3 a.m. and no matter how badly injured or sick they were there was always a 'thank you' after dressing even the nastiest of injuries.

After one particularly gruelling day at the CCS, as she tucked herself up in her rather uncomfortable camp bed, Madge thought to herself, *It really is a case of all work and no play here. They weren't wrong when they told us to expect to have to work our socks off.* There was the odd moment of fun and teasing at meal times, but there was not even the hint of a social life. When they weren't nursing the girls tried as much as possible to catch up on their sleep. And they certainly didn't get any mail, which would have helped to raise their spirits.

Madge was shocked early one afternoon, about halfway through their six-week stint at the CCS, when she heard two explosions that seemed alarmingly close. There was no way of finding out what was happening because she was in the middle of treating a soldier who had been shot in the thigh. An hour later she looked out of the tent to see two of the guards being cheered as they walked up the valley with several big, fat, juicy fish. They had thrown grenades into a deep stream in the next valley. She couldn't believe the size of the haul!

'One of our nurses has taught the boys in the kitchens how to make chips,' she told the wounded soldier, who could see the guards through the flaps of the tent. 'It looks to me as if there could be a treat on the menu,' she added. 'Good old-fashioned English fish and chips!' That seemed to bring a smile to the soldier's face despite the pain he must have been in.

The troops, out of gratitude for what the nurses were doing for them, told the girls they would be first in the queue for dinner that night before the inevitable blizzard of requests for the delicacy flew in. Madge and every other nurse, however, turned down the offer of fish and chips deep in the Burmese jungle that night so wounded troops could enjoy a little treat that would remind them of home.

The following morning, instead of the usual thunderous Allied artillery there was prolonged small-arms fire. It was a sign that the fighting was closer but Madge and Vera had no time to think about what was happening around them. They were kept busy dressing wounds of men who had been brought in at dawn on makeshift stretchers which had been hacked into shape from boughs that had fallen from trees. Two others had carved themselves such ornate walking sticks they took them back to the front line with them after their bullet wounds were patched up. The noise subsided around noon and the majority of the walking wounded had been treated and wasted no time in bravely returning to the conflict.

It meant the CCS was virtually deserted for the first time since the VAD contingent's arrival.

'The silence here is almost spooky,' Vera said when she joined Madge for some lunch after having been on duty with her from first light that morning. 'I don't think we've even had a moment's peace before now, and then this!'

'No,' said Madge. 'I can't get used to it either. It feels very strange.'

Phyl had overheard the girls talking and arrived at the table with her lunch. 'Well, girls, I say we just enjoy it while we can, don't you? You know it'll be absolute mayhem here again before we know it!'

The other two laughed in agreement before they all tucked in to their well-deserved meal.

Just as they were finishing, however, the afternoon calm was broken by the loud voice of a sergeant who appeared out of the blue. 'Excuse me, ladies, but everything in the camp must be packed up immediately. Please set to work without delay. We will be moving out in three hours,' he said.

The nurses weren't shocked or even scared, but put two and two together and decided that the Japanese were probably getting too close and that was the reason they had to get out at such speed.

'Thank goodness we have so little to pack,' said Madge.

Soldiers appeared to help move beds and medical equipment, and dismantle the tents. With fifteen minutes still to go before the three-hour deadline the convoy was ready to move out.

This time the nurses travelled in an army truck instead of the old green ambulance so they were able to look out at the rolling Arakan hills that were entwined with stretches of often impenetrable jungle. The fragrant wild flowers and beauty of the multi-coloured foliage provided the background against which the brutal hand-to-hand confrontations took place day and night. For the first time in days there was no rain and the journey made the most welcome of changes from the emotionally draining weeks they had spent nursing young men with life-changing injuries and the sheer intensity of dealing with increasing volumes of casualties.

During the journey the girls began discussing the time they had spent so far working at the CCS.

'The men are just so brave. Virtually every one I nursed simply wanted to get back alongside their pals,' Madge said as the truck shook and bumped its way out of the valley where their tented village had been home for the past weeks.

They thought they were returning to the coast and then north to Chittagong so when the convoy headed south instead of due west back to the Bay of Bengal, the nurses looked at one another in surprise.

The fact that they were told so little had always been a source of humour but they certainly were informed in this instance because their happy-go-lucky driver announced, 'We've got the Japs on the run, ladies, and the plan is to set up another CCS a lot closer to the action and a lot further south.'

'If we were moving home back in Blighty, talk would be all about the house and what the new garden would look like. Here it's all about changing one tent for another and the number of snakes and tarantulas and leaches that will be slithering around!' Vera said.

The camp was fully operational within hours of their arrival. Madge tried to pay special attention to the increasing number of troops who were being brought in to the new CCS after 'cracking up' following months of fighting in jungle territory. They hadn't been shot or wounded so there was no visible sign of the trauma they were experiencing, and as a result she felt a little out of her comfort zone. In general the poor souls who suffered from shell shock were taken by ambulance to the coast and flown to Calcutta military hospitals which had more qualified staff and better equipment to deal with their problems. But in the meantime Madge and the girls had to find ways to try to help them as much as they could.

'There's always the worry that one or two may be swinging the lead in a bid to get back to England,' said Vera one evening as the girls were getting ready for bed. 'You never can be sure, can you?'

'That's why we have to involve a doctor as soon as possible

for troops with emotional problems,' Phyl joined in. 'At least they get to make the final call and we don't have to.'

'I find it all very difficult,' said Madge, 'because they're so often vague about their worries. Not obstructive . . . far from it! They just don't want to talk about what happened.'

'You can't blame any of them for that, though, can you?' commented Phyl.

'No, I suppose not,' said Madge. 'When you think what they go through in the jungle where the rustle of a leaf or twig cracking could mean the difference between life and death, the real surprise is that there aren't many more being brought in suffering from battle fatigue.'

Madge, Vera and Phyl had been particularly impressed with the patience shown to emotionally troubled troops by Grace Padgett, a nurse they had always said hello to in Chittagong, but hadn't socialised with much. Madge had become concerned about the stressed soldiers and, one day, asked Grace just how she coped with it.

'Having three sisters and a brother and living on a farm in Yorkshire certainly helps . . .' Grace then became serious and said the key thing was to try and get the boys to talk about their problems. 'You need a lot of patience and time, which rather sadly we don't have here in the CCS. But in my opinion it is a major breakthrough if you can get them to share their worries because it's the first step, however tiny, on the road to recovery,' she added.

Grace's brother didn't want to work on the land when he grew up so their father sent Grace to agricultural college with the aim of getting her to run the farm when he retired. She however, chose nursing rather than farming. Over the next few days, Madge discovered that she really was also a good listener and when Vera was in full voice Madge felt that was a very necessary blessing!

During one of the very few quiet periods in the whole of their tour of duty, Vera, Phyl, Grace and Madge enjoyed an extended lunch. The main topic was a long weekend in Darjeeling that Phyl and Vera had spent at the very same time that Madge and Basil were in Calcutta.

'By far the best thing about the time Phyl and I spent there,' said Vera, 'was that it was full of men. Lots and lots of men!'

'We had the time of our lives,' laughed Phyl. Madge had heard her friends' stories before but she saw the glow that remembering the trip brought to their faces.

'The best day we had,' said Vera, 'started at two a.m. when we got up to watch dawn rise over the Himalayas. Then it was back to Darjeeling for an early breakfast, one or two pre-lunch gin and tonics, followed by a lengthy afternoon nap and then dinner and dancing in a nightclub until the early hours.'

In the end the VADs spent six weeks living under canvas, often waking to the sound of artillery units shelling the Japanese and the rattle of small-arms fire. They had also been drenched daily by endless monsoon rainstorms, but when the time came to leave the nurses were sorry their mission was coming to an end. Madge had seen first-hand what the soldiers had to put up with. There was no doubt in her mind, those boys were heroes.

The girls were thanked time and time again by patients, given bunches of divine-smelling jungle flowers and beautifully carved teak souvenirs. The finest compliment of all, however, came from a young corporal, barely out of his teens, who said he was going to let Madge in on a secret.

'That sounds really interesting,' said Madge. 'I've got two sisters at home and neither can keep a secret. Now, what's this one?'

'We looked on you as our lucky mascots,' he said. When she asked why, the reply was, 'Because very few soldiers died from their wounds during the time you girls were nursing here. So we decided you really must be bringing us luck.'

The journey back took almost a day and a half. After weeks of being on duty round the clock the weary nurses, once safely back at 56 IGH, indulged themselves in the ultimate luxury – hours of blissfully uninterrupted sleep. The only thing that was even better for Madge was a long, lazy soak in a tub that she loaded with Coty bath cubes.

On her first afternoon back working at the hospital Madge wandered up to the nurses' mess for a pot of tea and was given the warmest of welcomes by Sister Blossom, who rushed off to her office and reappeared minutes later with letters from Mum dating back to April, and one from Basil in Rangoon. Mum's first was written before Winston Churchill announced the German surrender on 8 May and was full of optimism and hope that 'once this is all sorted out we can get back to our own home in Dover'.

Happily the mail system from Rangoon to Chittagong had

been re-opened for the first time in almost three years and the letter from Basil said what a marvellous job the Pioneer Corps had done in cleaning up the place. There had been no running water and little food, disease had been rife and the streets had been coated in filth after the Japanese fled for their lives as units of General Slim's 14th Army fought their way into the city. The Japanese had left the place in an absolutely dreadful state, he said, but thankfully had not desecrated Rangoon's religious monuments like the Shwedagon Pagoda, an almost 100-metre high, gold-plated stupa with a diamond-studded spire. Basil said in the letter that although it had taken days to recover from the sunburn he had suffered on their wonderful last day together at Patanga beach, it had been 'nowhere near as painful as being without you'.

Madge went out on the veranda to be on her own and read and read those last few words time and again. *Oh dear. How silly*, she said to herself, after letting a little tear of joy drop on the letter which she carefully blotted dry.

Her happiest minutes since returning from the CCS came to an end when she heard an excited Sister Blossom asking, 'Has anybody seen Nurse Graves?' She was waving a little blue envelope in the air and as Madge appeared in the doorway of the veranda simply beamed with delight as she added, 'You've got another letter. It's just arrived and I think it's from Basil!'

Oh no, thought Madge, *another one so soon just has to be bad news*. She thanked dear old Blossom before returning to the veranda for a little privacy, her tummy turning over with worry. She took a deep breath and with very shaky hands opened the letter that looked so short at first glance that it worried her all the more.

Dearest Madge, it began. *After the wonderful time we enjoyed together I would love to have told you this face to face . . .*

She could hardly bear to read on and lifted her gaze to see a new group of Japanese soldiers, with Gurkha guards either side, being stretchered down to the POW ward.

Her chest pounded as she lifted the letter up again and continued from where she had left off.

. . . but circumstances deem it otherwise. I even tried to phone you without success. There has been absolutely wonderful news from home and because you are the most important person in my life I wanted to share it with you.

Madge's mood turned in an instant from the verge of despair to sheer joy and she was delighted to hear from Basil that all his brothers and his sister had survived the war. Not entirely without incident, but all were alive and well.

Bill got a nasty head wound in France, but has made a full recovery, and all the others have come through unscathed. It turns out Beryl was working at Brooklands, which was bombed by the Germans because Wellington bombers were being built there.

Young Bob is also OK after joining the Air Cadets and serving at Brooklands. Later in the war he moved to Fairoaks airfield at Chobham, where he helped repair Bristol Beaufort fighters and even went up on a couple of test flights. The Germans also had a go at the airfield but without much success.

I just wish we were together to celebrate this wonderful news.

Love Basil

Madge also wished that, more than anything else in the world.

The CCS nurses were given a forty-eight-hour pass to recover from the exhausting return journey to Chittagong but after that they were put on Matron's roster once again. Madge was listed for duty on the DI ward. Vera was on the Japanese POW casualty ward and said that the prisoner turnover was dozens every week.

'It's even busier than before because so many are on the brink of starvation when they arrive,' she told Madge over a pot of afternoon tea. 'But at least this group haven't yet started the usual spitting.'

The respite from being used as a human spittoon was more than welcome for Madge, who had been assigned to nurse one of the sixty-two Japanese POWs who had arrived late the night before. To her astonishment, it was a woman. Lieutenant Colonel Whittaker noted in the war diary of 56 Indian General Hospital (C) on 16 June 1945, that one of the Japanese POWs 'was a female . . . GSW back'. She was placed in a specially partitioned section of the DI ward that was as far from the Japanese POWs as possible.

She was suffering from a gunshot wound in her back which meant she had to lie face down on the bed. In spite of the constant pain she managed the sweetest of smiles at Madge's efforts to pronounce her name, which was something like Miho.

'She's beautiful and speaks passable English,' explained Madge to Vera and Phyl later that day, 'and always says please and thank you. She told me she is a journalist and learned to speak a bit of English on a holiday in New York. Her newspaper in Tokyo sent her to Burma and after a week with a Japanese unit somewhere in the Arakan she realised that they were desperately short of food, fuel and ammunition and actually retreating from our troops. When she tried to discuss the problems with an officer to obtain background information to write a story he went straight to the unit commander who issued orders for her to be taken from their camp into the jungle and shot.'

'Oh my goodness,' said Vera. 'That's horrendous.'

'All she remembers,' Madge continued, 'is waking up on a stretcher being carried from what was meant to be her jungle graveyard by two English soldiers and then being flown to Chittagong.'

'Well, she had a very lucky escape if you ask me,' added Phyl.

Over the next few days Madge spent as much time as possible with the lonely, frightened and badly hurt Miho, who apologised repeatedly for being such a burden. Madge washed her beautiful raven hair, cut and filed the nails of her elegant hands, and spoon-fed the perfectly mannered and quietly spoken woman at meal times.

Miho had been placed as far away as possible from the Japanese POW casualty ward for her own safety and as she began to regain a little strength she posed the same question as virtually every other patient. 'What is going to happen to me?'

'Hopefully you'll be flown to one of the big hospitals in Calcutta when you've recovered enough to be moved,' Madge said as she fluffed up her pillow and helped her move to a more comfortable position.

Later that evening when darkness had fallen, Madge checked on Miho and was pleased to see that she had drifted into a light sleep. Pain was still etched on those delicate features, but at least she was resting and hopefully would not be bothered by the noise coming from the next ward. *It's supposed to be empty*, Madge thought to herself, but the sound of footsteps echoed quite clearly. In fact, when Madge listened a little more intently she realised there were two sets of footsteps walking slowly towards the adjoining DI ward. She popped her head round the door, but could see nothing in the unlit interior and the footsteps stopped. A frightening thought crossed her mind; she began to wonder if the Japanese POWs had found out about Miho and were coming to finish her off once and for all.

Madge's mind went into overdrive as she walked back to Miho's bed to lift the top sheet over her head in the hope that the two POWs would walk past without noticing her. She lifted the sheet as gently as possible but the movement still woke Miho from her shallow slumber and Madge instantly put a finger to her lips to indicate silence. She then put a hand to her ear to try and get the now wide-awake patient to listen and within seconds the footsteps started again. *Hit them with anything you can get your hands on*, the self-defence expert had told the nurses, but there was nothing to hand and the footsteps were coming closer and closer. A vivid flashback to the scene in the kitchens at Stoke Mandeville when the troubled British soldier had held a knife to her throat crossed her mind. *You were just a teenager then*, she told herself, *so this time keep calm*. Madge was just a month short of her twenty-second birthday.

She peered under one of the shutters to see if any of the guards were close, but she was on her own and she decided to have one last peep round the corner before starting a rumpus that would wake the whole hospital. The *flop, flop* of two sets of footsteps was now frighteningly close, but she still couldn't see a thing until two huge, jet-black eyes set in a horned head turned to stare directly at her. *Surely not*, Madge thought. *This can't be real. I must be having a nightmare.* She looked again to see if the horns had been a trick of the light.

A sacred cow had found its way into the ward! By the time the beast actually lumbered past Miho's bed the two girls were laughing so much they were close to tears and thanking their lucky stars it hadn't left a very stinky visiting card.

Madge missed her gentle patient when Miho was eventually moved to Calcutta and often wondered what happened to the brave young woman.

24

The Himalayas at Sunrise

Within minutes of starting a shift one morning Madge was instructed to go straight to see Matron Olive Ferguson in her office. Wondering what on earth this summons was going to be about, she knocked tentatively on the door and was greeted with the usual cheery, 'Good day, Graves,' before being told to draw up a chair, sit down and listen.

'It has finally been brought to my attention exactly what you girls were up to at the casualty clearing station,' said Matron, with such a stern face that Madge thought she was really in for the high jump this time, although she still couldn't think what she'd done wrong. Matron Ferguson continued by saying that she had received a full report from the doctor who had been with them throughout the six weeks, and it left her with no option but to take instant action.

Matron drew a long breath, shook her head and told Madge with a very solemn face, 'I am instructing you to take a much deserved holiday as soon as you can,' then burst into deep, throaty laughter. 'You girls did us proud the way you worked round the clock without a single day off for six weeks. The

CCS crew thought you were all wonderful.' She went on to point out that the Japanese were on the run and everybody would be going home sooner rather than later. 'We are already well into summer so take the holidays you are owed and see a bit of India.'

Madge left Matron's office thinking of the week she had spent in Calcutta with Basil and wished he was still around so they could enjoy the Himalayas together. She was on a BOR ward that morning and, as luck would have it, Grace was nursing in the DI ward right next door. Their paths crossed late in the afternoon when they stepped out for a breath of fresh air and Madge told her about Matron's offer.

'Let's talk about this after work,' said Grace. 'I've always thought that to come to India and not see the Himalayas would be a very silly thing to do.'

Phyl and Vera inevitably got wind of the conversation in the nurses' mess later that evening and said that as somebody would be having a birthday towards the end of July, it would make the perfect celebration.

'Who's that?' asked Grace.

'Could be somebody with a birthday on the twenty-fourth of July and a name beginning with M,' said Phyl, who added that the best place to stay in Darjeeling was definitely the Windamere Hotel. 'The views from Observatory Hill are just amazing and the bar is always full of very wealthy and very handsome tea planters.' Phyl raised her eyebrows at Madge.

'None of that, Phyl! I've already got one man in my life and that's more than enough.'

Unfortunately, Madge discovered the Windamere was booked until November. It took some time for things to fall into place, but once flights to Calcutta, courtesy of the Royal Air Force, were confirmed, Madge and Grace had a week's holiday to look forward to.

Madge was kept busy in the weeks leading up to the holiday. One day, during her rotation on the British Other Ranks ward, she walked in to a heated discussion to learn that an election had actually taken place in the UK earlier in July. Two or three of the boys were kicking up merry hell as they had missed the opportunity to vote.

'Did Winston Churchill win?' asked Madge.

'Who cares?' said one of the soldiers. 'It's all a shambles anyway when they don't even take into consideration the opinions of the people out here fighting to serve our country.'

'That just about sums up the way the 14th Army has been treated throughout,' said an irate lance corporal, who had been brought in with a bullet wound in the buttock. 'It's a disgrace that the powers-that-be expect the military to lay lives on the line, but not to vote. It's bad enough being shot in the backside without getting a kick in the rump as well,' he added.

An RAF technician, who had a nasty bout of dysentery, said his squadron had heard about the election and there was a rumour that you could authorise a person back in the UK to vote on your behalf. 'But that disappeared up the Swannee, didn't it?'

However, later that week, with her twenty-second birthday just days away, Madge could barely raise a smile as she sat with shoulders hunched over a slice of toast that had long gone cold and a cup of tea in which she had not even bothered to put her usual splash of milk.

'Cheer up, Miss Misery,' said the ever tactful Vera, who stood and did an entertaining little dance as she sang, utterly tunelessly of course, '*The sun has got his hat on, hip, hip, hip hooray, the sun has got his hat on and he's coming out today.*'

Even that little bit of nonsense failed to lift Madge's spirits and it was clear from the faraway look in her hazel eyes that she was longing to be with a certain somebody. The rest of breakfast was spent in virtual silence with Madge polite as ever but far from her normal happy, joyful self.

They were seated at the end of the mess that was farthest from the office, where a phone could be heard ringing for an unusually long time. Finally Sister Blossom stepped in from the veranda and literally ran across to answer it. She reappeared looking breathless and shouted, 'Has anybody seen Madge?'

'She's over there,' one of the nurses replied, looking on in astonishment as Sister Blossom once again broke into a run, shouting, 'It's for you. It's for you.'

'Calm down, Blossom, old girl,' laughed the girls on the nearest table. 'And come on, tell us who the caller is.'

'It's Basil. He wants to speak to Madge. Is she still here?'

A mini whirlwind in a blue uniform and white apron swept past Matron as the mess ground to a halt. Half the girls were on their feet clapping and cheering as Madge raced into the office and slammed the door shut!

Basil had worked a minor miracle, thanks to his friends in the local Royal Signals unit who had navigated their way through the system between Rangoon and Chittagong, via Imphal – roughly 1,000 miles – and had actually managed to get a telephone call through to the main switchboard at the hospital. They, in turn, had patched him through to the mess where he had guessed, correctly, Madge would be having breakfast.

'*Happy Birthday to you . . .*' he gently crooned down the phone as soon as he heard Madge's breathless hello.

The conversation turned very quickly to the election and Basil said he knew nothing about it either, but while armed forces were fighting for their country overseas they certainly should have been given the opportunity to vote.

'It's a real shame,' he said, 'because we're both over twenty-one so it would have been our first chance to vote in an election, but because of the fighting still going on in the Far East, and the distance from the UK, it seems to have made the whole idea an impossibility. Still, I suppose there'll be plenty of opportunities for us to vote together in the future,' he added.

'Please repeat that as many times as you wish, especially the bit about the future,' laughed Madge.

'Enough of that,' he said, 'I'm ringing to wish you a very happy birthday and I'm sorry I can't be with you on the trip to Darjeeling because—'

The line suddenly went dead, but Madge was still full of smiles as she returned to her breakfast and couldn't help but laugh when Vera asked how many times Basil had said he loved her.

'You'll be surprised to hear for the umpteenth time, Miss Nosy, that it is none of your business,' said Madge, who was glowing with happiness.

On the morning of Madge's twenty-second birthday Sister Blossom performed another of her magic tricks at an early breakfast and produced letters from Mum and the girls from home, two from Basil, and one from cousin Ruby with the news that she was thinking seriously of emigrating to Australia 'now the war in Europe is over'. The ever kind and thoughtful Phyl told Madge to close her eyes and then produced an elegant royal blue silk headscarf that was a perfect accessory to the piqué dress Madge had purchased in Poona. 'It will be ideal for Darjeeling because the temperature can be quite chilly at that altitude once the sun goes down,' said Phyl.

After her birthday breakfast, Madge headed to Patanga airport with Grace for the flight to Calcutta. Again they were to take a DC-3, but this time it was a passenger flight and full of RAF boys instead of those very charming Americans. Within minutes of take-off the girls were bombarded with offers of dinner in Calcutta, dances in Darjeeling and told what to do and what not to do if they wanted to stay alive in the Himalayas.

'There's a big problem with several of the stations on the Darjeeling Himalayan Mountain Railway,' a handsome young RAF pilot told Madge, 'because tigers often eat people in the waiting rooms.'

His friend shook his head and laughed behind the pilot's back.

'Take no notice of his nonsense. The truth is, he read about a tiger eating a station master in a book by Mark Twain, but if you have time to join us for cocktails at the Grand Hotel in Calcutta this evening, we will tell you all about Darjeeling.'

Grace simply couldn't keep a straight face when she explained how disappointed she was to turn down the kind offer, but they had to catch a train to Jalpaiguri station in the foothills of the Himalayas.

In fact, they had little option but to stay overnight in Calcutta because the journey from Howrah station to Jalpaiguri was in excess of twelve hours and then another fifty miles or so up on the Darjeeling Himalayan Mountain Railway. Madge was delighted they had taken Vera's advice to travel as light as possible. The platform heaved with soldiers and RAF boys waiting for the locomotive to take them to the military camps around Ghoom and Darjeeling. The wounded were on crutches and walking sticks and several combat lads from the front line had arms in slings and heavy bandaging. Come hell or high water they were going to have a good time on their recuperation period at the most famous of all hill stations.

A loud hoot announced the arrival of the little steam-driven train and the passengers greeted it with a cheer. White smoke belched into the fading pink sunset and Grace felt a polite but firm tug on her sleeve. She turned to find a smiling, khaki-clad Scotsman with a leg in plaster leaning on a single crutch, and shouting above the noise of the approaching train, 'Pardon me, please. Is this the Darjeeling choo choo?'

She looked at the young man, who had been so badly

injured laying his life on the line for his country. The little train had finally shuddered to a halt as Grace instantly joined the fun and answered in her broad Yorkshire accent, 'Track twenty-nine, boy, you can gimme a shine.'

Within seconds the platform was in chaos as a huge Welshman, with the most magnificent baritone voice, boomed out, 'I can afford to board the Darjeeling choo choo. I've got my fare and a trifle to spare.' Injured soldiers pretended their crutches were trombones and a wheelchair-bound warrior completed a full circle in his chariot with Indian passengers laughing and applauding.

Madge was a huge fan of Glenn Miller and so was Grace who said that 'In the Mood' was her favourite. Then, as the warning hoot came that the train was about to start, there was one last serenade from the Welsh baritone. He looked directly at the girls and crooned a very charming invitation: 'Dinner in the diner? Nothing could be finer.'

'Sorry,' smiled Madge, 'but there isn't a dining car on this train!'

Madge realised, however, just how hungry she was and when the carriage quietened down the girls agreed that as soon as they arrived, instead of having an early night, as originally intended, they would go out for a meal.

The train rounded a bend on a steep incline with the wheels screeching on the single-track narrow-gauge line. Just then, one of the walking wounded passed out and cut his head as he fell. He couldn't have chosen better company because within seconds the two young nurses had loosened his tie and collar, turned him on his side and cleaned up a wound that was already starting to ooze.

By way of thanks to the nurses, water and a tumbler of very fine brandy was passed to them as they kneeled on the floor.

'That's a rather splendid-looking bottle of brandy,' said Madge to the young West Country boy who had so willingly filled the tumbler.

'Yes, miss,' he replied, 'I borrowed it from behind the bar of the hotel where we stayed in Calcutta. Purely for medicinal purposes, obviously.'

While the toy train built in Glasgow in the late 1870s heaved and rumbled its way above the clouds the lad who had banged his head regained consciousness. He perked up after drinking several tumblers of water and as the train finally pulled in to Darjeeling station he hobbled over to the girls to thank them.

'When I came to and saw you two looking at me I thought I had died and gone to heaven. But what happened to the tumbler of brandy my pal handed over?'

'Our need was greater than yours,' replied Grace with the sweetest of smiles.

They ended by having a very late night and were more than grateful the following morning for the first long lie-in they had enjoyed in weeks.

'You can have the bathroom first,' said Madge to a sleepy Grace, who instantly asked for a cup of tea.

'Milk and two sugars, please!'

'We'd better get a move on,' said Madge. 'Breakfast finishes at eleven and it's past nine now.'

There was suddenly an irate snort as Grace looked at her watch which was showing the time as eight. 'Ha, I'm not falling for that, young lady,' she laughed. 'You'd best make it up to me now and bring me that tea on the double!'

Phyl had told Madge about a shop in Darjeeling that was renowned for making shoes of any design so the first thing they did after breakfast was walk to the open-fronted stall where tourists stood and watched the cobblers. Madge gave the owner a page from an old copy of *Vogue* with the style of the shoes she wanted in gold lamé, and another pair in silver lamé, plus a pair of white leather shoes for work. She left the magazine page at the shop and was told all three pairs would be ready in forty-eight hours.

It was a beautiful sun-drenched morning and they had decided to take a mini tour of the town.

'It's surprising just how quickly the temperature warms at this altitude,' said Grace. 'I've never been this high and it was really surprisingly chilly first thing.'

Madge was overwhelmed by the view; verdant green tea plantations were perched above sweeping bamboo jungles. The predominantly Nepalese population greeted them with smiles and cheery waves as they wandered across the beautiful hill station, which was a remarkable piece of engineering in itself, surrounded by astounding views of the Himalayas.

'What amazes me about this lovely town,' said Madge, 'is that it's built into the side of such a steep hill. The waiter at breakfast this morning told me Darjeeling is close to seven thousand feet above sea level.'

Thousands of feet below the plains stretched for miles into a pastel grey horizon. The tour included a visit to the impressive Loreto Convent, which looked more like the main house of a French country estate than a boarding school. It was where the Macedonian-born Agnes Gonxha Bojaxhiu completed her novitiate before becoming known as Mother Teresa. Grace was impressed to be told that British actress Vivian Leigh was a former pupil of Loreto Convent.

'She was absolutely wonderful in *Gone with the Wind*,' said Grace. 'It's my most favourite film of all time.'

'Frankly, my dear, I don't give a damn,' quipped Madge, making Grace chuckle. 'I was far more impressed with Clark Gable.'

During a late lunch that afternoon, Madge and Grace met a pair of young army officers who said they were planning to see Mount Everest from Tiger Hill, the best local vantage point, early the following morning.

'We've been warned that heavy rain has made the roads far too dangerous so we're playing it safe and are going to go on mules instead,' one of them said.

'It will mean leaving at two in the morning if you want to see the dawn rise over the Himalayas, but apparently it's so amazing that it's really worthwhile making the effort,' said the other, a blond-haired lieutenant.

The girls asked where they could hire guides and mules and within an hour had booked the trip.

That night the girls were given a warm welcome when they went to dinner at a restaurant where the pianist heard that

Madge had celebrated her twenty-second birthday a few days earlier. As a treat he played and sang 'A Sentimental Journey', one of her favourites. The pianist, Tibor Stary, even bought them a birthday drink. He told them that he was Austrian and his father Elias had been so worried about the Nazis that he had changed the family name from Starykoff, which was Russian, to make it 'sound less Jewish'. Tibor said he had made his way towards India after escaping from Vienna, but his father had been arrested and he thought he may have been sent to a concentration camp.

'Tibor is such a lovely man,' said Madge as they waited for the bill to arrive. 'I can't begin to imagine the utter despair he must feel not knowing what's happened to his father.'

'So many people in Europe must be in similar situations right now. It doesn't bear thinking about really,' said Grace, after which both girls fell silent, contemplating the horrors they had been hearing about as news of the full extent of what the Nazis had done was slowly making its way around the world.

The girls left the restaurant to get a couple of hours' rest before their Himalayan adventure, but all too soon they were back on their feet and walking down to the meeting point with the guides and mules. It was a bitterly cold Himalayan night, but they had taken Phyl and Vera's advice and were well wrapped up. *This birthday scarf is a real bonus*, thought Madge as they began the eleven-kilometre ride to Tiger Hill.

A vicious wind whistled down from the mountains, which were shrouded in clouds and mist. It was so cold that Madge pulled her new scarf up to use as a face mask. The mules were startled when a ghostly and surprisingly large creature fluttered past to leave them in a grumpy, skittish mood, but as the guides spoke little English it was impossible to find out if it had been a bird or a bat. A smattering of rain, usually the prelude to a full-scale Himalayan downpour, didn't exactly lift the spirits.

With a 4 a.m. dawn approaching, the drizzle stopped and the clouds drifted away on the swirling wind that slowed to a gentle breeze. Tiny lights flickered ahead and Grace, who was used to night hunting on the family farm in Yorkshire, told Madge that they were within minutes of their destination.

'Those firefly lights are people smoking,' she said.

The girls were stiff and more than a little sore after almost two hours on bony and uncomfortable mules and when they reached the foot of Tiger Hill they simply couldn't believe the number of parked taxis.

'Well, Tiger Hill itself isn't exactly anything to write home about,' said Madge, as they surveyed the plateau that jutted out from the side of the hill on which they were standing.

'Absolutely right,' said Grace, 'but I am surprised that there's such a big flat area on such a huge slope.'

They continued to walk towards the car park when they spotted two men in a car with their feet hanging out of the windows.

'Just look at those rascals over there,' said Madge, as she pointed to the two men, who were holding steaming mugs of

Darjeeling tea in their gloved hands. 'Isn't that the two who told us it was far too dangerous to travel by car?'

The girls gave the chortling pair a fearsome telling-off but were placated by early morning brandies and hot tea – and the first hint of dawn. Within twenty minutes the sky was blood red and huge mountains sat under clouds that could have been bowls of cotton wool.

'You won't get a better view of Everest than this,' the blond lieutenant told Madge. But the rascal was up to his tricks again and his pal pointed out that it wasn't actually Everest, but the peak of Kangchenjunga, a mountain that was once thought to be the world's tallest. Madge and Grace were handed powerful military binoculars and the boys pointed to the real Mount Everest, which they were told was known locally as Chomolungma, goddess mother of the world.

As they gazed at the stunning beauty of the world's tallest mountains they noticed that they had suddenly been surrounded by a large group of fellow tourists.

'What's happening?' Madge asked the rascal. He told her it was a surprise for her birthday. 'But that was days ago,' she replied.

'They don't know that,' he laughed.

Then, with the tallest mountains on earth silhouetted by a blood-red morning sun and the snow-clad Himalayan peaks glittering like diamonds, the sound of a dozen voices resounded across the summit of Tiger Hill as they joined to sing 'Happy Birthday'. Madge couldn't help smiling.

Grace, however, was still far from amused at having made

the journey up to Tiger Hill on a mule. She gave the scally-wags a second and far more severe rollicking until, by way of an apology, they offered the girls a lift. They hummed and hawed for at least ten seconds before graciously accepting the men's offer of a drive back to Darjeeling.

'They should have done more to put it right,' Grace whispered to Madge. 'They didn't even ask us out to dinner or for a drink. Shame about that. The least they could have offered in addition to the ride back was a bottle of champagne – or two!'

There was no stopping her and she added, 'It may have been more than a hundred miles away from where we were but at least we saw Everest. Shame about the mules!'

Later that morning, Madge walked down to pick up the shoes she had ordered from the cobblers just off Chowrasta Square in Darjeeling, but there was a slight problem. Instead of copying the fashionable, high-heeled *Vogue* design in gold and silver lamé they had made three pairs of flat-heeled white brogues. There was no compromise to be had and in the end Madge decided to just leave the shoes at the shop.

This trip is turning out to be rather eventful, Madge smiled to herself.

25

The Japanese Surrender

Madge and Grace returned from Darjeeling to discover that Winston Churchill had been deposed as Prime Minister. The news had been released in London more than a week earlier that Clement Attlee's Labour Party had recorded a victory unprecedented in British political history and there was general sense of disbelief in the wards at 56 IGH. The election result was the first of two major surprises because days later rumours began to sweep the hospital that the Americans had dropped atomic bombs of enormous power on Hiroshima and Nagasaki. Then Emperor Hirohito, in a broadcast to the Japanese nation, confirmed Japan's surrender to the Allies on 15 August.

In London, King George V said, 'Our hearts are full to overflowing, as are your own. Yet there is not one of us who has experienced this terrible war who does not realise that we shall feel its inevitable consequences long after we have forgotten our rejoicings today.'

In Rangoon the news was greeted with wild celebrations when hundreds of troops cheered the attempts to drive a tank up the steps of Government House and in through the front entrance.

During this time Madge received a letter from Basil. *Since it was confirmed that the Japanese had surrendered it has been one long party through the night,* he wrote. *But we have been told to be on standby for redeployment from Rangoon to Saigon, so I still don't know when I'll get to see you.*

In Chittagong, Japanese soldiers continued to arrive at the POW casualty ward so it was still very much business as usual at 56 IGH. Madge had initially thought that the Japanese surrender might bring her and Basil back together, so she was sad to read his letter telling how they were to be driven even further apart. Basil's unit, which was responsible for running the Saigon docks together with other troops, was assigned the risky task of repatriating captured Japanese soldiers and sailors taken prisoner by the Allies in Vietnam. The Japanese had taken control of the colony, then part of French Indochina, in 1941.

From the moment the DC-3 on which he was flying to Saigon entered Vietnamese air space, Basil could hear the pilot's conversation with air-traffic controllers and realised that they were Japanese. When the Allied group landed in Saigon, heavily armed Japanese soldiers drove them in lorries to their billets. However, the Japanese, still fully armed, proved to be a godsend to the Allied forces who had fewer than five hundred troops to protect the French from the Vietnamese at that time and meant that the 20th Indian Division could focus on important day-to-day responsibilities. The Allied Commander-in-Chief told his

Japanese counterpart that they could temporarily retain their arms, and would be responsible for the maintenance of order among the French and Vietnamese populations. When the French military arrived, the Japanese would then surrender all their weapons and equipment.

It all went all right, Basil wrote to Madge, *though as often as the locals were disarmed, the Japanese probably sold, or gave them, more arms. We couldn't do anything other than warn them to stop, but I will give the Japanese their due because they are well disciplined, know how to work and don't need to be forced to carry out the new responsibilities. The Japanese officers, to the best of our knowledge, never took advantage of the situation even though they were fully armed. They actually came across as very honourable people.*

The letter left Madge with the same feeling of despair she had had on that last night in Chittagong. *I feel even more worried than ever that we'll never meet again,* she said to herself as she lay the letter on her bedside table.

The battle for self-determination and ultimate control of Vietnam, however, then burst into flames of such ferocity that in Basil's next letter to Madge he said, *I have seen more violence and killings here in Saigon since the war ended than ever I did when it was on. I suppose it all belongs to the hand of fate.*

Basil was grateful when full postal links were finally set up. He hadn't heard from Madge for some time and was longing to know that she was well and to find out if a date had been set for her return to England. When letters did start to arrive from Chittagong, however, there would be silent spells and then they would arrive in threes or fours. Reading them out of sequence was a bit of a nuisance but Sister Blossom, back at the hospital in Chittagong, was an expert in the vagaries of both military and non-military mail systems and suggested to Madge that she place a number on the envelope so the letters could be read in order. It worked and communication between Nurse Graves and Captain Lambert began to follow a well-worn route.

Although Basil was careful not to worry Madge in his letters, simply walking onto the second-floor balcony of his quarters at the Majestic Hotel was like Russian roulette because Viet Minh snipers would target unwary foreigners. In one letter he wrote, *Each morning I am working in my office in the Saigon docks to issue the day's duties to a Japanese officer who arrives with an escort. Both are always armed as that was one of the stipulations of their surrender. A couple of mornings ago the officer walked in and after saluting started hissing at me! As I was sitting behind my desk I could see my pistol in my drawer, but I was still very apprehensive as I had no idea if he was about to pull out his weapon and shoot me! Anyway, nothing of the sort happened and when I mentioned it afterwards, I was told that the hissing was actually a sign of respect!*

In another, he wrote, *We have all the necessary troops in now and they have taken over the guard duties so it won't be long before the Allies start disarming the Japanese. At present we don't know where we will end up, but it makes my blood boil to think that we have had to fight one war and after winning we may have to fight many more that don't really interest us.*

Good on you, Basil, thought Madge after reading his latest letter. *He's absolutely right because the last thing we need is to get involved in another confrontation.*

One evening, Basil was invited to the home of a wealthy and well-connected Chinese businessman, Charlie Choy, in the Cholon district of Saigon. Basil wrote that he had met Charlie and his wife in a restaurant where he was dining with Movements friends and the following week he was invited to join a multi-national group of fifteen who were treated to 'a veritable feast' that stretched to twelve courses.

The Chinese food was delicious and the conversation was fascinating because we all ended up discussing Vietnam's bid for independence. Charlie told us that Ho Chi Minh, leader of the Viet Minh, has declared himself President of the Democratic Republic of Vietnam. I suppose it's very similar to the Jai Hind movement in India – Vietnam wants the French out and an end to French-Dutch domination of Indo-China, and that is what the fighting is all about.

Basil went on to explain how one aged but highly articulate Vietnamese guest had said that there were many reasons the Vietnamese wanted the French to go home. There had apparently been a feeling in the country for many years that it was being exploited by the French. *They have tried to change the language and education of the Vietnamese, as well as their religion, and I have to say, by the end of the evening I was pretty convinced that the time has come for them to leave Vietnam and hand the country back to the Vietnamese.*

Early in 1946, Basil was then posted to Labuan Island off the northwest coast of Borneo to assist with the repatriation of Japanese POWs held on Papan Island to their homeland. He wrote to Madge that he had been appointed to staff captaincy and had been sent there to relieve the Australians who were either returning home or continuing their good work in Tokyo. *Labuan Island has been thoroughly destroyed by the fighting and bombing during the last few years and the only parts left of the old town are the foundations. It's really quite sad. But on the plus side, the island is beautiful and the bathing and the coconuts are excellent! Any inhabitants becoming ill have an excellent hospital to care for them.*

Good old Basil, thought Madge, who giggled at the thought of him sitting outside his tent in the sunshine in front of a little wooden table with tender chunks of coconut in a dish, although she knew he would be working hard on his army responsibilities.

The letter ended by saying that on a more serious note, one of the Australians told him that papers had been found at Batu Lintang, a Japanese internment camp on Borneo, ordering the execution of two thousand Allied prisoners of war to be carried out on 15 September 1945. Fortunately the official Japanese surrender had taken place just thirteen days earlier, and had no doubt saved all those many lives.

26

Homeward Bound

After months of rumours, the announcement on 1 April 1946 that a date had finally been set for the return of the 250-strong VAD contingent to England was treated as just another April Fool's Day joke. It was followed a month later, however, with letters stating that they would be leaving Chittagong in the first week of June. They were to travel by train from Calcutta to Bombay before embarking on the MV *Georgic* for the sea journey to Liverpool.

'Marvellous, absolutely marvellous news,' said Madge in the nurses' mess. 'I will miss it here but we've all been away from home for so long and the thought of seeing Mum, Doris and Doreen is just wonderful.'

'It really is,' said Vera. 'I can't wait to get home and see my parents.'

'And as we've all become accustomed to packing and moving within hours, it's also going to be something of a treat to have a little more time to get our things together,' said Phyl, to which the other girls nodded in agreement.

Madge had been summoned once again to Matron Ferguson's office the day before the initial announcement. *Surely it's not going to be another ticking-off*, she told herself after knocking on the door.

'Come straight in,' said Matron who had looked out of her office window to see Madge walking down from her basha. 'I haven't got much time, Graves,' she said, 'because there are a lot of things going on at the moment, but I just want to thank you for everything you've done at 56 IGH since you arrived. That includes some of your bloopers because even though I tried not to they always made me laugh.'

Madge was lost for words as Matron handed her an envelope and told her to 'have a browse through this when you get a spare moment. You're a bonza nurse. Even if you are a Pom!' With that she pointed to the door and said, with great affection, 'Shoo, go on, off you go. You're late for your shift!'

It wasn't until later in the morning when she had a ten-minute tea break that Madge had time to open the envelope and read the handwritten note it contained, which said:

Miss Graves has done outstandingly good work in this unit during the last eighteen months. She has gained a great deal of experience in surgical and medical nursing and has been called in to take heavy responsibility when there were few trained sisters. This she has accepted cheerfully.

She has had the management of busy wards, with the added difficulties of untrained nursing sepoys and ward servants as staff.

She has taken complete charge of a sisters' mess of forty

members and her book keeping was faultless. She will be
efficient at any work she chooses to undertake.
   Olive Ferguson
   Principal Matron
   56 IGH (C)
   Chittagong, 31/3/1945

Madge wiped a tear from her eye before placing the note carefully back inside the envelope.

After the initial excitement over the news that they would be returning to England, Madge set about sorting out what, and what not, to pack. She couldn't believe some of the things she had accumulated and ended up giving lots to Ahmed, her bearer, who had been so kind and supportive throughout her time in Chittagong.

That night of the official announcement she wrote to Basil at his address on Labuan Island, Borneo, to tell him the good news and added that she was counting down the days until his return to England. Next she wrote a lengthy letter to Mum, Doris and Doreen to say that she would be leaving India in June, but realised she would almost certainly walk back into the family home, 168 Union Road in Dover, before the letter arrived.

I'll leave a little bit of my heart in Chittagong, thought Madge as she packed up the last of her belongings. It was a bitter-sweet goodbye because there had been lots of very happy times as well as a wonderful team spirit at the hospital to make up for the dreadful injuries and illnesses the nurses had had to deal with on the wards.

Her happiest memory, of course, was of meeting Basil and she wished he could have been there at the farewell party that took place in the nurses' mess. Sister Blossom, the endlessly supportive, endlessly patient and endlessly smiling defender of her beloved young VADs, broke down in floods of tears when she was thanked for being 'the most wonderful foster mother to a group of very grateful girls who will be forever in your debt'. The nurses had secretly accumulated numerous boxes of dresses, skirts, shoes and jewellery that would be far from suitable attire back home in the UK where the average temperature was less than half of that in Chittagong. The boxes were presented to Blossom so she could share them with the rest of the hospital staff.

On a normal day in the mess the sister would be constantly on the go, but at the party, which was dedicated to 'Mother Blossom', the grateful nurses wouldn't let her lift a finger. There was one last surprise when she was told to close her eyes and hold out her hands, into which a large brown envelope, loaded with a volume of rupees that underlined the VADs immense gratitude, was placed.

The ever reliable Ahmed, Madge's bearer, made sure that the party ended with laughter instead of tears when he marched in wearing one of the dresses she had given him for his sister, a big floppy sun hat and bright red open-toed, high-heeled shoes.

The voyage back on the *Georgic* was very different from

when Madge had sailed out. They could sit and sunbathe without having to wear life jackets, people could smoke on deck at night and the boat was lit up like a Christmas tree after dark instead of operating under strict blackout regulations.

The girls travelled first class and Madge was delighted to find that the food was simply magnificent. Steaks, roasts, bananas and a huge choice of fresh fruit and butter were all available. There was a shortage of nothing. The war was over and this time the boat didn't have to keep zigzagging to avoid German submarines. Once the *Georgic* had cleared the Suez Canal and entered the Mediterranean they were on the last leg home and the girls spent exhausting days getting a proper tan.

'Where's your life jacket, Nurse Graves?' laughed Vera, as they relaxed with Grace in the early morning sunshine while the *Georgic* cruised gently on a surface that was as flat as a millpond.

'There's only one problem with all this,' smiled Grace. 'It's all too perfect!'

Indeed, within an hour the public address system burst into life with an announcement. 'We must inform you that a passenger has been diagnosed with smallpox and will be taken to hospital in Malta, where there will be a short stopover.'

'I thought that this was all too good to be true,' said Madge, 'but I'm sure there are worse things in life than being stuck on a ship in the Med for a few days.'

'The biggest problem for us is that sunbathing is simply so exhausting,' said Vera with a straight face. 'Sometimes I feel so tired after so many hours in the sun I really need to have a sleep!'

The rest of the voyage to Liverpool was virtually a luxury cruise, though Madge couldn't help but shudder again when they sailed over the watery grave of the *Strathallan* off the Barbary Coast of Algeria on the approach to Gibraltar. Even the Bay of Biscay was on its best behaviour as they continued north, and into Liverpool. There they had a stark reminder of the fearful destruction that had befallen the courageous city in the eighty air raids mounted by the Luftwaffe in a bid to cripple the vital northern port. Next to London it was the most heavily bombed city in the UK.

The northwest coast of England differed in a multitude of ways from the west coast of India, not the least of which was the weather. When the *Georgic* left Bombay in June 1946 the temperature was in the low nineties. By the time the boat docked in Liverpool a bracing wind was swirling across the Mersey and the VAD contingent were wearing coats, sweaters and cardigans for the first time since the outward-bound voyage that started from Gourock in July 1944.

Thrilled as they were at the thought of finally walking on home soil again, the VADs were far from amused to be greeted by medical authorities who insisted they undergo yet another smallpox inoculation, which for Madge was the fourth in just over two years.

As darkness fell and the girls were finally released to board buses waiting at the dockside, Madge turned to Vera and Phyl and couldn't help smiling at the end of a very frustrating last few hours. 'At least there's now light in our darkness,' she said.

'What on earth do you mean by that?' asked Vera.

'We're all too blind to see,' answered Madge. 'The street lights are on. There's no more blackouts!'

'Come on, geerls, yer supposed to be 'appy now youse all home again,' said a kindly old Scouse porter on the concourse at Liverpool Lime Street station, which was the end of the line for the 250-strong group of VADs. They had journeyed many thousands of miles to nurse soldiers with appalling injuries and woken to the sound of heavy artillery and small-arms fire on the front line in the Burma Campaign with a devotion to duty and unflinching courage way beyond the call of duty.

Now, suddenly, it really was all over. Addresses had long been exchanged on the voyage from Bombay and the time had come for the parting of ways. There were tears and emotional hugs as the very brave young women said goodbye and prepared for the next chapters of their lives.

'If you find another one like Basil, pop him in the mail for me,' said Vera before giving Madge and Phyl lengthy embraces. Along with Grace who was heading back to Yorkshire, Vera searched for the train that would take her to Manchester and then north to Sunderland.

For Madge and Phyl the journey from Lime Street to London seemed to take forever but Madge stayed awake to see towns and villages with street lights on at night. They said their goodbyes at Euston, with Phyl heading west towards Reading. There was one last change for Madge before she finally reached Dover Priory station on a crisp, bright morning and slowly made her way across the concourse. There was no hero's welcome for those returning from the Burma Campaign. No band playing. No parade with drums beating. No welcoming speech from the Mayor. Instead, the greeting Madge received was infinitely better because there serving tea on the station concourse in her green uniform and little hat at the WVS stand was Mum! The letter Madge had sent to say she was on her way home had not arrived so Lily was shocked beyond belief when her firstborn appeared on the concourse at Dover Priory.

'Mum!' Madge called. 'Mum, I'm home!'

Lily put a hand to her mouth in shock before the tears gushed and the two women ran towards each other.

Madge hadn't wept when she ran for her life to air-raid shelters as Dover was being bombed and machine-gunned by the Luftwaffe. Or when the town was shelled from across the Channel. Or during the deafening, terrifying silence when doodlebug engines cut out over London. Nor when the Japanese spat in her face. It had been important to be brave when she said that heartbreakingly painful goodbye to Basil in Chittagong. The rattle of small-arms fire near the casualty clearing station in the Burmese jungle hadn't upset her. But when Mum wrapped her arms round her eldest daughter, the tears finally flowed. Madge was home.

The last time she had set eyes on the family house in Dover, the front door had been blown in by a bomb blast, the wind was driving sheets of rain in from the English Channel and an air-raid siren had just sounded the all-clear, but even so, it had still been home sweet home. The feeling was quite the same as Madge stepped back into the house in which she had lived as a child. It made her think about the sacrifices and the wonderful job Mum had made of bringing up three daughters on her widow's pension.

'When do I get the pleasure of seeing my little sisters?' Madge asked with a smile.

'Well, for a start they are not so little now,' she replied. 'Doris is still working in the Land Army on the farm near East Grinstead, but Doreen is normally back from school around half past four.'

Mum asked what Madge was smiling about. 'It seems silly really,' she said, 'but the reason is that I've just enjoyed the simple pleasure of having a glass of water straight from the tap!'

'What did you do in India?' asked Mum.

'Boiled it,' smiled Madge. 'We boiled everything. Boiled water was even used when you cleaned your teeth.'

Lily realised in that moment how different life must have been in India for her eldest daughter and just how much they had to catch up on.

Madge was entitled to a long period of leave which helped her ease back into an England that was paying the price of six ferociously costly years of war. Food was still strictly rationed and supplies of bacon were actually lower than when Madge had left for India in July 1944.

The rationing worried her far less than the lack of communication with Basil, who said on that last night in Chittagong that whatever happened to him he would really appreciate it if she would spend time with his parents when she got home. Madge didn't even know if he was aware that she was back living in Dover, but once she had settled in, she contacted Basil's mother and father and was invited to spend a weekend at their home in Surrey.

Madge was told that there would be somebody to meet her off the train when she got to Woking, and she could hardly believe her eyes as she came out of the station, looked across the road, and there he was. Her heart leapt. 'Basil!' she shouted. 'Basil!' But she had another surprise when she realised it wasn't Basil, but his brother Bill. She was disappointed but was able to see the funny side. He introduced himself as Basil's eldest brother just as a group of people came out of a nearby pub to find them standing there doubled up with laughter.

'Goodness knows what those people must have thought,' Madge said eventually after they had composed themselves. 'We must have looked like we were cracking up!'

Madge knew from a letter she had received from Basil that Bill had been wounded by shrapnel in northern France in the spring of 1945, but nothing was mentioned and she decided it was better not to bring the subject up. Bill was very charming and it turned out that Madge was actually very lucky to meet him as he was still in the army and was spending a long weekend at the family home in Horsell for the first time in months.

'The kettle's on,' said Basil's mother Alys as she gave Madge the warmest of welcomes after Bill had guided her on the short walk to the house. When he told Alys and his father Herbert about the saga at the station the sitting room filled with laughter. The ice had been broken in less than five minutes.

'Ah, don't you go worrying about it, love,' said Alys as she poured the tea. 'Those boys look so similar from the back that even I've got them mixed up over the years – and more than once!'

She went on to tell her about her other children – Buster (Cyril), Beryl, Brian, and Bob – before Herbert asked if she knew when Basil was returning to England. When Madge replied that she wasn't even sure where he was, let alone knew when he was coming back, it made everybody smile again.

'Did you have a nice few days up there?' asked Madge's mum when she returned to Dover.

'They couldn't have made me feel more at home,' said Madge. 'It was like being one of the family and there was the loveliest of surprises just as I left because I've been invited to the wedding of Brian, one of Basil's younger brothers.'

After her Surrey visit, Madge received a phone call from Grace, who was living back in Yorkshire. Grace wondered if she would be interested in helping her eldest sister Hetty, who owned a maternity home in Birchington-on-Sea, north of Dover. Madge said she would be happy to do that for just two months.

It was such a change to nursing in the Burma Campaign, because in the main there was such joy and happiness when babies were born. She also had Grace, who was staying at her sister's nursing home for a few weeks, to show her the ropes, which made her feel very much at ease. Grace refused to let her stay down in the dumps and never tired of listening to her talk about how long it would be before she would see Basil again.

In Chittagong the nurses had been so short of bandages at one stage that they had had to tear sheets into strips, and they had had to make their own cotton buds as well as absorbent pads at times. So it was a major bonus for Grace and Madge to have everything readily available.

The two months soon turned into many more and along the way Madge spent a pleasant autumn weekend in Horsell with Basil's mother and father, who diplomatically never once brought up the great unaskable question. Unlike her much loved younger sisters Doreen and Doris, who drove her to distraction asking when Basil was coming home and when she was getting married.

They were told repeatedly that the subject of marriage had not been discussed with Basil in Chittagong and that she simply had no idea when he was coming back.

'It's none of your business anyway, you nosy parkers,' she found herself saying repeatedly.

One late afternoon as the nights began to draw in and autumn leaves carpeted the grounds of the nursing home, Madge was told by one of the hospital juniors that there was a telephone call for her.

'Thank you,' said Madge. 'Do you know who it is?'

'Sorry, Nurse Graves, but I wasn't told.'

It was such an awful connection that Madge didn't realise it was Basil until his voice suddenly came through loud and clear saying that he was in Singapore after leaving Labuan. Madge was so surprised that she could barely speak.

'I've no idea when I'm coming home, but the sooner the better because I'm missing you so much,' said Basil. 'I'm longing for the day when we can be together again.' He added that when he got an embarkation date he would let everyone know. Infuriatingly, before Madge could even ask how he was, the line crackled and cut out, much as it had done when he got through to the hospital in Chittagong to wish her a very happy birthday.

Because of the time difference it was already almost midnight in Singapore, but Basil sat down to write Madge a long letter to bring her up to date:

As I mentioned in our phone call, I have now returned to Singapore and the contrast between sitting in a tent eating British Army bully beef and beans for lunch on the war-torn beach of Labuan in place of having the most delicious roast served from a silver trolley in Raffles Hotel was remarkable.

The fact that I have had lunch in the most famous hotel in the Orient with two of my brothers was an absolute treat. We were so determined to make up for lost time that each ordered a Singapore Sling to start the proceedings. I hadn't seen Bill since 1942 and it had been almost two years since I had last met Brian at a Movements unit on the Brahmaputra River.

He's here on Troops Movement business as well. Bill didn't really say why he's in Singapore other than that he's been posted to the Allied Land Forces to help investigate Japanese war crimes. These organisations had major problems because of lack of staff and though there were almost 9,000 suspects under arrest fewer than 1,000 had been charged. Can you believe it?

I suppose this is as good a time as any to fill you in on a little of the family background. I loved the story about when you first met Bill and he has asked me to send his best regards 'to the lovely Madge'. I would have been surprised if he had mentioned his wartime adventures or anything about the head injury he suffered so here goes. Bill joined the TA in 1938 and enlisted for war service with the Royal Artillery in 1939. He was posted to northwest Europe on 6 June 1944 and in January 1945 suffered a shrapnel wound to the head, which resulted in him being evacuated from a casualty clearing station to Basingstoke Hospital, where he spent weeks recovering. Bill was promoted from lieutenant to captain and then major before being posted here to Singapore in October.

Lunch at Raffles wasn't exactly the time or the place to discuss war crimes and we didn't talk about Bill's injury, because we had so much to catch up on. Those Singapore Slings certainly helped! A very jolly waiter with a turban and rather splendid moustache told us that when the Japanese invaded Singapore the staff at Raffles had already buried the silver, including a beef trolley, and he pointed it out. He also claimed that when the Japanese marched into the hotel they

found guests enjoying one last waltz. After three Singapore
Slings each it almost sounded plausible!

At the end of a rather splendid afternoon we raised our
glasses in an emotional toast to the family and absent friends.
It made me yearn to be with you all the more.

Love,
Basil

It was November when Madge received the letter and the first thing she thought when she read it during a break at the maternity home was how marvellous it would be if Basil managed to get home for Christmas. Her mind ran riot for a moment wondering whether they would spend it with his family or with Mum and the girls, before she returned to the wards.

In fact, a few days later Basil's hopes of making it back to dear old Blighty in time for the festivities were given a huge boost when he received a message that he knew would be confirmation of his repatriation from the Far East. Others had received similar letters the week before. Basil opened it with a pounding heart to discover that he been given a berth on board the RMS *Andes*, but the embarkation date was not until 17 December 1946 so that put an end to dreams of a Christmas reunion. Try as he might, he could not get another phone call through to the maternity home where Madge was living or to his mum and dad in Woking. There was a small chance a letter might get through before he arrived home so he dashed a note off.

Coming home via the Suez Canal, RMS *Andes* created a

new record for a sea journey between Singapore and South-ampton of just sixteen days, fifteen hours and thirty-one minutes. From the moment it left to the time it pulled into the famous old Channel port, the *Andes* maintained an average speed of 21.66 knots and broke the previous best by almost three days.

All aboard the *Andes* expected their journey to take almost a week longer and for Basil it was the most wonderful boost because throughout the journey he was counting down the days until he could be reunited with his mum and dad and hold Madge in his arms again.

Wedding Bells

Basil could hardly bear the tension as he waited with hundreds of demob-happy troops to disembark from RMS *Andes* as it pulled in to Southampton with flags flying in early January 1947.

Raucous cheering broke out when an announcement came over the public address system to confirm the new record and this was followed by repeated singing of 'Rule Britannia', which was conducted with great gusto by a huge, red-haired Scot standing on top of one of the lifeboats with his kilt swirling in a lively breeze.

Two ear-splitting blasts from the ship's horn put an end to that, however, and signalled the start of an endless procession of hundreds of men from ship to shore that ended when they were marched to a demobilisation centre where they were issued with rail tickets.

As time wore on Basil became more and more frustrated because he had dreamed for days on the voyage from Singapore of how quickly he would phone his parents and Madge after setting foot back on English soil for the first time since

1943. He had even changed money on the *Andes* to ensure he would have coins for the call, but there was a problem. The queues for the phones were enormous and he became increasingly worried that by the time he did get through, her shift at the nursing home would be long over, so he simply got the train from Southampton Central to Woking. When he arrived at his front door, he gave his mother and father the nicest of shocks because the letter he mailed to them hadn't arrived and the boat had docked almost a week early anyway.

Almost as soon as he had greeted his parents and dropped his bags in the hallway, Basil picked up the phone to Madge, who ran to the telephone when she was told she had a call.

'Hello? Basil? Is that you?'

'Yes, it's me, darling Madge. I'm home!'

Madge held a hand over her mouth to suppress a sob of delight. 'Oh Basil, that's the most wonderful news ever! When can I see you?'

It seemed there were yet more obstacles in the couple's way when Madge remembered that she was supposed to be working all weekend. Grace, however, came to the rescue.

When Madge put the phone down from Basil, looking forlorn at not having been able to arrange when they could see each other, Grace asked her what was wrong.

'Oh, stop worrying, Madge,' Grace said once Madge had explained the situation. 'After what we've been through together, the least I can do is change my days off and fill in for you. I know you'd do the same for me.'

Madge practically squealed with delight as she threw her arms around Grace to thank her.

Madge called her mother and Basil and the big reunion was scheduled for late Friday afternoon at the Graves' family home in Union Road, Dover. However, it didn't turn out to be the big romantic scene Madge had had in her mind. When Lily told Doris that Basil was coming she arranged to leave the farm in East Grinstead early so she would be home when he arrived, and Doreen held top-level discussions with her school friends about the situation! The result was that when Basil knocked on the door just after 6 p.m. on the Friday evening there was an unholy scramble between the sisters to give him the once-over. He gave Madge a great big hug in spite of the audience, and that was that. They all loved him!

Basil had arrived at Southampton to a dry if somewhat chilly spell, but by the middle of January 1947 it had turned into the coldest winter of the twentieth century with heavy snow, and blizzards in the Channel. A month later there were three-foot-deep snow drifts and it became officially the coldest ever February, with March being the wettest.

Snow was the biggest worry in Kent, which was particularly badly affected, and because Madge and Basil could meet only every other weekend travel was a major problem. But whenever they were able to spend time together, the couple made the most of it, going on real dates where they talked and spent time getting to know each other in a normal environment, and during this time their love really began to blossom.

In a bizarre twist of events, however, an opportunity arose

in which they would end up staying under the same roof. It happened when Basil was being medically examined at Aldershot Garrison in connection with his discharge from the army. He was told that if he wanted an A1 discharge to show on his demobilisation papers, he needed to have his infected tonsils removed, otherwise it would be B2.

His biggest problem, however, was that he couldn't find a doctor to carry out the operation. A specialist surgeon connected to the maternity home in Birchington, where Madge was nursing, said he would remove the tonsils if he could use their medical facilities. The result was that Basil had his tonsils out in the maternity home's main delivery room, and because of a complication he wasn't released for ten days, much to Madge's delight!

Dr Bowie, the anaesthetist, told Basil the day after the operation that he had had such a problem getting him under that he had left the theatre and asked if anybody had a mallet! What he had actually done was to drip ether directly onto the mask.

'Isn't it wonderful to be able to spend time together after so many months apart?' said Madge, who had slipped away from her duties for a quick chat with her beloved.

'I'm far from a pretty sight, though, aren't I?' laughed Basil, who then winced in pain. The ether in the general anaesthetic had burned his lips and he had ended up with a big and very painful red ring around his mouth. 'I've been told all I can eat for the next ten days is ice cream, but I suppose that's no real hardship,' he said with a wink. He couldn't help thinking of the last time he'd been hospitalised, not long after arriving in Chittagong. He had been treated for malaria and diphtheria in 68 IGH, where he found that patients like himself, who were able to get out of bed, were put to work polishing and sterilising the lino-covered floors in their ward. On reflection, being looked after in the maternity nursing home was more his cup of tea!

The bitter and brutal winter was replaced by the most glorious of summers, with temperatures reaching 90 degrees Fahrenheit in the first three days of June. On the evening of 2 June, Basil took Madge to a Burma reunion concert. The heat in the Albert Hall was so extreme that the audience couldn't help but be reminded of the jungle conditions in which they had fought in the Far East.

'I just hope there's enough beer for everybody,' General Sir William Slim joked.

The show's line-up included Jack Warner, Lynn Burnett, Noël Coward and Tommy Handley, who paid moving tributes to the Forgotten Army. The performer who caught Madge's eye, however, was the fourteen-year-old daughter of Ted and Barbara Andrews who stole the show. Madge laughed when she reminded Basil that the girl's mother had actually asked the audience if it would be OK for her young daughter to sing.

'Remember the name because I think we are going to see a lot of that young lady,' she told Basil, as she praised the enchantingly pretty and talented Julie Andrews.

The headline act was forces sweetheart Vera Lynn, who

received a standing ovation after several encores, which included many of the favourites she had sung to the troops in Burma.

'That was an evening I will never forget,' Madge told Basil as they left the concert hall.

'It certainly brought back memories,' agreed Basil, who told Madge he had had the privilege of attending a Vera Lynn concert in Chittagong in 1944. 'She'd flown from London and even brought her own pianist and piano! Watch these steps, they're quite steep,' he said, as they walked hand in hand from the Royal Albert Hall.

'It was only two or three months before you arrived in Chittagong,' said Basil, 'and she wore khaki trousers and a long-sleeved shirt because the mosquitos were such a problem and it was an open-air concert. She sang non-stop for more than two hours, encore after encore. The whole audience kept chanting "We'll Meet Again" in an effort to get Vera to sing one more time, and hot and exhausted as she must have been, she nodded to her pianist and off they went again.' He smiled at the memory.

'Just like this,' asked a smiling Madge, who quietly began to sing, '*We'll meet again, don't know where, don't know when. But I know we'll meet again, some sunny day.*'

'Bravo,' said Basil.

Madge's life had settled into a happy routine. She was thrilled to find out, weeks later, that owner Hetty was so pleased with the way she and Grace had organised the maternity home she told them she had a surprise.

'This is my way of saying thanks to you girls,' said Hetty, as

Madge and Grace stood wondering what on earth she was talking about. 'I know you're both still young but I don't think you will ever get the opportunity again in your lives to see a future Queen of England being married. I'm giving you the day off so you can be part of the celebrations.' Madge and Grace clapped in excitement.

Not only did Hetty give them the day off to travel up to London for the marriage of Princess Elizabeth to Prince Philip, she also paid for return train tickets and a hamper full of goodies for their special day. They didn't really see a lot when the royal procession went past because there were such huge crowds, but Madge thought the atmosphere was amazing. It reminded her of that exciting week in London before the journey to Chittagong.

On the train back to Birchington, Madge asked Grace if she remembered the problems with trying to buy those three pairs of shoes in Darjeeling.

'I certainly do,' she replied.

'Well, just the other day I had a letter from a Darjeeling solicitor saying that I'm going to be sued for refusing to pay and I'm going to be arrested if I don't attend the court case!'

'Heavens above!' said Grace. 'What are you going to do?'

Madge said she was so upset she had asked the advice of a wily old lawyer who acted for the maternity home. 'He told me not to worry because he would write on my behalf saying that I would be only too happy to comply with the court ruling. All they had to do in return was send funds for my air fare. Oddly enough, neither I nor the solicitor have heard another word from them!'

The next day, Madge received an invitation from Basil to join him for a family weekend in Woking. He had settled quickly into his new job with Vacuum Oil in London. The invitation was just what Madge needed because she was concerned they weren't seeing enough of each other, even though they had had a vague discussion about a future together in the capital.

Oh, the thought of another weekend together has really cheered me up, Madge said to herself.

Basil told her there was going to be a big family dinner on the Saturday night and as it was going to be a special occasion, she decided to take her favourite dress from Poona.

'It looks so elegant and I love those stripes,' said Basil's Auntie Mabel. 'I haven't seen anything like it. Did you buy it in London?'

'It's a long story,' smiled Madge, as the evening drew to a close.

The following night there was a knock at the door of the single room where Madge was staying.

'Come in,' she said, and there was Basil with two cups of tea on a tray. He put the tray on the dressing table then turned and handed her a beautifully wrapped little parcel with a pink bow on top.

'Will you do me the honour of becoming my wife?' he asked. Madge had half opened the present but was puzzled because it certainly didn't feel like a ring and she began to wonder what on earth was actually in the delicate velvet bag. She shook the contents into her hand and out came three glittering diamonds. She placed her other hand over her mouth in surprise before beaming with joy.

'Basil . . . This is the most romantic and thoughtful thing that's ever happened to me,' she said. 'It would be a privilege to become your wife.'

Madge decided that there must be many, many wives who wished their fiancés had done exactly the same thing instead of being given rings that they secretly didn't like. But Madge was able to choose the setting that she really wanted.

A wedding date was set for the following October at St Mary's, an old Anglican church in Horsell, Woking. Stringent clothes rationing was still in force and there had even been a reduction from sixty coupons to forty-eight, but even when you had enough coupons clothes were difficult to buy. It was no secret, then, that everything was borrowed. Madge was loaned a beautiful, full-length wedding gown of white crepe with a figure-hugging bodice and a long lace veil with real camellia flowers that accentuated the elegant A-line skirt. Her sisters Doris and Doreen won admiring glances in their borrowed fuchsia-coloured bridesmaid's dresses. (When Madge and Basil returned from their honeymoon they decided they wanted to keep the dresses, in remembrance of their wonderful day, and paid their kind benefactor for them.)

Madge was hopelessly nervous as she approached the altar on the arm of Basil's father Herbert, who was giving her away. As she knelt alongside her bridegroom, Basil turned to her and said, 'You look absolutely beautiful, Madge. Do you know, I was just told about one of our wedding presents. Can you believe we've been given six green beer mugs from George Woodman!' It was a strange thing to say at the altar, Madge thought, but it made her smile and the jitters started to disappear.

When the reception was underway Madge's 'new dad' Herbert gave a speech in which he expressed great pride in the way Madge and Basil had served their country in the Burma Campaign.

'Madge's father Charles served in India in the Great War,' said Herbert, 'and had he been able to see his eldest daughter married, he would have said the same thing.' Basil's father was far too modest to mention his own wartime service in France but continued by saying that he and his wife Alys were equally proud of the way every one of their children had rallied to the cause. 'And it goes without saying that we are profoundly grateful that Bill, Buster, Beryl, Basil, Brian and Bob have all come home to us.'

Madge changed into a two-piece black bouclé suit, for which she had been saving clothing coupons for months, under which she wore a pale blue roll neck, long-sleeved sweater that she had knitted herself. She had splashed out on new black shoes when she and Basil had had that vague discussion about living together in London.

'You look just as stunning as you did in your wedding outfit,' exclaimed Grace. Sadly, Vera and Phyl had not been able to make the wedding because of travel complications.

'Oh, doesn't she just,' Doris agreed.

'Talk about something old, something new, something borrowed, something blue,' said Doreen. 'You've got the lot!'

Basil had also switched from his Moss Bros morning suit and waistcoat and changed into his Montague Burton double-breasted demob suit.

'I love that navy blue colour on you,' Madge whispered to him. 'You look ever so smart.' She took her new husband's hand and gave it a squeeze as they both smiled at each other affectionately.

As they left the Yorkshire Restaurant to catch the train from Woking to London for the first leg of their journey to Brighton, where they were going on honeymoon, they were hit with a blizzard of multi-coloured confetti. Just as they attempted to shake it all off on the platform, the whistle sounded and they hurriedly got into their compartment.

The train very quickly started to pick up speed as Basil tried to open the window in the hope that the draught would blow away the confetti that seemed to appear every time they moved. The window, however, was jammed so he decided to open the train door just a teeny-weeny bit to get rid of the confetti once and for all. It worked, but in doing so the train's emergency braking system was triggered and the Woking to Waterloo express screeched to a bone-shaking halt.

A moment later an irate guard was stumping through the train carriages to see who had caused the problem. Fortunately when he saw Madge and Basil, who were obviously newly-weds, he simply gave them a very cheery wave as he walked past and searched elsewhere for the culprit. Basil waved back and Madge blew him a kiss before resting her head on Basil's shoulder.

'Hello, husband,' she said, looking up at him with a smile.

'Hello, wife,' he replied, smiling back.

Then they fell into a contented silence as they gazed out of the window at a country no longer at war.

How different things are now from when Basil and I first met, thought Madge. *But whatever life may throw at us in the future, at least we will always have each other.*

Their life together was just beginning.

Epilogue

Nothing could have prepared Madge for the extraordinary events she would experience after she responded to Lord Mount-batten's appeal for nurses to serve in the Burma Campaign. She didn't even know if she would make it back to England, but many years later, as she celebrated her ninety-fourth birthday on 24 July and her sixty-ninth wedding anniversary on 16 October 2017, she said there was a very simple reason why she would do it all again.

'If I hadn't gone to Chittagong, I wouldn't have met Basil. We wouldn't have had such a long and wonderful marriage and we wouldn't have had Carolyn and Angela, our two beau-tiful daughters.'

Madge left the Birchington maternity home soon after the start of the National Health Service in July 1948 and worked in the commercial world until the arrival of Carolyn, her first-born, in 1951. Angela followed in 1953. It was only after a plea in 1958 from a close friend to help in an area branch of the National Health Service in Woking that Madge agreed to return to work – 'but just for a few months'. In a remarkable coincidence the office to which she reported was actually in the six-bedroomed home in Horsell that Basil's mother and father had sold when they downsized after their family of six children had grown up and flown the nest.

Madge was hard at work one morning when a secretary asked if she had a moment to step into what had been the lounge of the Lambert home. Workmen had been removing the fireplace when one had found an old Christmas card that had fallen behind the back of the mantelpiece. It was a card to Basil, Brian and Bob from a lady who had been their nanny in the late 1920s!

The 'couple of months' Madge promised to work for the NHS soon stretched to years and she became a key figure in organising school vaccinations and inoculations. She eventually retired from the NHS on 24 July 1988.

Basil joined Provincial (now United) Newspapers in 1948 and then in 1951, during the Cold War with Russia, he enlisted in the Army Emergency Reserve with the Royal Engineers, based at Longmoor Camp in Hampshire. He continued his annual camps until retirement in 1970 with the rank of major. His military awards include: the 1939–45 Star, the Burma Star, the Defence Medal, the 1939–45 War Medal, SE Asia 1945–46 and the Army Emergency Reserve Decoration 1951–70 with two Long Service Clasps.

In 1985, after thirty-five years during which time he became an executive on the management side, he took early retirement from United Newspapers. The next decade of Basil's business life was spent with Network Security, who dealt in corporate fraud, and whose retirement gift was slightly different from most. It was a round-the-world trip for two which enabled Madge and Basil to undertake a three-month journey down memory lane, to retrace the steps of a love story that had survived a war of unspeakable brutality. For both, the first port of call on their original journey had been Bombay, which had a population approaching 1.7 million. When they returned in 1994, Greater Bombay had grown to almost 13 million.

From Bombay they flew to Calcutta, where once again they made a point of seeing the good and the not-so-good. First, they were taken on a conducted tour of the poorer areas, which Madge found to be every bit as sad as it had been fifty years earlier. The hustle and bustle, kindness and courtesy hadn't changed, but there was one major disappointment. Firpo's was no longer a fashionable restaurant but had become a goods storage centre! The Grand Hotel was now the Oberoi Grand, but was still a haven of perfection. Last but not least, there was the wonderful sight of the Victoria Memorial, restored to its Taj Mahal-style white marble. At dinner the night before they left Calcutta Basil asked the pianist if he would be so kind as to play Madge's long-time favourite 'I'll Be Seeing You (in all the old familiar places)'.

There was certainly nowhere more familiar than Chittagong, the next stop on their journey. Madge and Basil found the small town they had left at the end of the Second World War was unrecognisable. From being an area of enormous natural beauty with lush green forests and white sandy beaches Chittagong District had grown into a city with a population of more than 5.5 million. The one or two cafes on the main shopping street where Madge and Basil had spent those tender and precious hours had long since been blown away on the winds of change.

One thing which hadn't changed in the half century since they had left was the natural courtesy and kindness which they remembered with great affection. When the manager of their hotel said it would be safer if he drove them in a conducted tour the offer was gratefully accepted. When they eventually got to the grounds of the old Governor General's residence there was a major surprise. The big house had been turned into a museum but it was closed on the day of their visit so they never did see inside. The grounds which had contained the basha hospital complex had been turned into playing fields and Madge said she was certain that every patient who had passed through the hospital would have approved.

Burma was renamed Myanmar and Rangoon became Yangon in 1989, but even after years in the international wilderness the sweeping elegance of the city's tree-lined boulevards and the colonial splendour of the dignified Victorian buildings were an eye-opener for both of them. The city was spacious and very impressive, and not at all what they had expected. Intense pressure during Basil's posting in Rangoon had meant there was no time for leisure visits to monuments like the Shwedagon Pagoda and gold-plated Chaukhtatgyi Buddha, which made seeing them during this trip all the more special.

The pair visited Ho Chi Minh City (once called Saigon) in Vietnam and had a personal look into the Cho Chi tunnels. There was a stopover in Australia, where they visited Basil's youngest brother Bob and his wife Esther. Then it was across the Pacific to places like Fiji, Hawaii and Los Angeles. Next they visited Vancouver, Memphis and Washington DC before spending ten days in Barbados, where Basil had arranged for their daughters and their husbands to be flown to the Caribbean paradise for a family holiday. It was a lovely end to the trip and Madge was equally delighted when they flew home business class.

Madge found the trip fascinating because it answered questions that had been at the back of her mind for fifty years. Basil had lived in a tent on Labuan for weeks and had told her there wasn't a single building standing when he left. When they visited together, the island was a happy, thriving community.

For Basil, rugby union was a way of easing the pressures of the Burma Campaign and after he was demobbed in 1947 he played for Esher Expendables, until he retired in 1985. He served as treasurer for many years and later became chairman before being appointed club president. He went on to become the first administrator of Aviva Premiership rugby club Harlequin FC. He also spent more than fifteen years as joint club archivist with Nick Cross and is still a founder member of Quins and life member of Esher Rugby Club.

Age has not wearied Basil and Madge, nor have memories of the Burma Campaign condemned them to the years of despair suffered by so many in the aftermath of the confrontation. At its height the Burma Star Association, which was founded in 1951, boasted a membership in excess of twenty-six thousand. By the start of 2018, Madge was one of just twenty surviving women members entitled to wear the coveted Burma Star on her left lapel. Her status as one of the last of the few resulted in a conversation with former Prime Minister David Cameron at the seventieth anniversary of VJ Day in August 2015. The service of remembrance took place at St Martin-in-the-Fields in Trafalgar Square, where Madge had attended her last Sunday morning worship before travelling to India.

Following the VJ Day service Basil and Madge took part in the parade down Whitehall with over a thousand other veterans and around Parliament Square to a reception in the grounds of Westminster Abbey. Madge wore the 1939–45 Star, the Burma Star, the Defence Medal, and the 1939–45 War Medal. Prime Minister David Cameron asked if the medals she was wearing were her own and was told very politely that if people wore them on their left breast, as she was, they certainly were their own. Medals awarded to deceased ex-service personnel may be worn on the right by relatives, she explained.

The following year the live audience of BBC's *Strictly Come Dancing* were in tears at the end of a moving tribute to Basil and Madge on the Remembrance Sunday show that peaked with an audience of almost 12 million TV viewers. The internet went into meltdown after the background to their love story stretching back more than seventy years to the Second World War was re-enacted by *Strictly* professionals AJ Pritchard and Chloe Hewitt. The dance routine included Leonard Cohen's 'Hallelujah' and the music of violinist Andre Rieu and his orchestra. The story of the wartime romance had been told with Dame Vera Lynn's wartime classic 'We'll Meet Again' playing in the background.

'It was marvellous to hear our favourite song sung by our favourite singer, who is also a Burma Star veteran. We had the pleasure of meeting her at the Burma reunion in 2005,' said Basil.

What very few people knew was that the show only went ahead after Madge turned back the clock to her Nurse Graves days and used the magic potion that brought light into the darkest of times in the Burma Campaign. Dancer Chloe was so overcome by the emotion of the part she was to re-enact that rehearsals had to be halted because she was in floods of tears.

'I can't do this; it's all so moving,' she told Madge, as she stood sobbing at the side of the stage. That was until Nurse Graves mixed a generous helping of compassion with TLC and the gentlest of cuddles to calm Chloe down and get her back on stage. Madge told her she danced so beautifully that all she had to do was take a deep breath and everything would be fine. Chloe and AJ performed with such grace and elegance that when Basil and Madge joined them on stage they were all given a standing ovation.

Several months later in the spring of 2017, the two veterans were invited to a garden party at Buckingham Palace. It was hosted by Prince Harry who had spent the morning at the Tower of London revealing the names of the ninety competitors to represent the UK at the 2017 Paralympic-style Invictus Games. He returned to the palace later in the afternoon, stopping when Basil told him that Madge had cheered his granny on the way to her wedding to Prince Philip in November 1947. Madge also told the Prince that it was almost seventy-one years since she caught a boat home from Bombay to England after nursing in the Burma Campaign, which he was fascinated to hear about.

'He was a real life Prince Charming,' said Madge, 'and after we'd thanked him for taking the time to talk to us, I suggested he should go and get a cup of tea and some cake before it was all gone. He burst out laughing.'

Before Prince Harry went to talk to other veterans, he made Madge's day by having his photo taken with her. What Madge didn't know, as the garden party drew to a close, was that her very own Prince Charming, husband Basil, had slipped on the lush palace lawn and broken his collarbone. Their daughter Angela went with him in an ambulance to St Thomas's Hospital and their son-in-law Chris drove Madge there. Madge made the nurses smile when she told them that when she was preparing for the journey to nurse in the Burma Campaign she missed curfew at Baker Street in July 1944 because a bomb had landed near the hospital and the roads became jammed with traffic.

'They were such interesting times,' said Madge, on a sunny afternoon in the early autumn of 2017. It was the same afternoon that she received the sad news from the daughter of Grace that her friend of more than seventy years had passed away in Yorkshire. Vera, who never married, had died several years earlier and Madge had lost touch with Phyl.

'They were all part of the abnormal life we led throughout the Burma Campaign,' said Madge. 'I know it's an odd thing to remember but one of my overriding memories is of the sheer tiredness. We all seemed to be constantly craving sleep because of the physical and emotional demands placed on us.'

'It was impossible to lead even the semblance of a normal life because those times were anything but normal,' said Basil. 'We were just grateful that we managed to live day to day although we lived with a constant worry about the Japanese. We both think about the brave souls who never made it back home and we pay homage to them every year.'

'What we all learned in those troubled times,' said Madge, 'was to compromise. There was no option in the Burma Campaign but to compromise. And I feel it is that ability to compromise that has really been the secret to our marriage too.'

Vivid as those memories of the past decade may have been, nothing compared to the peace of mind that Basil and Madge experienced at the end of a match in Brighton between South Africa and Japan in the Rugby World Cup. Both were on the edge of their seats in their bungalow on the south coast as the game thundered to a thrilling end. Then when New Zealand-born Karne Hesketh scored a try in the last minute for Japan to triumph 34–32 to complete the greatest upset in the history of the tournament, the Burma Campaign veterans burst into very raucous and very unified applause.

Her words were chosen with extreme care because under no circumstances would the atrocities ever be forgotten, but as they cheered the Japanese Madge suddenly realised something profound seventy years after the end of the Second World War. 'Basil, darling, we've forgiven them.'

Glossary

Anna (coin)   100th of a rupee
Arakan   an area in Burma
Basha   bamboo-built building
Bearer   servant or general worker
Bengal   now in Pakistan
Bhisti   an Indian water-carrier
BOR   British Other Ranks
Bully Beef   slang for corned beef
Burma   now Myanmar
Calcutta   now Kolkata
CCS   Casualty Clearing Station
CO   Commanding Officer
DC-3   Douglas Dakota-3
Dhobi or Dhobi-wallah   servant who washes clothing etc.
Dhoti   a long white loincloth worn in place of trousers
DI   dangerously ill
EMS   Emergency Medical Services
GSW   Gun Shot Wound
Havildar   Sergeant in Indian Army
HMS   His Majesty's Ship

HQ   Headquarters

ID   Identification Disc

IGH   Indian General Hospital

IGH(C)   Indian General Hospital (combined)

Jai Hind   Victory to India

L.O.   Hello, as spoken in London's East End by a Cockney

Memsahib   respectful word for European married woman

Mepacrine   substitute for quinine, used by British troops

Miliaria Rubra   prickly heat

MP   Military Police

NCO   Non-Commissioned Officer

NGL   Nurses Gossip Line

Pegu   now Bago

PSP   pierced-steel planking, used to make ground firm

Punka-wallah   servant who pulls large carpet-shaped fan to air room

QA   Queen Alexandra's Royal Army Nursing Corps

Rangoon   now Yangon

RASC   Royal Army Service Corps

RMP   Royal Military Police

RMS   Royal Mail Ship, used as a troop carrier

Sahib   friendly greeting to European male

Sapper   Royal Corps of Engineers (similar to an Army Private)

SEAC   South East Asia Command

Sepoy   Indian soldier (similar to Private)

SIB   Special Investigation Branch (of RMP)

Simla   now known as Shimla

SS steam ship
Tender small utility vessel
Thunder Box toilet pan
VAD Voluntary Aid Detachment
VD Venereal Disease
WVS Women's Voluntary Service

Acknowledgements

Looking back on my story of the past seventy-four years I became very conscious of the debt I owe to so many. My thanks go firstly to my husband Basil who has always supported me from the day we unexpectedly met during the Burma Campaign. Next I have to thank Bob Blair, a journalist whose intuition for a story came to the fore after a number of conversations he had with our younger daughter Angela. He spoke to us regularly over the following twelve months and wrote this fascinating story. Bob spent much time going through archives and other records to ensure that our recalled knowledge was true and accurate, before putting everything into chronological order – a massive responsibility!

During the past couple of years Carolyn and her husband Keith took a lot of the pressure off us, for which we are most grateful. The Burma Star Association through Phil Crawley MBE, and Helena Hamlyn and Tristan Nichols of the Royal British Legion, went out of their way to ensure that Basil and myself were able to attend the seventieth anniversary of the Burma Campaign on Horse Guards Parade in Whitehall, London, and we're very thankful for the invitation from *Strictly Come Dancing* for us to be featured in a unique programme danced by professionals Chloe Hewitt and AJ Pritchard on Armistice Day 2016, which was seen by nearly 12 million BBC viewers, plus thousands on Facebook.

To all our friends who went along with our moods and the necessary changes made in their diaries, for which we are most grateful.

To Rebecca Winfield, who looked after our negotiations with Macmillan; we thank her for the understanding and kindness she showed at all times.

To Ingrid Connell, Laura Carr and Zennor Compton who looked after our mood changes with much tact, consideration and every possible help.

We sincerely hope that everyone mentioned in these acknowledgements will continue to be friends for the rest of our sunny days.

—Madge Lambert

My thanks are due to Madge Lambert; I feel privileged that she trusted me to write the story of her truly remarkable life. Thanks are also due to her husband Basil for his guidance about life in the hell that was the Burma Campaign. Their patience and hospitality, which featured tasty cakes and most delicious home-made soups, was mirrored by the kindness of daughters Carolyn Blendell and Angela Elliot. The transcription of Madge's diaries by Angie was of immense importance.

John Giddings, MBE, chairman of the Burma Star Association, was endlessly supportive and the Rev Rana (de la Tour) Davies-James, vicar of the Magnis Group Benefice, Hereford, recounted with great pride the stories of her father Rev John Conway de la Tour Davies. He couldn't talk about the horrors of the Burma Campaign without weeping, she said.

ACKNOWLEDGEMENTS

David Blake, curator of the Museum of Army Chaplaincy, Amport, Hampshire, gave me a major boost at a time when my spirits were low, as I struggled to find an agent and publisher. He underlined how important it was that the courage and compassion of nurses like Madge Lambert and memories of Burma Campaign veterans like Basil were put on record before they disappeared into the mists of time. In an extraordinary coincidence it emerged that David went to the same St Andrews Church of England primary school in Bebington on the Wirral peninsula which I had attended many years earlier. His help was reflected by that of William Spencer of the National Archives at Kew, Abigail Cornick, curator of the Museum of the Order of St John, Clerkenwell, London, and Terry Sutton, of the Dover Association. Kashif Ahmed's advice on cultural nuances of the sub-continent and help with translation was invaluable.

The reality, however, is that without the advice and expertise of my agent, Rebecca Winfield, at David Luxton Associates, it is highly unlikely that this book would ever have appeared. I am deeply in her debt. The guidance of Oliver Holt of the *Mail on Sunday* was also much appreciated.

To Ingrid Connell and Zennor Compton, who edited the book at Pan Macmillan, your patience and expertise was invaluable from start to finish.

Surprisingly I will, for once, get the final word in with my wife, Gaynor.

Thanks for everything you did to help over the past two years.

— Robert Blair